The Answer Is Never

The Answer Is Never

A Skateboarder's History of the World

JOCKO WEYLAND

arrow books

Published by Arrow Books in 2003

1 3 5 7 9 10 8 6 4 2

Copyright © Jocko Weyland 2002

Jocko Weyland has asserted his right under the Copyright, Designs and Patents Act, 1988
to be identified as the author of this work

Published in the US by Grove Press

First published in the United Kingdom in 2002 by Century

Arrow Books Limited
The Random House Group Limited
20 Vauxhall Bridge Road, London SW1V 2SA

Random House Australia (Pty) Limited
20 Alfred Street, Milsons Point, Sydney,
New South Wales 2061, Australia

Random House New Zealand Limited
18 Poland Road, Glenfield,
Auckland 10, New Zealand

Random House South Africa (Pty) Limited
Endulini, 5A Jubilee Road, Parktown 2193, South Africa

The Random House Group Limited Reg. No. 954009

www.randomhouse.co.uk

A CIP catalogue record for this book is available from the British Library

Papers used by Random House are
natural, recyclable products made from wood grown in
sustainable forests. The manufacturing processes conform to
the environmental regulations of the country of origin.

ISBN 0 09 943186 6

Printed and bound in Great Britain by Cox & Wyman Ltd, Reading, Berkshire

For my parents, John F. and Cecilia Joan Weyland
Who have always supported and never questioned the left-handed path

Contents

*Outside the local grocery I was stopped
for skating on the sidewalk. The man wants
to know when my type is going to learn our lesson.
Skating away I know the answer to his question is never.*
—Lowboy (C. R. Stecyk III), 1981

The Answer Is Never

Introduction

I learned how to skateboard on a half-pipe in a meadow seven thousand feet above sea level in the Rocky Mountains of Colorado. The ramp was about a hundred yards from our house and my only companions were the rabbits, squirrels, coyotes, deer and goshawks whose natural habitat I was trespassing on. Besides the half-pipe and the house in the distance, it was a scene not much changed from what is shown in the romantic landscapes Albert Bierstadt painted in the late nineteenth century. I skated until it got dark in the summer, and if the temperature went above freezing in the winter I would sweep and scrape the snow and ice off the ramp for gloved, hatted and down-jacketed sessions.

I progressed from running up the curve of the transition and jumping on the board to gyrate higher by successive turns, to dropping in from the top, nine feet above the forest floor. I learned the basic tricks then—180-degree turning frontside and backside aerials and handplants; one-armed handstands on top of the ramp in which I went upside down with one hand balanced on the protruding coping and the other holding the board to my feet above my head. I was supremely satisfied spending my days in the rhythmic motion from the top of the ramp across the flat bottom to the other side, learning moves and frequently slamming to the wood to lie there listening to the sounds of nature and staring up at the canopy of pine trees. There were no other skaters in my town so I was always alone. Sometimes a herd of elk would congregate nearby to munch on the grass and occasionally look up in puzzlement.

I was thirteen when I acquired the half-pipe. The summer before that, I spent hours each day riding a twenty-foot stretch of sidewalk in front of our town's municipal pool, where until recently I had swum back and forth countless times in swim practice. Even though I was only skating a narrow sidewalk surrounding a rock garden, I had already fallen under the spell. Skating was all that mattered. My former swim coach would come out to talk, shaking his head at my folly and asking me when I was going to return to the fold. No time soon, I'd reply. Actually, never. He had ridden skateboards in the clay-wheel era of the sixties and liked to tell a story about two friends of his who had been riding down a sidewalk, one sitting on the shoulders of the other.

"They hit a crack," he'd tell me, "and they stopped dead. They ate it. The guy on top went flying onto his face. We looked down and saw two white lines on the sidewalk."

"Yeah, what was it?" I would ask.

"It was his two front teeth, they were ground down to his gums."

The story resonated; it was riveting and oddly inspirational, and there was something about the dental carnage that skating had wrought on that poor unfortunate that was powerful and enticing. I'd laugh with my ex-coach and then push off to attack the sidewalk for the hundredth time that day.

Twenty years later I'm still at it. I'm not entirely sure why, though I do have some theories. The primary one is that there is an inexpressible freedom in the act of skating and also in the culture of skateboarding. It has influenced and affected many of the choices I've made in my life, informing almost everything I've done. I'm under the spell of an athletic activity that lies at a unique junction of sport and art. There are no coaches, no rules, no one telling you what to do. It is a solitary pursuit that engenders intense camaraderie. There are no limits to what can be done or imagined except for the ones you impose on yourself, because skating is open-ended and always evolving. It can be done anywhere there is concrete, and reconfigures the public spaces of modern architecture, using constructed areas in imaginative ways that become second nature to the skater but are not understood by the nonpractitioner. Skating is a narcotic that offers release and a negation of self that defies analysis. Skating is different.

But what really matters is actually riding. So at the age of thirty-three, I'm skating alone in front of a building in downtown Manhattan that has a set of five steps I'm trying to ollie over. The ollie is the basis of almost every move in street skating; it involves popping the tail of the board off the concrete so the board is propelled upwards into the air, its path directed by the feet of the skater without any hand-to-board contact. After ten tries I manage it, flying six feet out before landing on the sidewalk and rolling off the curb into the street, where an oncoming garbage truck almost runs me over. I then try to ollie onto a foot-high cube of concrete and wheelie across it, falling on my face in front of the tourists and business-people, oblivious to passersby. I try again and again but keep falling, chasing my board when it shoots into traffic and getting scraped up and grimy from my bodily encounters with the cement.

That same June of 1999, Tony Hawk is completing his first nine hundred at an "extreme" sports lollapalooza called the X Games, organized for optimum television viewership. At thirty-three, Tony has won more skateboard contests than anyone in history. He is close to winning when he decides to try the nine hundred, a Holy Grail of skating. It has never been done before, but what it theoretically consists of is flying out of the twelve-foot-high half-pipe and spinning the body three complete revolutions before landing. His fellow competitors stop and watch as he tries it a number of times, coming closer with each attempt. Then he rides across the ramp and launches and spins, holding the board with one hand, his body tucked as he twirls three times through the air . . . and makes it, sketching out on the flat bottom but riding to the other side. He gets mobbed by his friends and the other contestants and wins the contest. His accomplishment is shown on television repeatedly, helping Tony further his position as the public face of skating's frontiers, at the apotheosis of what is possible in vertical skateboarding.

A few months later a skater from England named Geoff Rowley is riding across a plaza in Southern California at about fifteen miles an hour. Unlike the skaters in the X Games, he isn't wearing any protective gear, just shoes, pants and a T-shirt. He rolls toward the edge of a fifteen-step staircase flanked by a waist-high angled concrete ledge. A few feet from the threshold he snaps the tail of the board onto the cement and in one fluid movement ollies three feet into the air, the board seemingly glued to his feet. Floating almost halfway down the ledge, he lands on it at speed, the two trucks of his board screeching as he grinds down the edge to the bottom where his wheels slip out and he is catapulted off his board onto the pavement. He picks himself up and climbs the stairs to try again. This time he goes airborne and grinds off the end of the ledge onto the sidewalk and rides away nonchalantly. The whole time he is balanced on a thirty-inch-long wooden board with four wheels attached, the same kind of tool that Tony Hawk is using on the huge U-shaped ramp at the X Games.

The skating of ramps, pools, marble plazas, handrails, ledges, curbs and every other skateable terrain has been an ever present element in my life for the last twenty years. I have skateboarded all over the world—parks in Colorado, drainage ditches on Oahu, backyard pools in California, the streets of London, New York, St. Petersburg, Russia, and Santa Margherita Ligure in Italy. I've even skated in Cameroon. There is so much concrete and wood in the world that riding a skateboard is possible almost anywhere.

Why skating has had such a profound effect on so many people might be because it is a kind of play that defies any practical purpose—that is, it's fun. Play is a manifestation of an atavistic legacy that can be traced back to the propensity for the animals of all higher species to cavort and roughhouse. Humans inherited these impulses and used early transportation like rafts, chariots and wagons for more than just practical purposes from the time of their invention. Then they came careering down snow on skis and riding waves on surfboards. At some point in the middle of the twentieth century, the apple cart broke off the front of some anonymous kid's homemade scooter and the skateboard was born. Skating has now progressed from these humble beginnings to Hawk's and Rowley's feats, and along the way, what began as a toy gained tens of millions of adherents, spawned magazines and would change our culture, influencing music, fashion, art and film.

The essence of skateboarding is an urge for speed and a desire to manipulate the board and the body in a release of energy that combines skill with voluntarily induced danger. Skaters simultaneously draw on elements of the death wish, thrill seeking and meditation, using gravity as a fulcrum for propulsion while defying it to soar into the air. This breaking of the bonds of the laws of physics enters the skater into a rarified zone where the body and mind are fused in poetic, balletic action. There is an infinite variety of possible maneuvers but there aren't any rules that say who has to do what trick when, or that anybody has to do them at all. There are ways of expressing oneself on a skateboard that aren't possible in other sporting activities, a confrontation of physical and mental limitations that lead to gracefulness and style and transcendental moments.

Concrete has become humanity's natural habitat, and this is what skaters utilize in a way no other group does. Because of this appropriation of the physical world, skating is inherently in conflict with authority. This taboo aspect fuels a "The more illegal they make it, the more attractive it becomes" mind-set and has spawned skating's trademark rebellious behavior and ethos that other segments of society have increasingly come to emulate over the last twenty-five years. There are solitary challenges of skill and technique that make skating resistant to regulation and an element of total participant control at its core that cannot be judged or quantified. No matter how much acceptance it has gained or how much the media has exploited it, skating has stayed true to its rebellious roots—and on many levels always will.

The history of skateboarding goes back forty years. Henry Ford said, "History is bunk," and for the most part skaters dislike nostalgia and historicizing. But skating is built on precedent and oral tradition, and no matter how much the typical skater may disdain the past it can't be ignored. History is varied, and it's not just about the deeds of the "great men," of the Torger Johnsons, Steve Caballeros, Jason Lees and Bob Burnquists. There is a succession of advances in tricks from Mike McGill's 540 to Mark Gonzales's first frontside boardslide and the evolutions in board and wheel manufacture. And there's also the unknown kid doing his first fifty-fifty on a rail today. Skating's history is complicated and fluid because it is diffuse and constantly changing. There is a confluence of the many strands of history—the known and the unknown, the official and the forgotten. How they have influenced each other and crossed paths is what this book is about. This is a melding of those strands, an attempt to paint an accurate picture of what it means to skateboard and to follow a path in life that incorporates its unique appeal.

Being a skater means a life lived differently, in pursuit of something elusive. Skateboarding is misunderstood because it is outside the normal scheme of things. The rest of the world often watches, follows and imitates aspects of skating without really getting it. It is a singular activity with fluctuating and contradictory philosophies, a true subculture that has resisted attempts at going mainstream. Skating isn't nice. It's ugly and beautiful at the same time, a physical activity that isn't really a sport but is definitely a way of life.

Skateboarding is about getting towed behind cars, about riding off of picnic tables and ollieing onto them, about the sound of wheels carving on tile and trucks barking on coping. It's slamming onto cement and getting purple hip contusions that stick to your pants for weeks, riding on rain-soaked sidewalks and arguing with old ladies and running from cops. It's breaking your arm and getting your ramp burned down by hostile nonbelievers. It's skating the pools of abandoned houses or riding a good spot in a gang-infested neighborhood. It's boards breaking and wheels falling off when you're doing twenty-five down a hill. It's getting eggs, rocks and bricks thrown at you while doing ollies off a sidewalk bump late at night, or putting Bondo on cracks in rails so they can be slid down. It's inventive and often obscene board graphics, a way of dressing, a way of acting, of being.

Skateboarding has become part of culture through its linear history—the nuts and bolts of skating's path from the early 1960s to now—and the millions of personal stories that have made that progression possible. "*Traduttore traditore*" (translator=traitor) is the saying in Italian, and there is the worry that any attempt to represent and translate something that has been such an inexpressibly important part of my and other's lives is a betrayal. That to try to make an outside audience understand what is so special about skating will compromise it. But there is a clear imperative to tell about the history and cultural impact of skating, along with some of the great moments it has spawned, while staying true to its soul in a way any person who has fallen under its spell would appreciate. My version is only one of many, and it is intertwined with the larger narrative of skateboarding's objective history. This isn't a textbook; it is biased, prejudicial and discriminating, while also trying to be inclusive and wide-ranging. It's about the allure of scummy backyard pools and off-limits full pipes, of marble ledges and triple sets of stairs, of practicing an activity that has never really been understood by a public that is unaware of the rich rewards and inexplicable pleasures that start with the simple act of rolling.

Chapter One
Noble Pursuits

From the instant of the singularity that began the universe, movement has been a constant. Clouds of matter became stars and planets that were propelled away from each other, a scenario of unstinting expansion that continues to this day. Hundreds of millions of years after the big bang, the earth coalesced into a planet, spinning and moving along with the rest of the universe. The parts of this particular planet mimicked the entropy of the larger reality. Plates of rock shifted, mountains rose, volcanoes erupted. Moisture turned to vapor that became clouds and then rain, which fell to the earth to become streams and rivers that emptied into seas and oceans that sent waves crashing to the shore. Unending, eternal movement.

With the arrival of life the movement continued. In the beginning it wasn't planned or desired—the amoeba unthinkingly jostled to and fro—but by the time of the original amphibian crawling out onto shore, propulsion had become willful. Evolution led to more intricate creatures, moving, always moving, now with self-determination. Locomotion in the service of obtaining food, of seeking out new habitats to escape predators. At some point there was a development of movement that didn't have any clearly useful purpose. The baby cubs rolled and tumbled, the ancestors of dolphins jumped and splashed. They were play-ing; their actions didn't have a practical or easily decipherable reason.

Down the line, humanity evolved and had to move like all the other creatures. Except during sleep and infrequent periods of rest, they had to hunt and chase game and run away from fiercer fauna. The new species also traveled, leaving its birthplace in Africa and spreading out across the globe. At some point, humans came up with ways to move themselves along that didn't rely on their two feet. Floating rafts pushed by sticks and paddles and sails, then most im-portantly, the wheel facilitated this movement of the human body from one place to another. In addition to this, there were domesti-cated animals that were eventually ridden for transportation. And some of these, the horse in particular, could go much faster than humans could on their own.

The harnessing of the domesticated animal to the wheel led to the rounded object as an engine of recreation, and the pri-mal urge for speed blossomed. The mechanical advancement of the wheel allowed humans to figure out ways to ride in chariots and wagons, gliding with the forces of nature to become one with them, and in doing so to experience the joy of unshackled propulsion.

In myriad ways, the mechanical device married to natural forces enabled this urge for movement and unlocked the purely psychological reasons that were behind it all—a need for release, uncertainty and fear induced on purpose at high speed. All over the world, the ways of doing it emerged and multiplied. The horse was ridden faster, initiates jumped off of towers with only a vine attached to their feet, rafts shot rapids, and ships were flung for-ward by the power of the wind. A singular relationship to the earth based on independent movement came into being, to risking death in the pursuit of vertigo and using speed as a destroyer of perception's stability, creating simultaneous panic and tranquillity in ordered minds. Whether thrill-seeking, fun-making or an attempt to clear the mind of prosaic concerns, these urges fed a hunger to test balance and the body's ability to stay upright under adverse conditions.

Surely from the very beginning of the wheel or the sled, somebody was going too fast, using the device in a way that wasn't commensurate with its purpose. There is archaeological proof that points to later developments in the recreational use of wheels attached to a platform. Skis found in a bog in Hoting, Sweden have been carbondated to five thousand years, and prehistoric rock drawings at Rodoy in Norway and in northern Siberia from around 2500 B.C. show skis being used for hunting and traveling across snow-covered land. Later there are reports from the Tang Dynasty of Mongolian tribes riding *MuMu* (wooden horses), and Bishop Adam of Bremen in 1000 A.D. described *skridfinns* (sliding Finns) who "borne on bent boards . . . traverse the heights which are covered with snow." The Norse sagas tell of contests that document less disciplined and dreamier uses for skis. In the nineteenth century, a poor Norwegian farmer named Sondre Overson Norheim began experimenting with ski and binding design. He almost went bankrupt, and his wife was reduced to begging for food, but by 1868 he went to the Molmenkollen ski competition where his technical breakthroughs helped him win in both the jumping and style skiing events. Skiing took off soon after as an arena for physical flights of fancy that had nothing to do with work.

But the roots of skateboarding are found far away from the mountains of northern Europe, in the much warmer climes of the

Pacific. The Polynesians went one step further than the Scandinavians, using another kind of platform on an aquatic stage—the moving wave. The inspiration might have come from riding canoes in the surf, though before that, they were surely engaging in bodysurfing, one of the purest manifestations of a body acquiring speed via a natural force. Surfing waves with the body was going on in Tahiti, Samoa, New Zealand and New Guinea, but it wasn't until the eastern migration from the Society Islands to Hawaii around 500 A.D. that surfing developed the intermediary platform to balance on that bodysurfing lacked. By 1000 A.D., *he'e nalu*—surfboard riding—had been perfected in the waters surrounding the Hawaiian Islands.

By the time Captain James Cook landed in 1778, surfing was a cross between sport, leisure activity and religious ritual that amazed the Europeans with its combination of skill, talent, balance and daring. The Hawaiians owed much to the ocean; they lived by it and it had a profound influence on their lives. But surfing was special and mostly reserved for the royal classes, the *alii*. The *kapu* (taboo) system deemed it for the most part unvirtuous for commoners to engage in bowling, running, canoe races and especially surfing. It was the *alii* who had the time to really pursue surfing and who could use the lengthier and better *olo* boards, and it was their ceremonies that had the greatest religious import.

Building a proper *olo* board began by selecting the right tree with an offering of *kumu* fish and incantations by a *kahuna* (priest) at the base of the trunk. After the tree was cut down, the board was custom-built for a specific owner; shaped for the least amount of traction and maximum maneuverability. When it was completely carved it was polished with *oahi* stone rubbers, stained with the ash of burned *kukui* nuts and shined to reflection with *kukui* oil. The *kahuna* performed further rites upon the launching of the board. Then the *alii* owner paddled the *wiliwili-wood* board, fourteen feet long, five inches thick and weighing 150 pounds, out beyond the breakers to wait for a good set. As the wave approached, the rider got prone and paddled until the board was at enough of a slant on the incoming wave and in one feline, graceful movement, got to his or her feet. Standing upright, he or she rode the wave in, maneuvering by leaning left and right, rushing and gliding toward the shore with the power and roar of the curling wave. On these isolated islands in the Pacific, the *alii* were the avant-garde in rejecting mere transportation for a more transcendent connection to nature, one in which they tempted fate by going to the heart of the ocean's power to ride big waves.

Contact with outsiders following Captain Cook's arrival ripped Hawaiian society apart. The influx of explorers and then traders destabilized the civic situation and fostered a concurrent cultural revolution. Only fifty years after Cook's landing, the society was in such disarray that the taboo system was abolished. In 1820 the first Calvinist missionaries arrived from New England, and the war on surfing began. According to missionary Sheldon Dibble, "The evils resulting from all these sports and amusements have in part been named. Some lost their lives thereby, some were severely wounded, maimed and crippled, some were reduced to poverty, both by losses in gambling and by neglecting to cultivate the land; the instances were not few in which they were reduced to utter starvation. But the greatest evil of all resulted from the constant intermingling, without any restraint, of persons of both sexes and of all ages, at all times of day and at all hours of the night." The betting that went along with surfing and the scanty clothing worn in the water seemed to inspire particular horror among the missionaries. One of the first converts was Kaahumanu, King Kamehameha's widow, who had ascended to power as de facto prime minister. The missionaries saw the end of taboo as a sign from God that their mission had holy sanction. They convinced Kaahumanu and the other *alii* converts that surfing and other leisurely pastimes would offend heaven. The *alii* quickly decreed that these activities should stop.

So there were new taboos after all that coincided with the disintegration of Hawaiian society, a reshuffling of massive proportions. Some of the missionaries despaired at the passing of "noble" pursuits like surfing, but the damage was done. By the late nineteenth century, Caucasians were the important ministers in what was effectively a puppet government. The noveau-riche royal figureheads were so enamored with their newfound wealth and zest to acquire foreign luxuries that they taxed the commoners exorbitantly, forcing them to work harder and robbing them of any serious leisure time. Barter and trade replaced the subsistence-based economy, and the Hawaiians began to imitate the more technologically advanced Caucasians. The removal of the old gods and ways created a vacuum for a headlong rush to the new, in particular a mania for reading and writing. In Kauai surfboards were turned into desks for schools. The family and traditional crafts degenerated along with a catastrophic decline in the native population, from three hundred thousand in 1778 to forty thousand in 1900. The annual Makahiki sporting festival became a thing of the past. The cumulative effect of all these factors was that for all intents and purposes surfing was dead by the beginning of the twentieth century.

But some Hawaiians must have been surfing in secret, riding hidden breaks by moonlight; some rebels continued to hear the siren song of the crashing waves. In the early twentieth century surfing was resuscitated. Maybe atavistic longings could only be suppressed for so long. Maybe the example of skiing as pure recreation had echoed; perhaps the railroad and faster ships and the possibilities of aviation reawakened dreams of flight down waves.

After the turn of the century Hawaii's economy improved and with that came a resurgent interest in sports. Haoles (Caucasians) and locals alike began to surf again off of Waikiki. Around 1905, some Hawaiian boys started gathering around a *hau* tree at Waikiki Beach and formed a club called Hui Nalu, a poor man's fraternity whose name, roughly translated, meant "united in surfing." One of the boys hanging around at the *hau* tree was fifteen-year-old Duke Kahanamoku, who would later gain notice by winning a gold medal in the hundred-meter freestyle swimming event at the 1912 Stockholm Olympic games. After that he began to go around the world giving demonstrations on "speed swimming," and on surfing whenever there waves enough to do so. He brought surfing to Australia, New Zealand and the mainland United States, where his role as ambassador of surfing would have furthest-reaching consequences in California.

Surfing in California between the wars was a matter of a small brotherhood riding redwood or hollow "cigarbox" boards at places like Corona del Mar. In the early thirties, before the harbor entrance was dredged, surfers were riding a quarter mile from the jetty down to China Cove. A few schoolboys hitchhiked to the beach wearing custom-sewn white canvas trunks to partake in an idyll of uncrowded waves and unrestrained aquatic pleasure.

World War II slowed things down for surfing, with most of the able-bodied men and potential surfers away. The Allies' 1945 victory led to an American cultural ascendancy over the rest of the world. And much of that cultural hegemony radiated from the golden state of California, its massive filmmaking industry producing movies with their all-persuasive ability to transmit directly ideas and ideals through the retina to the brain, to entice people to covet a way of life and a notion of freedom and possibility.

In this state by the Pacific, the caldron of postwar change was roiling. Returning GIs were joined by an influx of new immigrants in fueling and benefiting from a booming economy. Working-class people now had more time for leisurely pursuits. Freeway networks were constructed that made these activities easily accessible. Fun became a goal, a way of life, a birthright. With these changes also came the advent of the modern American teenager. Kids with their parents' disposable income had time on their hands for fun and rebellion, time for being bad and a nascent repulsion toward their parents' world and its value system.

The confluence of these factors meant an upswing for surfing in California. GIs coming back from Hawaii drew on Duke's example and made surfing part of their lives. The new freeways, along with films of Hawaiian wave riding and the development of the light foam surfboard at Windansea in La Jolla (by Bob Simmons, who later drowned there), expanded the visibility and potential of surfing. A new type emerged who yearned for the sensation of speed that surfing provided, who saw the riding of waves as a lifestyle that was a rejection of the civilized land and its society, an escape to the last frontier. They had a spiritual attachment to the ocean and "the life," an ethical conception of what they were doing as a communion with nature that harkened back to the Hawaiians of two hundred years earlier.

They used the beach as a base for what was beyond. Surfing was challenging, a melding with the ocean's power. In life it was an art, a movement. They were doing something odd and transgressive and new. It was an obsession that was antisocial while having its own underground communities, a culture distinct from what was sanctioned. At the right place and right time, the gestation was happening. California had the adherents of surfing, and they were about to start a revolution.

Chapter Two
When the Waves
Are Flat

Down the street from Jack's house in Santa Monica lived a neighbor who was different. It was the ten-foot surfboards he glimpsed in the garage that first caught Jack's attention. He found out that the man who owned the house had been stationed in Hawaii during World War II and was of an exotic breed. He was a member of the San Onofre Surf Club, an organization whose criteria for membership were unlike that of any country club. Something about the tan and fit subculture he belonged to represented freedom to Jack. And his daughter was very pretty.

In 1958 Jack was eleven, dark and bookish, not outdoorsy in the California way. His father had been sent west by the company back in New York. The allure of that house down the street and the people who lived there served as incentive to enter into an unknown realm. Soon Jack was getting rides to the beach with his mother or in a friend's parents' chauffeured car. At Malibu Jack and his friends encountered another world, a practically deserted beach with one thatched hut and some men out in the water riding surfboards. The men wore sandals and beards—and white and tan clothes because it was an era before bright colors. These older men looked down on the young kids as interlopers who didn't understand their bohemian lifestyle and the ethical implications of what they were doing out in the water and in life. The boy saw a forties-era delivery van with writing on the side. It was the first time he had seen customized writing on a car. It read THE CALIFORNIANS.

When Jack was thirteen, his parents gave him his first real surfboard, a balsa-wood Hobie Alter model that was ten feet long and weighed about thirty-five pounds. He started localizing the breaks at Palisades, Santa Monica and Malibu, getting better, doing head dips, hanging five and ten, walking the nose and shooting the tube. At Malibu, an older lifeguard they called "The Enforcer" helped them out by clearing the waves for them in exchange for boards. Jack and his friends took a trip down to Newport and saw people bodysurfing the Wedge, where big waves break right near the shore. It was the first time they had ever seen anyone using fins.

One of Jack's friends who was a little older started taking Benzedrine and hanging out at arty coffeehouses like the Gas House and the Blue Horn in Venice. The girl down the street became an iconic progenitor of what was to come; she had straight blond hair and the original two-piece bathing suit, at least as far as any of them knew. In a friend's swimming pool, they jumped off the diving board to practice their wipeouts for when they would need to do the real thing out in the surf.

The older friend got a driver's license, possibilities expanded and things got a little wilder. They drove down to La Jolla where the first contact was made. They had heard about kids down there abusing a toy called a Flexi Flyer, a sled with wheels made for asphalt. These kids were charging down small drainage pipes on Mount Soledad, lying on their stomachs while holding flashlights, corkscrewing upside down and flying out on the beach. Jack saw something else—a hybrid of the Flexi Flyer and the broken scooter. What had been a broken toy was combined with the thrill-seeking aspects of the Flexi Flyer to create something independent of its antecedents. The kids were riding the scooter planks, purposely not putting the handle back on.

The skateboard was born. No matter how primitive the equipment was, it wasn't a toy any longer. At first just a length of two-by-four with roller-skate wheels attached at either end, it soon became a distinct tool. There was a leap to standing up, balancing and turning without any contact other than feet on the precarious moving platform. Its development was directly related to surfing; it mimicked the feeling and action of riding a wave. It was something to do when the waves were flat. They were upping the ante, translating and expanding upon what they did on surfboards, taking it from something dependent on natural forces to a man-made landscape of concrete and asphalt.

It was another thing to do, another way of getting radical while practicing for surfing. They always skated barefoot, because they surfed barefoot. The unforgiving metal wheels caused the board to stop short at the slightest crack, and as they wore down, they developed flat spots. These had their advantages: they could be used to instigate turns like the ones on surfboards, except now they were doing them on banked driveways. They carved and hung ten toes over the nose of their boards on the banks at Bellagio Middle School and shot the sloped pavement of Beverly Hills.

The skateboards were new and fun, but surfing remained their primary obsession. Not only the actual act of surfing but their own elitist conception of what surfing meant and their place in it. They were the sons of well-to-do families, educated in private schools and instilled with a reverence and appreciation for the canons of Western civilization. They knew literature from Goethe and Proust to Fitzgerald and Hemingway; they were aficionados of Bach and Wagner. They set themselves apart; their erudition made them prone to connecting a romanticized past to their own lives. They had Sunday clubs where they sipped grenadine drinks, smoked cigars and imagined themselves as chivalrous Knights Templars bound for greatness, ready and willing to die with valor. They were serious about their mysticism and its possibilities of transcendence in the experience of nature. An *alii* of sorts, they had the luxury of these dreams and ambitions. They were at the end of an aristocratic tradition. In being revolutionary, they were also tied to the past and now were about to confront a new order ready to do battle, an emerging horde whom they thought of as hopelessly déclassé, the *untermensch* who lived over three miles from the beach.

These kids and the older guys on the beach were driving Woodys and had hair with increased volume before its time. More importantly, they were part of a nobility based on bohemianism and romanticism that would affect and then be subsumed by a burgeoning mass culture that was just around the corner. Did they know or understand that these esoteric urges to ride waves and get speed were going to be coupled with new technology and changing ideas and conditions? That they were setting the pace for a future that was in direct opposition to their ways and mores, a future that would co-opt and pervert their version of a cultural elite of the waves? Did they know they were starting a revolution?

As they wrote the script for what was to come they inadvertently wrote themselves out of it, though they might have had an inkling of what was happening. (The Benzedrine user was also an aspiring painter, and one of his canvases, titled *The History of the Twentieth Century*, showed a menagerie of rogues and punk rockers before they existed, degenerate victims of commercial culture.) Their influence would be wide but always successively distorted and neutered by the popular culture they despised. The end was nigh; their private party was about to be crashed. Maybe it was the release of the original *Gidget* or the Beach Boys' emergence on the scene. Whatever the causes, the rupture was plain sometime in 1963 when someone from the Valley showed up at the beach in cutoff jeans. A representative of the new breed, working-class with a New Jersey accent, a transplant at the advance of the wave of the future. Jack and his friends still surfed and skated but stopped going to the beach on Sundays because it was too crowded. The krill were coming, and they were on their way to winning.

Now a teenager, Jack saw the change manifested in the younger kids who were his neighbors. They were different, more hedonistic; they didn't have the same respect for the subtle metaphysics of surfing and life. They were closer in attitude to the unwashed masses. These kids had gotten into skating heavily and were innovating, putting a kicktail (a slanted wedge of wood) on the end of the board and doing kickturns by putting weight on the tail and turning with the front wheels off the ground. It wasn't all about surfing anymore. They were branching out, taking the skateboard beyond being a toy. And they went out into the world, disseminating the knowledge. Back at the beach, the originators knew they had lost and they were angry with the new kids for giving away the secret.

For a few years in the early sixties, there was a small buildup in skateboarding. Toy companies manufactured most of the boards while a few surf-related firms like Makaha, Hobie and Val Surf made slightly more advanced models shaped like miniature surfboards. In 1964 the boom began in earnest. Propelled by the connection to surfing and the mythology of California, skating became an interest to many kids (and adults) willing to "ride the wave" and try out the latest way to harness nature's forces with a mechanical device, to go fast and do something new and a little crazy. And there was more and more pavement to try it out on. As the surfing and skateboarding bard C. R. Stecyk III remarked, "Two hundred years of American technology has unwittingly created a massive cement playground of unlimited potential. But it was the minds of eleven-year-olds that could see the potential."

Up until 1964, the boom in skating had been grassroots and impromptu, marked by trial and error and improvisation. Spontaneously and in different locations around the country, the broken scooters and Flexi Flyers were giving way to makeshift boards put together with sundry nailing, gluing and sawing, with trucks and wheels borrowed from roller skates. At first they rode down hills sitting on the board until they advanced to standing. They had to beat the hill. Staying on to get down in one piece was a major accomplishment because the inflexible steel wheels catapulted riders off their boards when they encountered the smallest irregularity or pebble on the road. Skin and bones were the only padding then, and they were employed frequently due to the inexperience of everyone involved and the failings of the primitive equipment. Despite that, it was exciting; the wave didn't have to be relied on, and the wheel was being used in a way that it never had been before.

Soon companies with names like Sterling and Native Custom started producing higher-quality boards out of solid oak, ash and mahogany. Trucks made specifically for skateboards were manufactured by Sure Grip, Chicago and Leesure Line. Wheels shifted to clay composite and hard rubber, which made them a little more resilient than steel. Skateboarding was growing. The proof was in one of skating's first brushes with the mainstream media in the June 5, 1964, issue of *Life*. "Here Come the Sidewalk Surfers" gave national exposure to "a new gimmick called the skateboard" that was "the next best bet to shooting the curl on an oceangoing surfboard." Eleven-year-old blond Tommy Ryan of Ocean Beach, California, was shown doing the coffin (lying on the board like a luge) and riding a slight bank, doing his best imitation of being on a wave. Of course he was barefoot. He looked like he was having a great time; the expression on his face was one of wonderment mixed with fear and joy. The article reported that sales had "shot over fifty thousand" and that "the next market to be tapped is the Midwest."

Pioneers began doing recognizable tricks adapted from surfing. They progressed past staying on to variations of surfing gymnastics—handstands, nose and tail wheelies, 360-spins and imaginary head dips. In 1964 the inaugural issue of the *Quarterly Skateboarder* (published by Surfer Publications) came out and featured rising stars in its pages—Steve and Dave Hilton, Torger Johnson, Bruce Logan, Bob Mohr, John Freis and Woody Woodward. The first international championship with skaters competing in front of judges took place in 1965 at La Palma Stadium in Anaheim, and was broadcast on ABC's *Wide World of Sports*. It wasn't only children doing it and skateboarding was being considered by some as a kind of sport. The people who were committed definitely took it seriously. Later in 1965, possibly in Pacific Palisades, skaters entered an empty swimming pool, and skating went beyond going down a hill or doing a trick on flat land to challenging gravity itself by using centrifugal force to carve a vertical wall. It wasn't just sidewalk surfing anymore.

Skating took off and entered into the public consciousness and imagination—and very quickly became a cause for concern. Similar to the juvenile-delinquency hysteria that started in the fifties as a reaction to youth "problems" like crime and drug use, skating experienced a backlash. To most it seemed like good clean fun, but others saw something unsavory and subversive about it that demanded repudiation. Certainly there were valid reasons for concerns about safety: injuries, the wheels' lack of forgiveness and the reckless nature of youth being the main culprits. The equipment wasn't up to the demands put on it and kids were breaking bones and getting bloodied and scarred. The limits of capability were being explored on the rudimentary platforms, like a Model T being run in the Paris-Dakar rally. But it was something else, something less qualifiable about skating, that made it alarming. Kids were cavorting around without respect for authority, going unsupervised while engaging in an activity that most adults had never done and couldn't relate to. The kids were getting out of control.

A year after their bemused look at Tommy Ryan, *Life* set a new tone in May 1965: "Skateboard Mania—A Teeter-Totter on Wheels Is a New Fad and Menace." The article argued that adults needed to be warned and the kids required reining in for their own good because they were hurting themselves and innocent bystanders too. The pictures in the seven-page spread were an odd mixture of cute (a coed on a skateboard, a mother riding while being spotted by her son, two priests in cassocks smiling as they shot down a hill in Denver) and a somewhat serious treatment of skating's frontier (a slalom contest and a kid doing a kickturn). The main focus, though, was on danger, illustrated by photographs of skaters in New York City flying off their boards, running into each other and wiping out in traffic with cars and taxis menacingly close by.

The text brought the point home. Skateboards were "the most exhilarating and dangerous joy-riding device this side of the hot rod," and riding one "gives the effect of having stepped on a banana peel while dashing down the back stairs." But they were "also a menace to limb and even to life. . . . A Los Angeles hospital reports twenty-five skateboard cases a month, two-thirds of them broken childish bones, and the toll will get worse as summer sends a horde of youthful skateboarders out into the streets. In the past month two children have been killed in the East when they careened into traffic on their boards."

Beyond the mayhem and death toll was the alarming invasion of the streets. "In the park they take over paths made for peaceful strollers . . . and ride on the busy streets through, beside and all but under cars." Almost unconsciously, the article illuminated the appeal of skating when it quoted a mother who rode her son's board: it gave her "a very free kind of feeling." There was one page showing accomplished skaters in Huntington Beach that gave grudging respect to their "skill and coordination executing complicated maneuvers." But the main thrust of the article came through on the same page, the largest photo being one of a barefoot skater's bleeding shin. The verdict was in. Skating was dangerous and a public nuisance at best, practically a criminal act at its worst.

This hyperbolic treatment, along with other magazine reports offering the testimony of various safety "experts," combined with the real injuries that were occurring, had a dampening effect on the early skateboard craze. The result wasn't instant; skating continued to grow in popularity through 1965, more contests were held and innovations were made in equipment and tricks. A growing dedicated minority appreciated it for its unique character and challenges. This was at odds with the judgment handed down by the arbiters of what was an acceptable pursuit for the average person. The mandate was that something about skating wasn't quite right. It wasn't nice: it needed to be regarded with suspicion and probably declared illegal. The media cast a stereotype, and in the way that stereotypes are often somewhat grounded in reality, the media's assessment was correct in a general sense while being distorted in the particular.

"Skateboard Mania" and other articles of its ilk were right to a degree. What they didn't take into account was that these "bad" aspects—the thrill, the potential for danger—were precisely what made riding a board attractive. They constituted the freedom that made skating unusual and revolutionary. Tricks were changing daily, and there were no guidelines or rules. There was an inherent distrust of authority, which lured a certain type of person, and this type would pigeonhole skating as an antisocial act for many years to come. The shunned skaters reacted by being even more rebellious and anarchic than they were already perceived to be, and incorporated the myth and reality of their persecution as one of the main tenets of their lifestyle, a construct inseparable from its athletic essence.

Makaha alone sold $4 million worth of boards between 1963 and 1965, but by 1966 sales dropped drastically and the *Quarterly Skateboarder* ceased publication. Bad publicity didn't kill skating, but the lack of technical advancement, combined with injuries and the fickleness of the passions of American youth, laid it low. Skateboards gathered dust in garages or were thrown away. A select few ignored the winds of change. They kept at it, not caring that it wasn't an established sport or a big trend. In schoolyards and on the paved roads of out-of-the-way canyons, they continued to skate. The seed had been planted in the sixties, and the gestation had led to birth and early infancy. Then the newborn went into hibernation.

Chapter Three
The Urethane-Fueled
Cambrian Explosion

Where was skateboarding amid the momentous tumult of the late sixties? Basically, absent. Skateboarding had almost ceased to exist. But surfing, skateboarding's erstwhile parent, had become entrenched as one of the many subcultures that made up the new national fabric of a balkanized America. Bruce Brown's 1966 film *The Endless Summer,* in which two friends travel the globe in search of the ultimate wave, had conquered the minds and longings of many. The California ideal had continued to gain strength, and surfing was bigger than ever. It was such a part of the times that it insinuated itself into the recreational activities of soldiers in the Vietnam War, later immortalized in Francis Ford Coppola's movie *Apocalypse Now.* There were good breaks to ride in Vietnam, and as Lieutenant Kilgore said, "Charlie don't surf!"

Somewhere in the pervasive culture of surfing was its abandoned stepchild. Skateboarding was invisible to the outside world, but there were holdovers from that innocent time of shorter hair and striped shirts, outcasts who still skated on wooden boards with clay wheels. These transitional figures had mutated with everyone else into a new decade but continued to ride by the beach and cruise the hills in the canyons. Their hobby and their world were about to be altered forever by a word: *plastics.* The swimming pool behind

Benjamin Braddock and Mr. McGuire during this exchange from *The Graduate* prefigures future relevance.

Thermosetting polymers of high molecular weight had arrived by the start of the seventies, emerging from the technologies developed during World War II. The introduction of foam and fiberglass made a major impact on surfing, which led to it becoming a much more affordable and accessible sport. By the mid-seventies, plastic was part of everybody's life, from furniture, aerospace and automobile manufacturing to countless toys, baubles and pastimes. Plastic was part of the new arena of speeded-up trends, a culture that used disposable objects and ideas as part of everyday life. Lifestyles were becoming interchangeable playthings to be consumed and discarded, and they were coming and going faster than ever before. The ascendant demographic group of the American teenager, with its unprecedented surplus cash, was a leading force in the cycle, as were adults who were increasingly behaving like teenagers further into their lives.

Plastic transcended the life-and-death cycle of fads by becoming such an integral part of so many things that it achieved a figurative immortality—and a literal immortality in its propensity for never decomposing. Now plastic started playing a role in the willful resuscitation of old fads as new ones. Not long after being relegated to the past, they would come right back under the auspices of benumbed nostalgia—or historical amnesia. People had skateboarded, and then the trend died and was forgotten, but it was about to make a comeback, though its resurgence wasn't premeditated.

All those teenagers were out there and more curious and rapacious than ever. Most of them had only a slight memory of the wooden skate toy. They did have an ingrained ideal about California that had expanded beyond the beach and nubile girls in bikinis to include the Manson murders, Altamont and the Watts riots. These additions to the popular mythology just enhanced the appeal by giving the state a tantalizing sense of danger. It was a place where people chose what they wanted to be and how they wanted to live. It was where the action was. And a lot of people were living a close approximation of a life of ease and pleasure in a modern-day Arcadia that provided more excitement than the place described in pastoral poetry.

The permissiveness, the surfing, the cars, the tension and the population of teenagers converged in the Eden of greater Los Angeles. Kids who had grown up surfing (or had at least tried it) lived in a place where the car made mobility and freedom of movement defining characteristics. They were open to furthering the desire for speed and death-defying acts. With the rebirth of skateboarding, they would have an improved platform that could be experimented with and taken to unforeseen levels. The waves could still be flat, and all that pavement was still out there waiting to be taken on. What had happened in the sixties with skating was almost prehistory, the first stumbling attempts, somewhat quaint in retrospect. The modern history would come out of advances in equipment and social forces that set in motion an unprecedented boom in the popularity and significance of skating that was a hundred times larger than what happened in the sixties.

By 1973, as American losses in Vietnam reached forty-five thousand and two cease-fires passed with continued fighting; as the Watergate hearings began; as Salvador Allende was overthrown in Chile and "committed suicide"; as Pablo Picasso died; as Secretariat ruled the Triple Crown and the energy crisis was in full swing, a man named Frank Nasworthy started skateboarding's industrial revolution. An engineering student from Florida who had relocated to California, he wore his shoulder-length blond hair with a side part and sunglasses and later came to be known as "Captain Cadillac." He surfed, was aware of roller-skating and hadn't forgotten skateboarding. By combining these interests with his engineering prowess, he instigated a technological leap that changed skating forever. He applied his discovery at the skateboard's most sensitive point—where it met the ground.

The simplest analogy for the change in wheels is the introduction of foam into surfboard construction. As with surfing, a new element made skateboards easier to ride, increasing their popularity dramatically. And as with surfboards the improvement came from science developed for other purposes. In the human quest to make things easier for beginners, urethane wheels had been introduced for roller-skating, a pastime that moderately thrived throughout the sixties. These wheels simplified learning because they were softer and had more traction. But they didn't go over well, since most roller skaters were interested in speed and the older metal wheels were faster on the smooth floors of roller rinks. Frank Nasworthy made the cognitive jump that these wheels might work for the less than perfect surfaces that skateboards were ridden on.

With a company called Creative Urethanes, Nasworthy designed a wheel that used a cast-molding process in which the material was poured into a mold cavity and then cured in an oven. The wheels were symmetrically round (from being molded around a core), so they didn't deteriorate and lose their shape nearly as fast as the clay composite wheels. Most importantly, they had vastly improved traction and resiliency. The Cadillac wheel debuted in

1973 for the skateboard market—a market that barely existed at the time.

The innovation didn't cause an overnight sensation. The urethane wheel didn't change the basic structure of the skateboard. What it did was cause a shift akin to jet engines in aviation or the handheld camera in photography. The wheels fundamentally altered the basic machine by improving on one of its elemental components, opening up vistas of possibility. With those broadened vistas came a psychological leap concerning what could be done on a skateboard. Radical surfer and skater Larry Bertleman was quoted soon after as saying, "Anything is possible," and now it was mechanically and mentally true. It was fitting that this comment came from a man who was equally proficient in both activities, because the new wheels meant the beginning of the end of skating's dependence on surfing. It would soon grow up and start to challenge the dominance of its precursor.

The modern age of skateboarding began when Nasworthy's wheels met with the riders who rode them. These riders were often committed types who had been skating all along on the boards from the previous era, so they appreciated the import of the urethane wheel and started capitalizing on it immediately. Soon the word was out on the improved version of what the masses had flirted with ten years before. California was the site where a wave was generated that would crash over the country a year later, when it would suddenly be mandatory for every kid to beg, borrow or steal to get a skateboard. The initial manifestation of the change came from riders who ignored precedent and ran roughshod over questions of what surface was ridden, how it was ridden and what was done on the board while riding it. The rivalries and cross-fertilizations of disciplines and skateboard design in these years before skating became a international movement had profound effects on its path.

The board itself began evolving at this time as well. Today skateboards are standardized, with only cosmetic differences between the components sold by the various companies. Now the platform just is, and what is done on it is what counts. What was done on the board in the mid-seventies was just as important, but much more thought and care went into maintaining and customizing the board itself. The amount of effort that went into upkeep and the sorting out of ideas in product design was prodigious. Everything was up for grabs; the skateboard itself was a site of contention and flux. These technological growing pains would help forge what skating was and what it would become.

A skateboard is a whole made up of three important parts. The deck is the board that riders stand on. It's about thirty inches long by eight inches wide (though in the early seventies, it was slightly shorter and skinnier) and is shaped vaguely like a miniature surfboard. On the bottom of the deck are two metal assemblies called trucks, one near the nose of the board and the other a few inches from the tail. Protruding from the base of the trucks are cylindrical rods known as kingpins, which have bushings on them, and perpendicular to the kingpins are the axles. At each of the four ends of these is a wheel coupled to the axle with bearings.

By 1975 many choices faced the skateboard consumer. The primitive wooden plank was no longer the norm, though there were plenty of homemade and woodshop-shaped models out there, particularly where there weren't stores selling equipment. Skating supported a few specialized companies and offered a sideline for some surfboard companies and a couple of toy manufacturers in the sixties, then in the mid-seventies went from almost no sales to a late capitalist flowering of an industry geared to providing skateboard equipment. The number of choices went from the minimal to the maximum in a short span of time, something like the Cambrian explosion 540 million years ago with its evolutionary profusion of body types. And like the Cambrian explosion, this spurt of growth and divergent developments went on at a frantic pace for a while and then leveled off, with many of the species not making it.

The proliferation of forms led to a heightened emphasis on technological virtues. Advertisements were mostly concerned with proclaiming superiority over rival competitors, mixing valid-sounding technical information with deliriously pseudo-scientific claims. After the Cadillac wheel debuted (followed immediately by the Meta-Flex wheel, which was also urethane but used a different manufacturing process), options in wheels became legion. At first clear red wheels prevailed, looking like hardened strawberry Jell-O. Soon after, there were green wheels, white wheels, orange wheels, "mag" wheels with hubs, all sorts of hardnesses and sizes. Size was measured in millimeters indicating the height of the wheel and hardness, calibrated in the durometer scale of a hundred. Hardness ran from the marshmallowy (77–85), best on asphalt and the choice of downhillers, to the harder (90–98), better suited to smooth surfaces.

The bearings that kept wheels revolving on the truck axle were nearly as important as the wheels themselves. Sealed precision bearings were almost universally adopted by 1975. They allowed the wheel to spin better and faster than loose ball bearings, and they didn't fall out all the time. Bennett made the first axle specifically designed for the new bearings, and the rest of the truck manufacturers followed suit. Tracker was around from the beginning with their distinctive wedge-shaped axle housing. Independent and Gullwing came out a little later, and the three companies have survived to this day. There were ACS, the Pittsburgh truck, Apex, Pool Rats and many others that didn't survive. There were trucks with differently angled kingpins and exotic departures from the usual design, like the Stroker, which had a square torsion bar as an axle that provided a shock-absorber effect.

Boards became specialized for different disciplines. There were boards for downhill, slalom, freestyle and pool riding. There were also longboards. Everybody who could had a quiver with a variety of boards—the quiver photo was a mainstay in the magazines at the time. There was a lot of discussion about the merits of stiff boards versus boards with flex, a debate similar to the one between soft skis for moguls and powder and stiff skis for racing. Flex was supposed to be crucial for pumping through turns in slalom, though some used stiff boards and beat all comers. There were boards with adjustable flex. Cheaper decks were made out of plastic, often a bright banana yellow. There were serious attempts with metal and aluminum boards, but the evolution went toward wood boards of birch, cedar, ash or oak and then on to boards with five of seven plys. The choices were dizzying, and decks of wildly dissimilar quality for a number of specialties were all competing in the market.

Advances arose in minor components as well. What kept the trucks attached to the board went from wood screws to mounting hardware made expressly for that purpose. Riser pads (a block of wood, later plastic, about half an inch thick) between the truck and the board allowed for extra space between the wheels and the board so the wheels didn't "rub out" on the bottom of the board during turns. A major breakthrough was grip tape, a mild sandpaper applied to the top of the board to improve traction. Plain black grip became the standard, though along the way there were some abominations like pizza grip, which looked like its name and was imbedded with razor-sharp rocks that caused a lot of bloody encounters between skaters' skin and their boards. A very important ancillary development was the modification of the kicktail at the end of the deck. An angled tail that gave a rider leverage to unweight the front two wheels had been around as a concept in the sixties, but now it went from being a triangular piece of wood nailed on to an organic part of the shaped skateboard.

All of these innovations were vital and lasting. In some shape or form, they are part of every skateboard ridden today. The product profusion also engendered a bevy of forgettable gizmos and gadgets, along with claims in advertisements that read like testimonials for weapons guidance systems in *Aviation Week and Space Technology*. "Unidirectional fiberglass" and "strength beyond T-6" were probably legitimate, but what about "high-strength resin systems" and "hardcore isothalic polyester and silica cells"? Whatever panned out or didn't, it was a heady and exciting time of multiple choices and skater-driven advances. In its expression of individuality in design it followed the painted surfboard and the sedan customized as a work of art. There was a conceptual link to the Los Angeles delinquent underground of pinstriping cars as practiced by Von Dutch and Ed Roth and others. In the manufactured sense and in personal adaptations, skateboards carried on the Southern California tradition of throwing dignity out the window and riding forth to seek romance. The skateboard instilled itself in the fabric of the city as an artifact of a way of life, an activity that borrowed from surfing and applied it to the automobile's terrain.

All this progress was indispensable to skateboarding's development. But the most significant movement was happening on the skateboards. And that had to do with skateboarders, not manufacturers. The latter supplied the inert tools that the riders took from their source over the isthmus to worldwide contagion. The riders were the avant-garde who made the object sing and realized its potential.

Chapter Four
Dogtown Rising

S oon after World War II, Los Angeles underwent a massive transformation. Industry rushed in and the orange groves were lost to frenzied urbanization. Water became too expensive, smog began to affect the trees and the citrus farmers couldn't compete. There was an influx of new people, and new houses were built for them to live in. The suburbs drew closer and closer to the San Gabriel Mountains. Fires denuding the hillsides and seasonal rainfall that sometimes yielded as much as thirty inches in six days loosed vast mudslides from the mountains down on all those residents of the growing metropolis. The feature unique to Los Angeles that was so decidedly a factor in the rebirth of skating was its varied terrain, and it was partly through attempts to hold back the mountains that its geology and geography set the stage for the celebration of the extreme physical pursuit that is skateboarding.

The human defenses against these natural forces are multifold. They are replacements for natural river systems—two thousand miles of underground conduits, concrete-lined open stream channels and at least 120 bowl-shaped excavations. These pits are designed for the express purpose of catching debris (in the form of earth and boulders) as it slides off the hills, before it can get to citizens' houses and crush them. They were built by the Los Angeles Flood Control District beginning in the early twentieth century and are maintained by the Sedimentation Section of the L.A. County Department of Public Works. The oval basins can be as big as football stadiums, though they are usually smaller catchments, with capacities of about one hundred thousand cubic yards, that some people call reservoirs. They are made of smooth concrete. They are big stationary waves, and they are eminently skateable.

Above and beyond the efforts of the Sedimentation Section, L.A. had tens of thousands of the exact opposite of debris basins. These turquoise liquid receptacles of the American dream were status symbols, emblems of material success, totems of that search for physical perfection that Southern California had long excelled at. Swimming pools of all sizes, from B shapes to kidneys to the more extravagant rabbit-shaped pool of a Beverly Hills magician and the football form in the backyard of O. J. Simpson to other flights of fancy along the lines of departed wonders like Alla Nazimova's pool, built in the outline of the Black Sea to remind her of her childhood Yalta. In the middle of the seventies all these pools fell prey to a severe drought. Directives were issued to conserve water—shorten showers and water lawns only on allotted days. Water had become too scarce for pleasure. A lot of pools were left empty and dry.

Pools are normally drained for cleaning, but the drought of 1975 to 1976 caused an epochal shift in skateboarding. The shift and split that followed had some of its roots in the differences between San Diego and Los Angeles. Down south in San Diego, skaters were mostly doing freestyle, a trick-oriented style that hadn't changed much from the sixties. They kept their bank riding to mellow walls like Escondido's reservoir; there was a lot of slalom at La Costa and other hills. They utilized the southland's presuburban sprawl of freshly asphalted streets for subdivisions that didn't yet exist.

The focus of skating at the time was known as flatland freestyle. These were the same tricks that were done from 1961 to 1967, maybe done better now because of the upgraded equipment. Three-sixties (with the back foot perpendicular to the board and the front foot angled parallel, as many revolutions as possible), walking the dog (stepping the back foot over to the front of the board, turning it 180 degrees, stepping over again and repeating), nose wheelies (balancing the back wheels off the ground—one-footed, squatting, going in circles), headstands and handstands: variations on low-impact gymnastics using the board as a platform instead of a balance beam, manipulating the board with the feet while rolling. Many believed at the time that these tricks were the core of skating. And in a way they were, because variations were being invented daily. It might have been slow and unspectacular, slightly ridiculous and quaint in hindsight, but freestyle's legacy and reverberations keep coming back up through the present day.

But up north in the urban space of Los Angeles, the skaters weren't only skating the streets, they were often taking their surf-style skating to schoolyards with their banked walls, the debris basins and, most prophetically, empty pools. That these vertical walls were most often in private backyards didn't matter.

By the summer of 1975, skateboarding had exploded across the country. If it could still be called a fad, it was now a long-lived and pervasive one. *Skateboarder* magazine rose from the ashes and came out with the first issue of phase two in 1975. Not only were kids across the country clamoring for and riding skateboards, developments were brewing nearer the epicenter in Santa Monica, San Pedro, Carlsbad and Pomona pools.

At first glance what was portrayed in the magazine did not, besides the fashion and equipment changes of ten years, look much different than what was shown in the sixties. But underneath the surface, things were definitely different. The obvious outward sign was that the magazine was in color and much thicker than it had been in its previous incarnation. There were a lot more advertisements; skating had blossomed as a viable economic activity that would soon grow to an industry with hundreds of millions of dollars in annual sales. It had also emerged as a movement on its own terms. Though the clothes and style and references were still almost universally related to surfing, a new breed was coming up who didn't necessarily surf. The magazine's first issue was filled with pictures of people doing handstands, 360s and nose wheelies—the same old tricks. But the cover showed something else, and that said it all. Looking back, you can see the blueprint of what was to come.

The color picture on the cover showed a skater suspended halfway up the wall of an eight-foot-deep pool: barefoot with his arms outstretched, defying gravity, taking concrete reality and treating it like a wave while smiling with his long blond hair flowing. It was Gregg Weaver, soon to be one of skating's first celebrities. He was such an exemplar of the vibe and place that his renown extended outside of skating; there is a long-standing urban legend that the perennial favorite by the cocaine-fueled band the Eagles, "Hotel California," was inspired by him.

The continuum from swimming along the surface of water to surfing on the permeable face of a wave was now translated to a stationary, solid object. Surfing is balancing on a liquid that poses the danger of drowning. With a nod to skiing, a sort of surfing on water in its frozen state that has its own possibilities of submersion by powder and avalanche, surfer Gregg Weaver was taking that skimming over wave and snow and bringing it to the opposite of liquid—concrete; hard, static and unforgiving, at once made with water and paradoxically a container for it. In pool riding, the strange combination of natural urges and nature subdued by them, the desire for flight combined with the wave is taken to the man-made.

The picture of Gregg Weaver on the cover of *Skateboarder* is a defining image, announcing to the larger world the shift that had occurred before the issue hit the newsstands. Two years after the urethane wheel, the fire was raging and multitudes of people were skating, especially in Southern California. There was an epidemic— streets, spillways, schoolyards and pools were all being assaulted. The Bahne-Cadillac skateboard championships (also known as the Del Mar Nationals) were held in the summer of 1975. The events were slalom, downhill and freestyle. It was the first time in skating's revival that people from all over, four hundred contestants in all, converged in the same place. Those who hadn't had exposure to other skaters were brought together (there had been no magazine or media coverage up to that point) and saw what everyone else was doing. The isolation period came to an end, and future truths were revealed. The truth was a shock.

Some of the skaters who came to the contest weren't into the muscular flatland-freestyle trip. They wore a semblance of a uniform, with their team T-shirts and Vans shoes, but their ripped jeans and unruly hair contrasted with the other competitors' clean-cut looks. With a tangible ghetto swagger they pushed their way through the crowd to the registration table led by their "manager," who was carrying a briefcase and wearing a fedora, white dress shoes and a purple Hawaiian print shirt. The first team member to ride in the freestyle event was a fourteen-year-old with long, scraggly blond hair. He pushed toward the edge, picking up speed while staying low to his board. When he was almost at the brink, he crouched even lower and slid frontside with one hand on the ground and the other in the air, his body practically touching the surface, turned 180 degrees and continued his run. He went just as fast for the rest of his two minutes and didn't do a single handstand or pirouette. The spectators in the bleachers were audibly astounded. What they were seeing was almost unbelievable. There were now two diametrically opposed sensibilities. It was as if a Willem de Kooning painting suddenly appeared in a nineteenth-century Paris salon. Or as team member Nathan Pratt later said, "It was like Ferraris versus Model Ts."

Needless to say, minds were blown. The modern age of skateboarding had started. The skater was Jay Adams, the association was the Zephyr Team and the manager was Skip Engblom. They were the Z-Boys, and they were from Dogtown, *ese.* And Dogtown was about to be ascendant.

Dogtown was a byname for Venice and Santa Monica. Its skating roots went back to the surfers of the late fifties and the original skaters who had come from the area in the sixties. Dogtown was a part of a real metropolis that dated back at least a hundred years, not a recently sprouted contrivance like San Diego. Added to that was the area's place in the national psyche: it was where Route 66 came to an end, and pilgrims parked at the pier after crossing the country to the promised land and ran into the sea. It had a symbolic significance, the end of the road, the focal point of a manifest destiny of leisure and escape. It was also the location for thousands of movies and television shows; it signified the California dream and still does. There was a self-awareness in the locals of their hometown's place in the world's dream consciousness. And the nascent Dogtowners had grown up exposed to a population that had been surfing and skating for a long time, people who had skated the roads in the Hollywood Hills when there were brush fires raging, who had carved down the off-ramps of the still-under-construction 405 freeway into traffic full of new Mavericks and Valiants, who had skated past surfing champion Peter Peterson's surf shop in the sixties and been appraised and looked at as little kids who didn't know anything. These were people who were aware of history, of skating's roots.

After 1973, Santa Monica and Venice had a bunch of kids who were surfing and skating the debris basins and the banked walls at the Kenter, Bellagio and Paul Revere schools in Beverly Hills and Brentwood. Torger Johnson, Davey Hill, Danny Bearer and other luminaries of the Makaha and Hobie teams from skating's first wave were still riding and passed their knowledge on to the younger set. The new kids skated the eternally glassy banks at the schoolyards and looked up to the Australian surfers who were pioneering the short-board aggressive style—Wayne Lynch, Nat Young, Midget Farrell and the Hawaiians Barry Kanaiapuni and Larry Bertleman. The link with these surfers was so strong that some of Dogtown's prime movers referred to their low, fast cutbacks and off-the-lips adapted to concrete as "Bertleman style."

They surfed and skated a lot. That was almost all they did. They also had a big advantage in location. Besides waves, they had the banks, the reservoirs, the pools. But it wasn't only the terrain that was the crucible; it was the culture of Dogtown itself that produced this group that was to have an immeasurable impact on skating. Dogtown was a place where the main surf spot was a dangerous break next to the Pacific Ocean Park Pier, a ruin that had once housed an amusement park under which bums lived, gay men had encounters and junkies went about their intravenous business. It wasn't Gidget's beach. The scene was territorial, to put it mildly. Interlopers were met with a punch in the face or had their cars sabotaged to dissuade them from coming back. The skater kids surfed and also performed "rat patrol" duties to earn their place in the lineup, sitting on the pier throwing rocks and bottles at outsiders who made the mistake of trying to surf there. Away from the pier, downtown Santa Monica was a desolate collection of liquor stores and boarded-up storefronts. In school, the skaters dealt with riots and heavy gang activity, from the cholo sets of Barrio Sotel and Santo to the black Bloods and Crips. This atmosphere undoubtedly contributed to their manic combative energy. Nathan Pratt summed up the Z-Boy attitude as "screw you": "The skate style follows the lifestyle, when you're dealing with bikers, vatos and Bloods every day, you've got to have your shit together."

The Z-Boys were Jay Adams, Tony Alva, Stacy Peralta, Shogo Kubo, Bob Biniak, Nathan Pratt, Paul Constantineau, Wentzle Ruml, Jim Muir, Peggy Oki, Chris Cahill and Allen Sarlo. Their hangout was the Jeff Ho and Zephyr Productions surf shop, owned by surfboard shaper Jeff Ho and vagabond surfer Skip Engblom. Part of the shop served as the studio of longtime surfer and skater C. R. Stecyk III, a writer, photographer and self-described cultural anthropologist whose texts and images became defining documents of the skating ethos. The shop sold their own surfboards and a clothing line. They also served as vendors for quaaludes and firecrackers and other sundry items that made their way into the inventory. At night bands played and the shop turned into the local social club. Alva, Adams, Kubo and Peralta were on the shop's junior surf team, the team that "You didn't try out for, you just belonged," which evolved into the Zephyr competition skate team. Out of this came a way of skating and living that was to have effects of epic proportion in skateboarding.

It was the beginning of what Stacy Peralta would later characterize as "the good times, to-the-max times, everybody was pretty crazy." They became what can only be described as stars to skate urchins the world over. They had a primary impact on those who actually saw them ride and saw how they behaved. In a broader and ultimately farther-reaching way, their style and image galvanized incalculable numbers of people who never saw them in person. Their appeal was based on a healthy disrespect for authority, a sort of antisocial radicalism and the avant-gardism of their skating. It was a combination of rabid skating and living with a backdrop of surfing historicism and cholo iconography. They were a coterie that was hard to ignore. As Tony Alva put it, "You could never find a more aggressive, arrogant, rowdy, perhaps ignorant bunch of people than me and my friends." It was the era of the skater as obnoxious rock star, maybe infuriating but simultaneously irresistible. And this was when rock stars really acted the part.

Jay Adams was a primal force, with his mouth twisted into a contemptuous snarl as he grinded coping blocks so hard they were jolted out of place. There were also his outrageous forward-looking tricks. He was all instinct, all id. Alva was his complementary ego, the leader of the pack, not only as a skater but as an ideal. Alva's insouciance seared itself into the minds of countless would-be skaters: braggadocio tempered by an articulateness that offended and endeared; a prototypical antihero, a distorted acrobatic Holden Caulfield with exotic part–Native American looks under a cascade of dirty-blond dreadlocks. His first interview in *Skateboarder* was an ex post facto confirmation of his importance. The cover blurb was

"The World's Hottest Skater." C. R. Stecyk did the interview and hit the nail on the head in his introduction: "Alva is the one skater with the across-the-board appeal to surpass the boundaries of the skateboard sport/art."

Alva was also presented as "The Prototypical Z-Boy, Mr. Electric, Mr. Man of the Moment" and, more precisely, as "The Man of the Movement." For those who didn't read, Stecyk's photos made it clear. Alva, with his big hair, wearing a white pantsuit with a red arrow on his chest pointing southward while throwing a bucketful of red paint toward the camera—what more needed to be said or shown? He was pictured in his more characteristic gear—shorts, striped sports socks and no shirt—kickturning backside on coping, the height of radicalism at the time. Under the photos were captions taken from his own words: "I just skate and don't talk bullshit" and "When I skate, it's towards the Nugent, Hendrix, Zeppelin style." He explained what had occurred at the Del Mar Nationals and after as the Dogtowners "not doing bullshit tricks . . . people are just now starting to flash on how heavy it all was."

In a period when everyone was "flashing" on something—a trick, a concept, a worldview—people were definitely flashing on Alva and his cohorts. All of that could have been just hot air, an after-the-fact burnishing of his reputation. Surely some of the Dogtown rhetoric was overblown, but there was no doubt that they had done something, or stumbled upon something, unprecedented. When asked, they all tried to come to terms with it. Nathan Pratt, the most enigmatic and intellectual of them, offered a succinct appraisal: "We were obviously more evolved . . . we blew their minds." He was right—their intense impact continued in skating for at least ten years and after that was disseminated in a less overt but still pervasive way, often into areas outside of skating, to people who didn't even know where the influence came from. Dogtown was almost a religion in the way it touched converts.

The Dogtowners had a mission at the midpoint of the decade. Along with skaters at the L pool in the inland empire east of Los Angeles, in the San Fernando Valley and everywhere else in Southern California, they began a wholesale invasion of private pools, an act of mass trespassing and athletic civil disobedience. It was a full-scale, inherently criminal assault. As longtime editor of *Thrasher* magazine Jake Phelps put it, "It was the ultimate buccaneering sport . . . we're in your backyard, we're grinding your pool, you're not here." Pools were everywhere, and their owners weren't always home, and skaters were addicted to skating pools, so the obvious happened. Aside from a few tile rides in the sixties, this was an unprecedented new frontier to be explored. The pool invasion was unstoppable, and it pushed skating forward to an irrevocable break with its surfing and freestyle past.

Though some pools were at abandoned houses, most were on private occupied land and needed to be infiltrated. There were many inventive methods of doing this. Stacy Peralta drove the alleys of Beverly Hills with Jay Adams on the roof of his car, looking over fences into potential backyards. Alva hired a chauffeur to drive him around and search. The ones who could got into the city hall of records or hired planes to fly them over likely territory. Other schemes included asking a female accomplice to pose as the wife in a couple interested in buying a house that had a pool, or using a fake sheriff badge to impersonate an undercover officer. Some went legitimate as pool maintenance men to gain access. Pools were drained during the night while a family slept in the house and were skated the next day. Pools might be skateable for months, days or less than an hour before the police came and the skaters were forced to run for it. The owners of the house might show up, or too many people would hear about it and overcrowding and graffiti would result, or some kook would break his arm and insist on calling an ambulance, leading to a pool's demise. Whatever happened, whatever the obstacles, there was no stopping the onslaught.

The early stages weren't that different from the unknown skater's carve a few feet above the scum line in Pacific Palisades ten years earlier. The antecedent was quickly surpassed. Initially it was carving, going up the wall and making an arced turn with all four wheels staying on the surface. It was a big deal if the tiles were gained. Soon they went beyond the tiles to the coping, the rounded protuberance of an inch or so at the top of the pool. They hit the coping with their wheels, then got one wheel above the top, and the grind was born. It is a simple primal act, the scraping of the back truck on the coping, creating a loud barking sound. From there the next step was the kickturn, lifting the two front wheels at the apex of momentum to turn 180 degrees, a way of turning from straight up to straight down, either frontside (with the skater's back facing the bottom of the pool) or backside. Just gyrating back and forth, pumping from wall to wall doing forevers (consecutive kickturns), was a trick at that point. Waldo Autry claimed that he did the first kickturns in pools, though it easily could have been someone else. There was also the fakie—going backward—which came about out of improvisation: going up to the top, not turning and, in an instant of seat-of-the-pants inspiration, just rolling down backward. That was probably done first by Nicky Vlaco in San Pedro, but again it might have been someone else. There are no precise records for how these basics of vertical maneuvering came about. They'd figured out how to get around the pool, to the top and back down again in a number of ways. They'd consummated the marriage of centrifugal force and the skate platform. Next came the use of the walls as a stepping stone.

These seemingly simple and primitive basics became the building blocks for everything that followed, for every aerial twelve feet above coping. The fact that they were doing it at all was so incredible it beggared comprehension. A lot of people didn't get it, as an encounter between Stacy Peralta and local television newsman Ray Duncan at a skatepark in 1977 plainly demonstrated.

Duncan told Peralta, "I've never seen anything like this."

Peralta replied, "There's never been anything like this."

Not only had people never seen anything like it, the riders had never done anything like it. Skating pools was an extension of what had been done in the past, but it was straying into a realm that wasn't derivative of anything. The grinding got harder and longer. There were carves over the steps and then grinds over the "death box," the foot-long and six-inch-high rectangular hole at tile level where a pool's filter is located. After that, pools couldn't contain the riders. They started skating up and out of the pool onto flimsy wooden extensions set up above the coping, kickturning two or three feet above the top, or flying out past the lip and bailing. The inevitable happened: the break with gravity and surface, the break with accepted mental concepts. Riding to the coping and blasting out, the speed of the skater propelling his body above the perimeter of the pool, the momentum off the coping bouncing the board up and into his hand. Momentarily suspended, with one hand grasping the board and the other extended for balance, he achieved flight before falling back into the pool and riding to the other side. Like the kickturn and the fakie, the air was born of expanding ambition. The kickturn and the fakie were important, but they were no match for the dramatic effect of the air. With the development of the aerial, skating literally made a leap off the surface into controlled flight.

Before these "real" airs came plenty of foreshadowing. Skaters dropping off of picnic tables, flying out of bowls, Nathan Pratt's and Paul Hackett's "assisted" (using straps across the feet to keep the board attached) experiments, Tom Inouye's almost backside airs at Skatetopia skatepark. These were serious attempts and precursors but not the real thing. The first genuine frontside air to be seen by the public was in a spread of Tony Alva in the January 1978 *Skateboarder*. In a color Glen E. Friedman photo, he was suspended a few inches above the legendary Dogbowl in Santa Monica wearing a fedora. The caption was "Tony Alva, Transcending Planes." Again, whether he was the first is a point of contention and not really important. He certainly was the first to be shown above the coping in the midst of an independent directional aerial. The photograph brought the concept and reality of air to many others and added to Alva's already growing reputation as an innovator.

There were other things going on. Berts (frontside slides with one hand down, via Larry Bertleman and the Z-Boys) were being done on vertical, most notably by Jay Adams. He was also photographed doing backside proto-handplants, grabbing the board with one hand and going upside down with his other hand on the pool's wall. This was beyond belief, whether or not he was making it. Just seeing the attempt opened up minds to multiple possibilities. The rupture with gravity and freestyle had transpired. Whether or not they were just for kids, tricks in pools were gaining currency. They were the future of skateboarding.

Chapter Five
Play and the Futility
of Competition

Older than humanity is the irrationality of play, the freedom of no discernible purpose. Play is eternal in skateboarding, from the child on the scooter in the forties to the best trick scientists of today. No matter how intense it is, skating is play. With the explosion of skating's popularity in the seventies, a culture arose around that inner core.

Dogtown at its height defined the most attention-getting part of the emergent culture. But outside of that was an inclusive wider spectrum with the common denominator of riding a board with four wheels. Millions of people had skateboards and were using them in ways that might not have equaled the frontside air in radicalism but were no less important. They were riding them to school and to the store, cruising down sidewalks and carving driveways. The freestyle that the Z-Boys had rejected and on one level made obsolete, at least temporarily, was still very popular and the most accessible aspect to the majority of skateboarders. The extremism of the Z-Boys and the other vertical pioneers was slow to filter down to the regular skater—the usual scenario of the vanguard taking a while to become acceptable and attainable to a larger populace. Most people didn't have the Dog Bowl or the Vermont Drop to skate; they were riding cheap plastic boards and turning down the sidewalk. Skating was serious play to some, a not so serious, fun fad to others. People from both camps fell under the spell of skating and its possibilities. In the blooming years of 1976 and 1977, there were three main types of skating besides vertical: downhill, slalom and freestyle.

Downhill is the most basic facet of skating, harnessing gravity to achieve speed going down an incline. On a skateboard the ante is upped quite a bit, since falling on asphalt can have a lot bloodier result than on water or snow. Skaters in the sixties were going up to fifty miles an hour, a feat that boggles the mind considering the equipment they were using. By the mid-seventies, velocities near the fifty-five-mile-an-hour freeway speed limit were not uncommon. Somebody on a thirty-inch-long wooden board going that fast on asphalt, even with the improvements of urethane wheels and sealed bearings, enters a realm of dementia and nerve that is hard to find a comparison to. Yoga teacher and downhiller Dennis Shufeldt put the attractions of speed into words in a 1975 *Skateboarder* article: "The feel of the wind, the sound of spinning wheels, and my vision blurred at the sides trigger a rush of adrenaline that excited me to the point of ignorant bliss." Ignorance is bliss when all that matters is staying on top of your wooden plank while rocketing down a backcountry road. Speed has an allure that is hard to match.

Shufeldt's yoga leanings may seem a little silly in the context of skating, but they were very much a part of the period. Skating was new and radical, but it was also happening at the same time that transactional analysis, birthstone rings and interest in the Bermuda Triangle were flourishing. It isn't surprising that in this climate, many skaters listened to Santana and extolled the virtues of health food and tai chi. Shufeldt's attitude was just a reflection of the uniquely Californian worldview that was prevalent. "Harmony of mind and body must be required by individuals so that they may clearly consider all the variables" was followed by "Witnessing harmony in a self-created situation is mastering the moment. Freedom in the NOW." Shufeldt called the hill the "energy source," and whether it sounds corny or not, it's true, just as the wave and the ski slope are the energy source for the surfer and skier. The absolute mental confidence and lack of analysis required during downhill are still at the heart of skating.

Early on, downhill was central to skating in a way that it never would be again. It hasn't disappeared entirely though, and the current revival is yielding intriguing anachronisms like frontside air innovator George Orton (he went airborne at almost the same time as Alva) reaching stand-up speeds of fifty-five miles per hour at age forty-one. During its golden age, Shufeldt, John Hutson (arguably the greatest; he won the most races), Guy Grundy, Bob Madrigal, Mike Williams, Dave Dilberg, Tommy Ryan, Bruce Logan and others were pictured rushing down hills in a crouched position with their arms either forward or behind to present an aerodynamic profile. There was a lot of discussion of equipment, in particular which wheels were fastest. There was a correlation with the then underground rise of speed skiing, the quest for the highest velocity on skis going straight down extremely steep slopes. (An early practitioner was Steve McKinney, the first person to reach 125 miles per hour, a speed that has the skier literally flying on a cushion of air. A little while later he was killed by a semi that crashed into his car as he slept in it on the side of the highway.) McKinney and the downhill skaters were into pure speed—and on the scale of near insanity, a skater going fifty miles per hour is at least the equal of a skier going 125 miles per hour. Downhill is the antithesis of freestyle; it is a pursuit where turning is superfluous and quickness of motion is the goal.

The Signal Hill contest in the summer of 1977 was downhill at its best and worst, and also a swan song for that kind of organized racing's popularity within the skating community. Mike Goldman had the fastest time of the stand-up riders with his arms behind him, but the real excitement and attention went to luge riders lying down on long boards and modified "enclosed fairing" skate vehicles that had more in common with Bonneville Salt Flats rocket cars than skateboards. There was a lot of experimentation with equipment, a lot of speed and a lot of spills. "Get a skateboard!" was yelled quite a few times from the sidelines as non-stand-up vehicles went by. Some of the riders were going down on their stomachs, wearing leathers and steel-tipped boots, and Terry Nails's brakes failed on his streamlined "car," sending him crashing into hay bales and flying thirty feet into a nearby intersection. Certainly this made it exciting for the spectators, and the "riders" had to be at least applauded for their derring-do—though the questions of what exactly they were doing and whether or not it was skateboarding went unanswered.

Concurrent with the heyday of downhill was an equally vibrant slalom scene that has almost entirely disappeared—though it certainly lives on in spirit, for what else is the skater going from ledge to rail doing than some kind of slalom steeplechase? Slalom's roots were in ski racing; it is the combination of downhill speed with the intuitive act of turning. Slalom racing used small orange cones (or soda cans or rocks or whatever else was available) placed a few feet apart, and skaters rode in a narrower stance or with both feet together on the middle of the board, parallel to its sides, pumping turns with their hips swiveling, timed against a clock or head-to-head. There was much deliberation over how much flex a board should have, and the speed possibilities of different wheels and bearings were also a big concern.

Bobby Piercy, Bob Skoldberg, Henry Hester, Chris Yandall, Bruce Walker, Danny Trailer, Stacy Peralta, Conrad Miyoshi and

Lance Smith were some of the leading lights of slalom, though there was a lot of crossing over with downhillers doing slalom and slalomers riding pools and vice versa. The skater-organized races were emblematic of skating's seventies vibe, with people racing barefoot in short shorts with their hair flowing in the wind, vans parked nearby and girlfriends looking on. It was laid-back and souled-out. Winning or losing wasn't too important, it was do your own thing with people getting together and having fun.

Freestyle was broadly defined. It was "free" so it encompassed everything besides downhill and slalom. Strictly speaking, freestyle was (and is, though like downhill and slalom, it has all but disappeared as a separate entity) comprised of the flatland tricks that were the legacy of the sixties: 360s, nose wheelies, handstands, high jumps and barrel jumps—jumping for distance from one board to another over barrels. There were new tricks like one-handed handstands and two-board 360s; some people did up to a hundred with a board under each foot. The most advanced maneuver was the kickflip, in which the rider used a toe under one rail to lift the board into the air and flip it 360 degrees before landing on it. This was the board trickology that pointed toward an unforeseen future. In the late seventies, freestyle opened up to include more and more variations of previous tricks and the combination of new maneuvers with movement.

There were many contests with skaters doing routines to the Beach Boys, Aerosmith, Chicago and Boston. Long-lasting nose wheelies led to 360s and a moving handstand before maybe flying off a small ramp. It was loosely choreographed rolling gymnastics, introducing as many moves as possible with quick footwork in the allotted forty-five seconds. The contests continued, but as time went on, freestyle was featured less in the magazines. This was partly because it wasn't as visually stunning as vertical riding. A picture of someone doing a stationary nose wheelie couldn't compete with a skater one-wheeling on a plank above a ten-foot-deep pool. The contests were held through the mid-eighties, but freestyle increasingly came to occupy the role of the geeky, uncool younger brother in skating. There was something to the answer Jay Adams gave in 1977 to the question of what he thought the future of freestyle was: "Everyone will give it up 'cause pools and parks are more fun." Whether they were more fun was an opinion, but there is no doubt that freestyle got relegated to the margins.

There was a time, though, when everybody engaged in flat-land freestyle, including legends like Torger Johnson and all the Dogtowners. A partial list of other notables includes Steve Cathey, Desiree Von Essen, Russ Howell, Ty Page, Ellen O'Neal, Doug Saladino, Chris Chaput, Paul Hoffman, Robin Logan, Skitch Hitchcock and Ed Nadalin. All were freestylers, and they pushed skating forward with their innovations, as well as taking these advances to other terrains besides flat ground.

Freestyle was universal because it could be done by anybody, anywhere. There was no need for a pool or even a hill, just some flat pavement. There was variety in the tricks and ideas to build upon. There were certainly more things to try in freestyle in 1977 than the basics of kickturns and fakies being done in pools. Its allure lay in possibility and accessibility. The problem, particularly in contests, was the constraints put on riders. In some contests there were even compulsory routines. This made freestyle a sort of antiskating; it made it not free. Putting up barriers to what could be done went against the skater's prerogative to do whatever he or she wanted in whatever style they chose. There was something incongruous about freestyle dying out in part because of its stifling of exuberance.

Though skating had these divisions, with leaders in each category, there was a lot of interdisciplinary back-and-forth. There were specialists like Russ Howell, who was known for doing numerous 360s. That was no mean feat, but it was a very specific skill, like that of the designated hitter in baseball or the placekicker in football. Twenty years later, the divisions in skating have fallen away; they've been recombined and hybridized. All the different parts have mostly melded into a somewhat organic whole.

The most groundbreaking aspect of skating was undoubtedly vertical riding. It bears repeating just how incomprehensible, even to the skaters themselves, it was at first. Stacy Peralta relates how he and Bob Biniak were skating a keyhole pool in Beverly Hills in 1975 and got into a debate over whether it was possible to do a frontside kickturn on vertical. Peralta said it could be done, while Biniak thought it was impossible. No one in the world had done it yet; they weren't even sure the human body could move that way on a vertical wall. Needless to say, Biniak did it two days later, with Peralta egging him on. It was this newness that added to vertical riding's inflammatory nature. Its defiance of improbabilities inspired many. More pictures of bowl riding appeared in the magazines, crowding out photos of other types of skating. The images that vertical provided were intoxicating, they were iconic, and they impregnated minds all over the world.

The urge to compete is ancient. It is the measuring of achievement, the testing of limits, an inclination ingrained in the human psyche. It isn't too far-fetched to see it as an extension of the contest to survive, albeit in a form where life usually isn't at stake. This will to compete is an awkward fit with skating, which is a realm where competition is an intensely personal, often solitary, affair. Yet contests have always been a part of skating. There are contests when a few friends get together, big media spectacles where a lot of money is at stake, and contests like the Del Mar Nationals of 1975 that are historical turning points. Most smaller contests are humble affairs, with a minimum of competitive zeal and a maximum of camaraderie. Typical prizes are free boards and other equipment. Bigger contests have cash prizes and get magazine coverage, but until recently they have been the exception rather than the rule.

In the old days with slalom and downhill, who won was easily quantifiable, since it was a matter of times in getting from the start to the finish line. Assessing performance for freestyle or pool riding or street skating is another matter altogether, since it involves "judging," which is inherently subjective. As in ice skating or any other "interpretive" sport, the whole idea of judging can be a little ridiculous. Beyond that problem is the very nature of skating itself. Its freedom of spirit is what makes it antithetical to controlled contests and regimentation. Skating is too nuanced to be judged well. Many skaters bring a bone-deep wariness and skepticism to the whole contest concept, making them a somewhat compromised phenomenon.

Competitions have been and always will be important in a number of ways. They're a way for skaters to make a name for themselves; a gathering of the tribes where people make new friends and see new tricks unveiled; an open forum where limits are pushed. Skating is also exposed to potential converts, and manufacturers get to promote their wares and be identified with their riders. But contests, no matter how good they are, represent everything many people get into skating to avoid—rules and the mentality of judging and one-upmanship that competition fosters. That is why skating is the only sporting activity where someone will get the crowd's (i.e., other skaters) support and cheers for wearing a wig or a dress during their run, for skating drunk, for falling spectacularly, or for any other action that subverts the tenets of organized competition. No matter what contests do for the "sport," many skaters feel indifference or a deep-seated ambivalence toward them.

Chapter Six
Hot Action

I n 1975 the culture that had grown up around skateboarding gave birth to its own media. The *Skateboarder* of the sixties was short-lived, more of a simple, homey hobbyist newsletter, especially compared to the color and frenetic graphic energy of the new version. With the magazine's reemergence, it became more engaged and aware than its predecessor. It was more expansive; it had become the window to a real subculture. And the writers seemed to have an understanding of skating's power and visibility, a self-confidence that reflected how many people were skating and how many people were about to be, across a wide spectrum of society. Skating now had an impact on the mainstream world, and that world was about to take notice of skateboarding in a big way.

The pages were full of advertisements for decks, wheels, trucks and clothes, not to mention ads for crocheted bikinis, puka-shell necklaces and "Primo Beer" and "Ski Stoned" T-shirts. On the cover were sunset-silhouetted skaters doing nose wheelies, and inside were ads for boards with one size wheel for the back truck and another for the front truck. Surf shops ran full-page mail-order ads picturing a plethora of complete boards and accessories, a tantalizing profusion that included surfboard leashes and sandals, to be ordered by unfortunates outside of California. There were new faces, new tricks, new spots, all displayed and written about and photographed in a magazine that was being sent out into the world, into the hands of greedily curious and enthralled neophytes who pored over the articles and photographs and fingered the pages into pulp.

There was something prescient about it, as if the publishers knew that skating was going to expand tremendously, that it would become an irrevocable part of culture and history. Skating was about to be a hothouse flower existing within a fishbowl of attention, so pervasive that it couldn't be ignored. It was about to lead to other magazines and books, to movies and to an episode of the television show *CHiPs,* involving criminal activity at a skatepark. Katharine Hepburn and Bing Crosby were now riding skateboards; soon there would be competitive organizations and professional skaters living off product endorsements. Many different segments of society investigated skating, and it was brazenly reaching outside itself. These were the salad days, the boisterous teenage years of skating. It was giddy with its own potential and ability to compel millions to roll on a four-wheeled wooden board.

There were other magazines, but *Skateboarder* was predominant. It was the internal organ of skateboarders everywhere, their color Bible. In format, it was the blueprint for all skateboard magazines to come. That consisted of an editorial, a letters section, information on new products, how-to descriptions of tricks with sequential photos, stories on contests and road trips, interviews with leading skaters, profiles of up-and-comers ("Who's Hot"), pictures sent in by readers and a "gossip" page. The color-photo gallery in the middle of the magazine was paramount, and this reliance on photography was as understandable then as it is now. Given the audience and content, visual communication had an obvious advantage over the written word.

The gossip, or "society," column in *Skateboarder* was called "Off-the-Wall," and it and its successors in other magazines cover the minutiae and internal conflicts and happenings within the cloistered world of skating. They are a mixture of gossip, items on who's riding for whom, and the goings-on of "industry" players, such as who's bought a house or a new car. "Off-the-Wall" and the others are the *New York Post*'s "Page 6" adapted to skating. There are a lot of "blind" items and nicknames; information is given in a slightly opaque, allusive style that can be deciphered only by hardcore followers of the scene. Besides these fairly trivial matters, the columns often include some kind of philosophizing on the state of skateboarding.

An item from "Off-the-Wall" in the first seventies issue of *Skateboarder* is a good example of skating magazines' dialogue with (and admonitions to) their readers: "Negative vibes are starting to prevail in the Southern California media. The radio has picked up on accidents in a pretty sensational way. It looks like the whole movie is repeating itself ten years later. Skateboarding can be dangerous, but so can aerosol cans, so can walking, driving and living." Aware of the past and foretelling the future, the item is a succinct rebuttal to the enemies of fun, and it speaks to skating's troubled relationship with broader society, a state of affairs that hasn't really changed since the sixties.

That first cover featuring Gregg Weaver was accompanied by type that read "Hot Action, High Speed, Radical Runs, Slalom, Tricks, Freestyle, Equipment Info." The concerns of the magazine were plain, and there wasn't going to be too much intellectualizing.

But the first editorial did manage to analyze skating's appeal and background intelligently: "For the last ten or fifteen years, man has come closer and closer to finding pure modes of expression just for the joy and the challenge. Surfing's pattern of constant equipment refinement made wave riding on short, responsive boards closer to flight than ever before. Surfers started snow skiing and sailing swift multi-hulls for the same rush. Then came hang gliding; as close as you could get to unencumbered flight. And now, most recently, skateboarding has joined the ranks of serious, artful, downhill motion sport; yet another form of physical and mental release in which you glide and swoop and experience the wildly exotic sensations of speed."

The general attitude was fairly clean-cut, portraying skating as a viable sport and downplaying unseemly behavior by skaters. Skaters were every bit as unruly then; their antics just weren't reported and celebrated in "Off-the-Wall" the way they would be in the magazines of today. There was an undercurrent of good intentions in those early issues, usually from older "industry" people and the magazine editors themselves. They were on a quest to earn legitimacy for what they understandably saw as a great "sport" that wasn't getting the respect it deserved. On a benign level, this was a well-meaning desire to see skating appreciated for what it is by a large audience—an athletic activity with interesting characters doing incredible feats that are incomprehensible to the general public. But there was another side to that desire for legitimacy, an attempt to sanitize skating's culture for mainstream tastes. A classic example of this attitude was spelled out in the first seventies issue of *Skateboarder:* "If skateboarding is to earn its acceptance as an ongoing form of sport, it will be necessary to demonstrate to parents, city fathers, and the world at large that it is indeed a genuine healthy and valid athletic activity with a surprising degree of depth, and that it deserves its place alongside other accepted recreational/sport activities." A nice sentiment, and true enough on one level, but in many ways wrongheaded or at best disingenuous. Certainly skating is great, but does it need or want acceptance? Therein lies the conflict between the do-gooders and the skaters. It is a forty-year-old unresolvable dichotomy. The noble or perhaps self-serving efforts of skating's defenders and saviors are often at odds with the reality of true skateboarding.

Many of the people who appeared in the early "Who's Hot" columns had been prime movers in the sixties, and several were to become influential practitioners in the seventies and beyond. Torger Johnson was an especially resonant figure who was ripping again in 1975, practicing "the new grand-prix style, which consists of doing everything you can, tricks and slalom combined, in a fluid, overall approach, which pretty well exemplifies Torger's whole lifestyle." He was a legend even then due to his nonspecialized riding, a harbinger of what would be crucial in skating two decades later. His mythic status was sadly compounded by his death in 1983 in a car accident on the island of Maui.

Tom Sims, known for his longboarding, went on to start Sims Skateboards and was also instrumental in the early manufacturing and drive for acceptance of snowboarding. Paul Hoffman would later do some forward-looking moves in freestyle; at this early stage he was being towed behind a bus at forty miles per hour and getting a ticket for his trouble. Danny Trailer was skating and "just enjoying flowing energy . . . celebration is what it's all about." Lonnie Toft was riding a much wider board (with "outrageous" engraved on the bottom) than most, a "pig" nine and a half inches wide with four sets of trucks and eight wheels. His and others' experiments with wide boards would soon become the standard. Gregg Weaver offered his respect for Larry Bertleman and Gerry Lopez, signifying how influential these two surfers still were, especially the Fu-Manchu-goatee-wearing Lopez, a master of Hawaiian big-wave riding. Surfing still cast a long shadow; there was a palpable anxiety of influence that emanated from skating's link to wave riding. Almost all the Dogtowners were in "Who's Hot" at some point, including Jay Adams, who was reported to have gotten a ticket for skating on the freeway and to have skate-snatched an old woman's wig as he passed her on the street.

One noticeable aspect of "Who's Hot" and the general coverage in the magazine were the numbers of women skating. Ellen Berryman, Laura Thornhill, Robin Logan, Kim Cespedes, Desiree Von Essen, Peggy Oki, Robin Alaway and Ellen O'Neal were just some of the women who made a name for themselves in the early days of the renaissance. In an undoubtedly male-dominated arena, their involvement stood out—though at the time, it didn't seem that strange as skating was more inclusive then. By the end of the seventies, women skaters would almost completely disappear from the pages of magazines, a situation that has barely changed twenty years later, though there has been a resurgence with many women skating and getting attention for their skills instead of their pulchritude. In those more sexually balanced early years, there was a mixture of feminism and references to Billie Jean King with an acceptance of women's minority status. Ellen's sister Cindy Berryman, in "Let's Hear it for the Ladies" in the August 1976 *Skateboarder*, made a case for women to take advantage of their differences from male skaters. Ladies were "smooth-flowing, not sharp; graceful, not forceful." In just writing the article, she was acknowledging that there was something different about women skaters but that their grace and balance and rhythm were important. The certainty of this faded over the next few years, and women skaters all but vanished. These early pioneers should not be forgotten, and their successors are now occasionally becoming integrated into skating. Then again, a letter in 1977 is more accurate in summing up most skaters' attitudes toward women: "Ellen Berryman is a stone fox and I wouldn't mind meeting her."

By the summer of 1977, there were a reported twenty million skateboards in circulation and rumors of the U.S.S.R. ordering twenty-five thousand red boards with red wheels for "inexpensive transport." The band Sneakers and Lace released an album with the songs "Skateboard U.S.A." and "Little Skateboard Queen." *Skateboarder* went monthly with an issue whose cover showed Gregg Ayres high up in a huge Arizona full pipe. The magazine addressed the basics of skating, including articles on how to fall and turn and other rudiments. These concerns might seem laughable now, but skating was young and there were a lot of newcomers who had no precedent in doing these fundamental things. There were advertisements for Cadillac Wheels with a Maxfield Parrish–like illustration of a pirate with a parrot on his shoulder next to a treasure chest of sparkling golden wheels. Another Cadillac ad used a Jim Evans illustration of a blond barefoot skater in a graffiti-enhanced drainage ditch—an iconic image, the melding of the California surfer with the realities of urban decay; the new, less sanitized California dream. Chris Yandall opined, "Sealed bearings are happening," and there was a lot of soul carving, like Dennis Shufeldt's graceful "impressionistic asphalt stroke" on the cover of volume two, number three. OJs were the spawn of Road Riders; they were orange and would be the standard in wheels for some time to come. Makaha made a shoe expressly for skating, following Vans, whose popular red and blue canvas shoes actually dated to 1966. Skate pads for the knee and elbow evolved from volleyball-style pads, with no plastic caps, to ones made expressly for skating; the most notable manufacturer was Rector. Pads were seen in photographs more and more, since they were mandatory in skateparks, where liability insurance demanded their use. There were also padded skate shorts, a defense against "hippers"—contusions on the hips from falling on concrete from a ten-foot height. An advertisement by Hobie showed a lilac-suited Gregg Weaver wearing a straw hat next to a vintage Rolls-Royce, with a comely brunette woman sitting inside and a rack with a surfboard and skateboard on the roof. There were motorized skateboards with tiny gasoline engines. Things were getting pretty ridiculous.

Some staples were already evident in the early *Skateboarder*s. There were the letters from faraway places seeking information: one from New York told of a "South American friend" who wanted to locate a "land surfing training board." Purism reared its head immediately with a letter complaining, "Have you seen anyone doing a handstand on a surfboard lately? Leave the gymnastics in the gymnasium." The sentiments and concerns expressed in the letters are not that different from the ones in today's magazines. A standby is the antipolice, antiauthority letter. One in the first issue of 1975 referred to "our ever-loving law enforcers" who are "giving tickets for riding skateboards on the streets." Chris Yandall wrote to the magazine with the entertaining advice, "If given a ticket, keep from laughing." The struggle with authority trying to keep skaters off public and private concrete environments has always been part of the bedrock of skating, a powerful, healthy spur to skaters transgressing barriers and being on the constant lookout for new terrain.

The epic struggle with the keepers of the peace that started in the sixties was resumed in the seventies to be fought into eternity, always and evermore.

Besides tickets, the biggest threat was the authorities' efforts to make skate spots unskateable. In California, the Vermont Drop was one of the first to go, with "speed bumps" put in to make skating impossible. The Super Bowl was outfitted with bumps at a cost of twelve thousand dollars. La Brea Spillway, the Reservoir, the Edmonton Bowl, the Toilet Bowl and the Bird Bath were rendered unrideable soon after, leading Stacy Peralta to complain, "What are they trying to do, protect us from ourselves?" Skaters' incessant search for spots led them to find and ride new terrain, a lot of which was on government property. L.A. Flood Control and other agencies responded with whatever deterrents they could, including speed bumps and rough cement. If there was a concrete playground out there, skaters had no choice but to abuse it and adapt it to their needs. Dennis Shufeldt put it well: "It's a matter of society's fault over a lot of years of having a concrete jungle created, and all the young people have discovered it, and using it because they have no other place to skate." Aaron Chang put this idea of redemption through concrete adaptation into an earthy New Age ode: "Cement became the earth /Plants do not grow on cement/Cement is not beautiful/Children are beautiful." The last line commented on how the life-deadening ugliness of cement had given rise to a beauty that used it as its medium: "A new joy was rising out of man's cement creations." A little hokey, but it did address the transformation skating can work on man-made environments.

And then came a big change: the development of environments built specifically for skating. The idea for skateparks had been there from the beginning. The problems of the "natural" spots—

vandalism, liability, run-ins with the police and the installation of antiskating impediments—forced people to look for alternatives. The potential profitability of spaces where people paid to skate was also a factor in the impetus to build skateparks; there was a market in "centrifugal recreation." Brian Gillogly, an editor at *Skateboarder*, wrote an article called "Skateparks: Fantasy or Reality?" in which he observed that "many people within the sport see the creation of new skateparks as important, if not vital, to the future existence of skateboarding." The writing was on the wall: skating needed to be taken out of the dangerous "natural" terrains that it had grown and flourished in and put into a safer environment. It started with Derby Park in Santa Cruz, a little dish of a bowl that was actually public. Then came plans for Carlsbad, the first commercial skatepark.

A series on skateparks began in the magazine and ran uninterrupted for the next three years. Carlsbad opened in 1976, and everybody went. The magazine was filled with luminaries doing berts and frontside kickturns on the lip. The park had no vertical or pools; it had "snake" runs—long, slightly downhill S-curved runs with walls that got to about a fifty-degree steepness. These snake runs would be the standard for the first generation of skateparks. Carlsbad was hugely popular. There were so many skaters that there was a traffic problem—people running into one another, snaking one another left and right. It was a demented Grand Central traffic jam.

By the end of 1976, photographs taken at skateparks were the main ingredient in the magazine, both editorially and in advertisements. The parks that had been built by that point (Carlsbad and Derby in California; Skateboard City in Port Orange, Florida; and one in Corpus Christi, Texas) were primitive compared to what was to come. Gillogly wrote, "On a surreal plane beyond that which cannot as yet be explicitly known, within the imaginations of many, though within the financial grasp of few, lies a manner of skatepark quite unlike any that now stand." The existing parks were of inferior design and difficulty compared to the "natural" terrains of pools and ditches. The most important thing about a park, its design, was unfortunately left in the hands of architects and landscapers who had never set foot on a skateboard. There was a surfeit of bad design, unnatural curves, Astroturf between bowls and illogical runs that sometimes hindered skating instead of fostering it. Tom Inouye bluntly stated the obvious: "People who build parks don't really know much about skating."

The horizontal surfaces were made of poured concrete, while a concrete mixture called Shotcrete was shot under pressure onto the banked sections. There was a lot of trial and error, much of it done by businessmen trying to get the most economical design for their money. By the middle of 1977, there were fifteen parks in the United States, and others were being poured as fast as possible. The skatepark boom was on. Many people agreed with Bruce Logan, who had been skating since 1958 and was (along with his brother and sister) the owner of the Logan Earth Ski company. He had skated through the dark years, and his attitude toward parks was unequivocal: "Skateparks are the greatest thing to ever happen to the sport."

The incongruous involvement of engineers and construction companies was evident in an ad for the Campo Construction Company: "A national recreational construction company offering a team of experienced track engineers coupled with a team of field supervisors who hand-sculpt each skatepark." Another advertisement by Solid Surf of America promised "a highly profitable skateboard park built in thirty days for $40,000!" Both ads listed projects under development in numerous states. These ads were definitely not targeted at skateboarders. At a skatepark conference in San Diego, the reality was impossible to ignore. The people at the conference were, in the words of the author writing about it in *Skateboarder*, "interested because skateboarding represents an already huge—and still rapidly growing—industry . . . which translates into 'money to be made.'" As expected, the majority of people at the conference "had never seen a skateboarder in action." The sharks were out; there was a palpable get-rich-quick mind-set in the air. It went along with other advertisements and gewgaws, like the "Dirt Board" and the nonfunctional "Wheeler Board" with three trucks, to "replace all other conventional boards!" There were a lot of exclamation marks, a lot of unfounded claims and rampant hucksterism.

The parks kept coming. Skatercross opened in Reseda, San Fernando Valley's first park. The Pipeline opened in Upland and gave the Inland Empire skaters a proving ground. It was built with more sensitivity to their needs and operated by Stan and Jean Hoffman and their son Don, whose dedication to skaters over the next ten years was unswerving. The park had a full pipe and a huge fifteen-foot-deep bowl. Skatepark Paramount opened and took the bigness factor to an absurd extreme with a sixteen-foot-deep bowl that had eight feet of vertical. Absurd, considering the equipment of the time; even now that much vertical would be unwarranted. Things did improve a little when skaters were belatedly brought in on the design process, as Waldo Autry was with Campo at Paramount. It wasn't until late 1977 that the first real pool was built in a park at Spring Valley in San Diego.

All these parks had an undeniable effect on the evolution of skateboarding. They pushed skating forward in an even more significant way than had the drought that caused all the empty backyard pools. Skaters now had a controlled, somewhat safer environment to experiment in, and they took advantage of it. The parks embodied skating in the late seventies, and they were the petri dish for the tricks of the future. But there was a downside—a concentration on only one kind of skating, and the stifling of creativity that comes with the pay-for-play paradigm. There was a conflict between skaters' behavior and most skatepark owners' visions of control, exemplified by the caption under a picture of Jay Adams at Skatercross in *Skateboarder*'s June 1977 issue: "Thrown out later this day for his usual radical behavior."

Besides parks, there were a lot of other spots being skated. Pools still figured prominently; they were in the magazine as much as parks for the first couple of years. Later they were certainly being skated, even if they weren't photographed as much. There were the hills and ditches, and a man-made structure put to good use: full-pipes. Arguably the first one ridden was the infamous Mount Baldy pipeline, a fifteen-foot cylinder for run-off from the San Bernardino Mountains in the Inland Empire east of Los Angeles. It was ridden as far back as 1969. In pipes, riders got over vertical, free-falling or sliding back down to the transition. Mount Baldy is still skated and continues to be a site of pilgrimage. After Baldy came the Camp Pendleton full-pipes that the photographer James Cassimus discovered (his father had been an engineer on the project) and then the twenty-two-foot pipes in Arizona constructed by the Ameron Corporation. Out in the desert, at least forty sections of pipe were sitting above ground, waiting to be buried as part of a $2-billion project to bring water from the Colorado River to the burgeoning city of Phoenix. With expanses of the sun-bleached desert dotted by saguaro cactus in the background, Southern California rippers were photographed high up at ten o'clock, with their leading hands touching the curving ceiling above them. These images became icons of the expansive nature of skating's ability to surpass itself—in this case, to go beyond vertical.

There were other kinds of terrain developing besides the natural spots and the parks. In October 1977, an article appeared about how to build a wooden ramp, an at-home alternative to paying to skate. A year later, ramps were becoming more commonplace, including wooden bowls that mimicked parks. These first ramps were rather primitive, like Skitch Hitchcock's six-foot-high portable fiberglass wave, something like a pool's shallow end that he set up in parking lots. It was just big enough to carve once through. Most of the ramps were very narrow, eight feet wide, with no flat bottom between the opposing walls, no coping and no rollout decks (the platforms atop each side where people can stand between runs); the polycarbonate Pepsi ramp was a portable example of this type of ramp, used in demonstrations. Its transparency afforded the opportunity to take pictures of riders kickturning from directly behind. Rollout decks weren't strictly necessary at the time because everybody fakied up the transition to get going—there was no standing on top yet. These articles subtly encouraged the possibility of having your own playground to skate on. The proliferation of ramps was slow to start, but these exhortations were just the beginning. It was hard to fathom at the time just how big a role backyard ramps would play in the future of skating.

One aspect of coverage in *Skateboarder* was provided by the skaters themselves. Warren Bolster wrote an article about how to take pictures of skating action, his main piece of advice being to use a wide-angle lens. This and other articles encouraged the average skater to document his or her friends and their scene, a do-it-yourself exhortation that was itself subversive, since in a way, the magazine was fostering its own competition. Even the "big" magazine wanted readers to contribute. This idea of self-documentation became a central tenet in skating, in lieu of more mainstream coverage, and predated the self-revealing photographic and video frenzy that has become part of larger society with the advent of webcams and reality TV. Skaters were getting a lot of attention but it wouldn't last forever, and this predisposition to record their actions would serve them well in the future. It also led to an early embrace of and reliance on video technology as a way to document skateboarding in a cheap, accessible, homegrown fashion.

What could be pictured was changing dramatically. There were glimmers of the aerial revolution early on. Skitch Hitchcock was doing "unassisted aerial hopping," using his toes at either end of the board ("Evil Knievel–style") to hop into the air and do 360s. Rodney Jesse, with his long, bleached-out Afro that was one of the largest hairdos of the time, was shown going too far during a frontside kickturn at Carlsbad—not making it but flying out enough on the board to allude to the possibility of airs over the lip of the bowl. Jay Adams was again ahead of his time, shown in a Z-Flex ad flying out a bowl frontside, one hand holding the board, the other about to land on the coping. This was the beginning of a trick that would be known two years later as the layback air. There was a sequence of Paul Hackett going from a vertical pool wall, over the coping, to rolling on the deck. The next logical step was doing the opposite and rolling into the pool, riding from the deck over the coping and changing the body's orientation ninety degrees in an instant to ride down the pool's wall. Rick Blackhart and Doug Schneider were the first two to make this leap of faith and skill. Vince Klyne was pictured at Wallos in Hawaii turning frontside with his hands up, riding on the rocks that abutted the top of the ditch. Wallos was described as "perhaps the most demanding and most unique spot. It is a roller coaster ride of drops, jolts, and switchbacks in all directions with a thousand possibilities." Tom Inouye was on the cover flying frontside out of the Pipeline's full pipe, with no hands and no straps, another harbinger of unassisted flight. A kid named Wilson Fair, never to be heard from again, flew a six-foot-long backside grab over six kids prostrate underneath him at the Gaithersburg, Maryland, park, a bowl-to-bowl transfer that was very unusual for the time. Pool-and-park-bred Chris Strople went beyond grinding to get all four wheels out and stall on the tail of his board. Grinds were getting lapped over the top, the board slapping against the coping. All kinds of slides were happening, like Stacy Peralta's 720 slides and the cess slide, an alley-oop (going up frontside and then doing the trick backside, traveling backward) maneuver where the skater slides backward, parallel to and just underneath the coping, before riding down the wall. Scott Senatore was shown doing a backside air-grab hop in Florida, paralleling the frontside aerial evolution. Not long after, Alva's frontside air centerfold announced the real aerial age. Shortly thereafter, Mark Lake and Greg Meischeid were doing frontside grab berts, going almost upside down with one hand on the wall and another holding the board. There were tricks bubbling up, variations, and the basics—grinds and slides and now airs—were being taken to new levels. In November 1977 *Skateboarder* ran a "Skate Tips" article featuring Curt Lindgren doing a 180 kickflip—kickflipping the board and turning it and his body 180 degrees to land rolling backward. And in 1978 Paul Hoffman was on the cover doing a nose wheelie on a curb, grinding his front truck. Nobody could have guessed at the time how prescient these moves were.

The interviews in *Skateboarder* were revealing. They let personalities come through in a fairly uncensored fashion and also evoked the mores and concerns of the skaters and their times. Russ Howell unfavorably compared fly-fishing to skating, dismissing it with "They call it a sport—stand for six hours and drink beer." Commenting on the emergence of footwear as a viable alternative to going barefoot, he said, "Shoes, I've found, give you more confidence." He ended the interview saying, "If elected, I'll put two skateboards in every garage." Stacy Peralta was described as quiet and unassuming, the person responsible for introducing the modern surf-skate style to Australia, and conversant on such diverse subjects as Bessie Smith, English sea chanteys and the life story of Arnold Ziffell— the pig on the television show *Green Acres.* "Tube Monster" Waldo Autry was shown high up in the Arizona pipes and was reported to have shot Signal Hill inebriated while doing a handstand, not to mention pulling a knife on the Crips at his high school. Tom Inouye was the epitome of Southern Californian mellow, with his long black hair and flip-flops, drinking a beer next to his Porsche. He belied his image with the statement "I guess I've always been radical. When I was two I jumped out of my crib and fractured my skull." He mentioned being influenced by his Dogtown peers and the Hal Jepson films and rued the fruits of skate stardom, complaining that people expected him to be ripping when he just wanted to have fun.

Bobby Piercy was the flashiest slalomer around and the closest thing skating had to a freestyle-skiing-type star. He wore straw hats and his clothes were tight, and he was photographed long-jumping over a bevy of Playboy Bunnies. He was an advocate of the feet-together-in-the-middle-of-the-board slalom technique, with a lot of hip swiveling. Although he coexisted with the Dogtowners and the park riders, he represented a dying breed, an anachronism by the time he was interviewed in January 1978. "I owe it all to my mom," he proclaimed before explaining his success. "My skating, surfing and dancing help my love life, and my love life helps my skating."

Bob Biniak was interviewed between his morning round of golf at the Rivera Country Club, a luncheon photo shoot at the Dogbowl and a night out at Gazzari's on the Sunset Strip. His frontside kickturns in the full pipe at the Pipeline were insane and almost upside down, and he made a good point about the dangers of "all the dime-store cheap equipment" that was getting people hurt and "ruining the name of the sport."

Rick Blackhart came down from Santa Cruz, where he rode a wooden bowl in the mountains with his friend Kevin Thatcher. He blew minds by being one of the first to roll into pools and do fakie 360s (riding up backward and turning 360 degrees at the apex of momentum) above vertical in the Pipeline's full pipe. He announced, "I just want to ride with everybody who thinks they're worth anything in the most outrageous place possible . . . and see what comes down," proving that the Dogtown–San Diego rivalry wasn't the only one happening.

The idea of Dogtown held sway over the letters in "Skate Post." Letters pro and con abounded concerning Tony Alva, Dogtown's lightning rod. Invective flew back and forth between Down South and Dogtown. "Alva's a good skater, but his mouth is too big"; "I cannot understand how come Scumtown gets so much coverage"; "What's with these Dogtown dudes, do they think they invented the skateboard?" were typical of the San Diego position. Jim Muir wrote in on the Dogtown side: "You guys couldn't even do a kickturn in a pool until T. A. [Alva] stayed down there and laid down some lines at the Soul Bowl." There was certainly acrimony, though some of the rivalry was probably media-induced.

In one issue, three letters demanded a Jay Adams interview. He was at his peak, ripping and causing trouble everywhere. One sequence of photos showed him shirtless, tanned and scarred, signing autographs for a group of teenage girls at Skateboard World in Torrance. In one part of the sequence, he signed something on a girl's body, which provokes a demonstrably shocked reaction on her part. His board came out on Z-Flex in 1978: a thirty-inch-long board with a slight tail and a middle core, it was one of the most popular boards for a while. Newer members of the Dogtown contingent surfaced, including a twelve-year-old named Eric Dressen in a Park Rider Wheels ad; and Shogo Kubo, with his long black hair halfway down his back, on a board with the Dogtown "cross," doing the most laid-out layback slides on vertical yet. There were also Marty and Gary Grimes, two of the first black skaters pictured in *Skateboarder* magazine. Dogtown's makeup reflected skating's racial diversity—it was multicultural long before the term came into vogue.

Alva was, without a doubt, the biggest star in skateboarding. To nobody's surprise, he won the first annual *Skateboarder* reader's poll in 1978. Alva was not only up there with the best skaters, he was also the most photogenic and outrageous, and he knew how to sell himself. The first ad for his own company, Alva Skates, was a milestone of graphic freshness in which image completely superseded product. The Alva logo was distinctive, a kind of slash font. The ad didn't make any assertions about equipment performance or contest results; it was a full-color shot of Alva wearing his fedora, standing in an empty pool. His image and the mystery of the photo were in sharp contrast to most ads' technical gibberish. A later ad, almost elegant in its simplicity, showed a parking garage with puddles on the ground reflecting greens and reds, and the shadowy figure of Tony in the background holding a board with the barely discernible logo cut into the grip tape. The moody and almost foreboding advertisements were shot by the photographer Raul Vega and were more along the lines of Helmut Newton or Guy Bourdin than the typical skateboard ad. They were a break with tradition; they stood out.

There were other developments as well. Kryptonics and Powell arrived on the scene as board and wheel manufacturers, both to be major players in the future. Kryptonics used advanced foam technology from skis to make boards and had some of the best wheels. Powell had the Quicksilver board, an epoxy-filled fiberglass and aluminum composite that was an attempt at a lighter and stronger board. Powell also came out with their Bones wheels.

Though skateparks continued to proliferate, their value as investments would soon be challenged. An advertisement for the "Skiboard" appeared. It was a sort of snow surfboard with a complete skateboard attached to the top. It was part of the early evolution of snowboarding, an activity that would be very much connected to and influenced by skating, and was in an even earlier stage of development. Stickers promoting skate companies became the deriguer board decoration, especially on the bottom, where they would show up in photographs when the bottom of the board could be seen during tricks. High-top shoes were seen on skaters for the first time and soon became mandatory. Bob Skoldberg, Mike Weed and Ed Nadalin went on a European tour, were mobbed by enthusiastic kids and met the mayor of Portsmouth, England. Skaters were not as advanced in Europe but were just as into it. More and more letters came from places as varied as North Carolina, Canada and Europe. Sports painter and *Playboy* mansion habitué LeRoy Neiman came out with an impressionistic ripoff of a Gregg Weaver photo in an edition of five thousand sold by the Knoedler Gallery in New York. Mike Weed bought a house for eighty-two thousand dollars. By the end of 1978, skating was big, profitable and exciting. But times were about to get tough again.

Chapter Seven
Frontier Tales

Skateboarder magazine was a mirror of the times and is now a historical document—one of the few, since there aren't many books or other primary sources covering skating from that time. It also had a writer who was in a category altogether different from the norm. Most writing in the magazine is just what would be expected for a periodical whose main audience was fifteen-year-olds: workmanlike. Not that there was anything wrong with that; it fit the market and the audience's mind-set. But somehow because of the whole wide-openness of the time, something besides that slipped into the pages of the magazine.

In a series of articles over a five-year period, one particular writer got to the core of the skating ethos in a distinctive prose style, accompanied by equally unorthodox and important photographs. He turned out to be the bard of skateboarding and has continued to make unique contributions to this day. It's doubtful he was appreciated at the time, but his articles and photographs communicated to anybody interested that something new and special was going on in a way that would stand the test of time. This was a singular voice describing a singular subculture, and one uniquely suited to do so. Whether the people reading his articles knew or cared that their author had written for *Surfer* in the sixties, was an expert on duck migration and California custom-car culture and many other arcane subjects, was an artist with a career completely outside the realm of skateboarding and, more importantly, had been a part of skating's inner workings in Santa Monica, that crucible of skateboarding, was beside the point. The man's name is Craig Stecyk or, as he is more commonly known, C. R. Stecyk III.

Stecyk's name is probably unknown to the majority of people who have skated in the last thirty years, but his influence has been extraordinary. Pundit, philosopher, friend and confidant to top skaters and industry types alike, he holds sway in a way no one else has. Stecyk's photographs are always credited to him, but his writing has appeared under numerous pseudonyms, adding to the mystery of just who he is. Whether they appear under Carl Izan, Sam Fernando, John Smythe or Lowboy, his writings and photos have always represented skating in a literate, complicated way.

Starting in the fall of 1975 with "Aspects of the Downhill Slide," Stecyk set out his personal vision. His combination of text and photography is unmistakable and makes for an utterly original whole. The photos are more artful than the usual skate photo, with a melding of intense action in the foreground—real "sports" photography—and sociological concerns in the background. The sensibility combines a "*consofas*" (a Hispanic gang term that translates loosely as "Such is the nature of things; if you don't like it, fuck you") attitude with a deep background of Hollywood and surfing history. His oft-quoted pronouncement about "two hundred years of American technology" was the beginning of his broad-based, eclectic, erudite, informed polemics, stories and rambling theses. His work hybridized an innate knowledge of the art of Robert Irwin and Ed Ruscha with that of Von Dutch and Ed Roth. Tom Mix met Shogo Kubo; the surf world melded into the sphere of skating.

"Aspects of the Downhill Slide" begins with a full-page photo of Tony Alva compressed at the top of a schoolyard bank that lays down the Dogtown style. The other photographs are of Nathan Pratt, Wentzle Ruml and Paul Constantineau from a low vantage point, showing the texture of the asphalt. The man-made environment is represented as much as the culture itself—the clothes, the look, the style. Near the surface and sometimes blurred, the skaters are shown in a way that illuminates the real speed and motion of skating. The dual concerns of sport and art are in sync without prejudice in Stecyk's photos.

The article starts with what was to become Stecyk's trademark, the clash of the outside world with the particular subversive subculture of skateboarding: "Somewhere in the Arizona desert lies the estate of Barry Goldwater. In his front yard, amidst the rock and cactus garden, stands a flag pole topped by a spotlight, an electric fan and a screaming gold eagle. . . . Tourists make the pilgrimage to this opulent shrine of patriotism in air-conditioned, Gray Line tour buses. . . . A few miles away in one of his department stores, clerks and clerkettes sell skateboards hand over fist. The manager tells that they can't keep enough skateboards in stock; he also confides that Senator Goldwater feels them a public hazard, and consequently is moving to have them outlawed in the Arizona legislature." The particular blend of erudition, intellectualism, slang and eccentric turns of phrase impeccably evokes a specific time and place.

From there it moves to the Lucky Market in Ocean Park Heights—Skatetown. "In street gang logistics, Skatetown is located between Dogtown, Ghost Town, Smogtown, Downstream from Frogtown and south of Kosher Canyon," where "the kids skate with undeniable aggressive proficiency." Then to Malibu where a scruffy figure—Bob Dylan—is skating down a canyon road at night. Speed is "downhill somewhere past forty-five, the fine line fluctuates." Beyond that line there is "an entity you don't want to look at, yet have the urge to see." Stecyk acknowledges the arcane nature of his reportage. "Most people probably won't understand some of this, but that doesn't really matter since the intrinsic elements are meant for those who really skate." He is talking to a select group, a select society that *understands*. The difference between the sixties and the seventies in skating was that more people were closing in on the advanced levels, and the degree of acceptance was growing in the larger public. "The big breakthroughs are yet to come, since the current practitioners really haven't even begun to hit their mark." He is uncannily prophetic when he extols bank riding as a three-dimensional opportunity. This is classic Stecyk, a voice that is both historically aware and far-reaching in its analysis.

This combination continued in his articles in *Skateboarder* and its short-lived successor, *Action Now*, and later in *Thrasher*. Stecyk's next piece (as Carlos Izan) was "Fear of Flying," which began: "In the final analysis, truth always evolves from the state of total madness." Not the musings of your average illiterate skate rat— or the "literary" writer's take on sport, either. He predicts the future again, using a quote from Steve McKinney, "Riding the substance of dreams, a magic carpet of air, into which our willpower was sensuously intertwined," to make explicit the connection between extreme speed and the breaking of the bonds of gravity. There is an "other side of there," and it is air. "In actuality, the only limiting factor is that of your imagination. . . . After you leave the realm of traditional preconceptions, you enter the area of endless freedom. There exists no right or wrong, rules are unheard of, and the course is uncharted." This is the poetry, mystery and indefinable mysticism of skating as it can best be described by the written word.

In the August 1976 issue, Stecyk's (now John Smythe's) definitive Dogtown article appeared: "The Westside Style, or, Under the Skatetown Influence." The full-page photo of "El Thumper" said it all—a hardcore *cholo* wearing sunglasses and a bandana on his head, holding a board with his middle finger extended over the grip tape, the Dogtown cross spray-painted at his feet and Stecyk's "Rat" crossbones graffiti on the wall of the ditch behind him. This was not nice. It was scary and threatening and gnarly. Stecyk posited the "Origin of the Species" argument—since skating had started in the mid-fifties with the Malibu surf crew, it followed that people in the vicinity were naturally more proficient. He used a Buckminster Fuller quote in relation to the Dogtown phenomena: "In any given situation, new approaches invariably precede the new technologies."

The photographs have an almost mystical quality. They show the doings of a secret, advanced yet down-and-dirty urban society, an elite corps. There was something about them that was more "classic" than the usual photos in the magazine; they had a combination of Walker Evans's simplicity with Weegee's taste for the bizarre. They represent the paradox of Los Angeles, the dystopian, abject darkness of John Fante, Nathanael West and Raymond Chandler; a darkness suffused with "light," the light of youth and skateboarding in the imploding metropolis. El Thumper handstands down an empty spillway with a tunnel leading into oblivion behind him, a swastika, "skate town" and "Victor de Santa" written on the wall and the brush in the background gothically hanging down. There's a shot of Nathan Pratt's bert at Bellagio with the schoolyard empty, the sun glinting in the evening. Then one of Jose Gallan, L.A. cool with the surfer look in front of hardcore *cholos* Danny, Payasa and Chaco leaning on their mean lowrider, a wall completely covered with *vato* graffiti behind them. These pictures show otherness—true skating turning into and begetting its own culture.

Next came "Frontier Tales or . . . Any Resemblance to Any Persons Living or Dead Is Purely Coincidental," in which the virtuoso photographs are paired with a meditation on the conflict between skating's newfound popularity and its true nature. A single day is recounted in which Tony Alva and Stacy Peralta were taped on the *Tony Orlando and Dawn* television series, Fred Astaire broke his wrist skating and the *Howdy Doody Show* conducted an audition for a skating part with 326 crying child actors dressed up in Howdy Doody wigs, flannel shirts and boots, all with recently issued cheap plastic boards. "What does it mean? Probably nothing. . . . Except that here in the seventies, a lot of outsiders are recognizing skating as a way to commercial profit." The ill effects of the do-gooders' efforts and the fly-by-night operators' misdeeds are examined. "Whether you skate for pay or play, it's all interrelated and interdependent. At present, in certain quarters of the skate phenomenon confusion, greed and dishonesty threaten to displace the essential essence of skating itself . . . enjoyment." The antics of the "shuck and jive masters" and the factions (i.e., "governing" bodies that put on contests) that supposedly represented skaters, along with the media blitz of the moment, were making for a climate in which skaters were being exploited left and right and the representation of skating in the mass media was straying far from roots and reality. Stecyk rightfully criticized the parks as being no match for existing skate spots, and ended with "Somewhere beyond the formalized spectrum, street skating reigns supreme." So very true, even if it wasn't to happen for another ten years.

Another article began with a session at the Dogbowl, where two L.A.P.D. officers were just watching and it was "total dementia in the deep end, ranging from complete upside-down aerial assaults to four-walled off-the-lips." The photographs were an innovation, one that was to become a standard for skateboard photography as well as all sports photography—the motor-drive sequential. The sequence makes it possible to represent a trick with microsecond lapses, to show a move from start to finish like in an Edward Muybridge motion study. It was a breakthrough in representation that helped demystify what was going on and brought the pictures into another realm of explication.

"Vicious Lies and More Interplanetary Communications" brought you into another zone that somehow aligned itself with and was a portal to the world of skating. Celestial events coincided with a mummy stolen from the Living Desert Museum that ended up reclining next to an empty pool atop the old Pasadena Hilton Hotel as Danny Bearer was stopped by the police for going fifty-five miles per hour on Diamondback Peak, riding a Team Hobie board with clay composition wheels, while Paul Constantineau skated a flood-control ditch and sighted (and took a photograph of) a UFO. These were the new Knights Templar, the progeny of the sixties skaters and surfers, though a different, more modern sort. Coupled with street slang and references, a real walk on the wild side; but these happenings didn't have anything to do with heroin or transvestites. Plus there was a sequence of Constantineau on the lowest, raddest bert yet, with his hair to the ground, and Adams's frontside edger with only the minute edge of his wheel touching the coping. The caption read: "Episodic discontrol."

In "Things Are Hot in the Valley," the mix of strangeness continued with a full-page photo of a twenties cowgirl starlet packing two pistols. Stecyck poked fun at the surfer attitude that maligned the San Fernando Valley as a hotbed of interlopers and kooks: "While you can argue the San Fernando Valley isn't by the sea, you've got to admit that the pit is paved, and quite possibly depraved." He acknowledged what was becoming a reality, that skating didn't have to be connected to surfing. Not only did the Valley have pools, mountain roads and concrete spillways; it also had rippers like Bobby Barbore and Kathy Reese in the sixties, and Kent Sentanore, Jerry Valdez, Marc Smith, and Bill Border in 1977; and it was the home to Val Surf, where Mark Richards sold the first complete boards in 1962. It was also home to Bob Hope, Clark Gable, Dinah Shore, Lucille Ball and Gene Autry. Stecyck made the claim of a rather bizarre and unique precursor to skating—cowboy star Buck Buchanan's standing ride on a horseless buckboard wagon down the Chatsworth Drop in a 1936 *Three Musketeers* movie—a precedent as valid, no matter how weird, as the kids on scooters were at the time. The caption accompanying a picture of Buchanan on one of his horses somehow summed up the combination of deviant seriousness and humor that was Stecyck's trademark: "Buck Buchanan, buckboard slalom expert, astride one of his many kicktails."

In "The Season of Divorce," John Cheever wrote of children who have "built something out of an orange crate, something preposterous and ascendant" in the attic. Was it a skateboard? Maybe so, maybe not. Whatever it was, that magical creation of children was at the heart of skating, and had grown up quite a bit by the end of the seventies. Stecyk's arcane musings, the color action photographs, the ads for ridiculous gimmicks, the pioneering moves were all there in *Skateboarder*—a world unto itself of preposterous ascendancy.

Chapter Eight
Massive

The mass media, books and movies capitalized on the immense popularity of skating in the mid-seventies. The books came out by 1977 and had the marks of being rushed into print to take advantage of the fad, while showing skating in a way that neophytes could relate to. They showed the same things that were in the early *Skateboarder* but from a less knowing perspective, as they were meant for a broader audience. One immediate problem was that the books were out of date as soon as they were published, since skating was advancing at such a quick pace. They were about freestyle and the basics and barely touched on pool riding, where the real excitement was happening. They included tips on weighting and unweighting, getting on and off, coasting and foot placement, how to do "wheelie stops" and "down curbies." As how-to books, they were concerned with the fundamentals, and they actually did a credible job of describing these things for beginners—though the enterprise is futile, because skating is not really something you can learn from reading about or seeing pictures of; it just has to be done, with advancement through trial and error.

Skateboarding: A Complete Guide to the Sport mixes pictures of a skating Katharine Hepburn (apparently a friend of author Jack Grant's) with references to tai chi and yoga. It opines that skating "gives you a great chance to discover and perfect your personal style of gracefulness." Gracefulness is probably not the first thing that comes to mind in regard to skating, but the quote alludes to grace not only in a physical sense but in its theological meaning: the transcendent moments that instigate a step beyond the mundane to enlightenment, clarity and the negation of self that comes with leaps of faith into the abyss.

Pahl and Peter Dixon's *Hot Skateboarding* is dedicated to "that first young person who fastened steel skate wheels to a board and pushed off to click-clack along the pavement." The book starts with "All that smooth surface lies waiting to be explored and ridden for the sheer purpose of having fun. Skateboarding is fun, and adventure. It's inexpensive and non-polluting, and healthy and the way to go if you live where there's more pavement than dirt." It gets specific with "Our great corps of engineers . . . have provided skateboarders with countless curved retaining walls, storm drains, flat spillways, flood control basins, yet-to-be-filled reservoirs, and other banked and contoured surfaces to ride on." The Dixons state that skating "allows sensations of gravity-defying motions not found in any other sport" and that "there's art out there on the sidewalks." Skating is definitely more than a sport and it isn't a stretch to call it an art. It's an activity that goes outside the parameters of sport. It is ever evolving, enters into all parts of a skater's daily life and is so varied that it becomes second nature, like walking and breathing, an art that is a by-product of living.

Hot Skateboarding is a good example of something from the "outside" (though the authors did skate) getting to the heart of the matter on two things that are crucial to skating: terrain and style. The search for new terrain is a driving force for skaters, always on a search for structural forms to subsume to the skating urge. Then it was drainage ditches and pools; now it is more often marble ledges and triple sets of stairs. The impetus is the same: "Hardcore skate explorers travel hundreds of miles following vague and unfamiliar directions and rumors in hope of finding new challenging banks and bowls to ride." Not only will skaters go anywhere to ride something new, but there is a good chance that it's off-limits. A fresh place to skate is attractive because it is new and because, like Mount Everest, it's there. The book also includes the amusing advice that "there's a good chance you won't get busted if you stay cool, quiet and act with reason." Maybe, but maybe not. That's the fun of it, running from The Man sometimes.

Hot Skateboarding tries to tackle the subject of style, which has been inextricably linked to skating since the beginning but is difficult to pin down. Is it "a manner of expression characteristic of an individual" or "overall excellence, skill or grace in performance?" The question of style hinges on if it is smoothness or personal "style." The surfers had smoothness, especially Gerry Lopez, who was casualness personified on the face of huge, grinding Pipeline waves. But then there was Larry Bertleman, whose way of moving on a wave was more aggressive. They were polar opposites, but both definitely had style. It can be smoothness, and give the impression of lack of effort; or it can be personal idiosyncrasy, personalized movements and thrashing around. It is inexplicable, like art. You know it when you see it. Defining style in skating is impossible, akin to Leo Tolstoy's failed attempt to define what makes good art in "What Is Art?" Style is hand positions, lack or an abundance of sketchiness, details, an intimate relationship with the board. Great skating takes something from the inside, something creative and different. Style could be considered the application and finesse of the drive to skate.

Ben Davidson's *The Skateboard Book* touches on some elemental truths, and his attitude toward competition is in keeping with many skaters' ambivalence: "Competition skating is neither desirable nor undesirable in any absolute way. It's strictly up to the individual. There are plenty of outstanding skaters who have never competed." He touches on some of the ulterior benefits of skating: "The pleasure to be derived from skateboarding is enough of an incentive to get into it. But there is an additional value: while you're having fun, you're doing your body good. Not only does skateboarding afford basic exercise—because it's a speed sport that incorporates elements of balance and grace—but it can also help you confront and accept your physical limitations. . . . In addition, the confidence you attain in mastering the various skating skills can give you a foundation for self-confidence in other areas. . . . Who can explain the importance of that? Suffice it to say that challenge is the stuff life's made of." It might be a little simplistic, but there is much to be said for the self-sufficiency of skating acting as a catalyst in people's lives.

Outside of the trade magazines and these books, skating also appeared in magazines like *Time, Rolling Stone* and *National Geographic,* and in many advertisements for products that weren't related to skating. Skating also made its way into impressionable minds through the medium of television and included celebrities slaloming on the *Battle of the Network Stars* and Ponch and John taking on skating felons in a *CHiPs* episode. In film, there were the grassroots documentaries made by sympathetic aficionados; they might have leaned toward corniness, but the exploitation level was low. Noel Black's seminal trippy sixties film *Skater Dater* was the precedent. These films proselytized and spread the fever. They could represent skating in a way that still photography couldn't, showing the motions in a linear fashion. Spider Willis and Gregg Weaver were involved in *Downhill Motion*, and Hal Jepson did *Skateboard Madness* and *Super Session* (with music by Daryl Dragon of the Captain and Tennille), which featured surfers Rory Russell, Gerry Lopez and Larry Bertleman along with Jay Adams and other skaters. This was shown at junior high school auditoriums and community centers and undoubtedly enthralled and inspired many kids.

On a larger scale were feature-length films made for theatrical release. The first was a crossover attempt called *Freewheelin'*, directed by Scott Dittrio. It is a time capsule of the possibilities and excitement of 1975, and also a precursor to the skate videos so prevalent in skating today. *Freewheelin'* isn't a good film—the love story is an inopportune narrative addition—but it is good ethnographic look at a subculture just getting under way. Narrated in a doleful tone by a young woman named Camille, the story serves as a vehicle for her take on a summer spent with her boyfriend and his skater friends. She is seen running along the beach while she says in a voice-over, "Wherever there's a hill and concrete, skaters will ride it till they have it wired . . . the speeds are amazing, they call it freewheelin'."

The interesting aspect of the film is the skating. Camille's boyfriend is played by none other than Stacy Peralta. When he's not acting, which fortunately is for the majority of the film, the movie is exceptional, since it shows one of the major figures at the center of the skating revolution being himself and just skating.

What transpires in *Freewheelin'* is akin to Lou Gehrig playing himself in *The Pride of the Yankees*. This is skating's living history. The footage of the skaters at Paul Revere and Kenter—the Kitty Hawk of skateboarding—is the equivalent to having film of a nineteenth-century baseball game. The environment is a flat asphalt space about half the size of a football field, with thirty-degree banked walls on the sides, ranging in height from two to fourteen feet. Two skaters roll along the top and then drop in diagonally down the wall to carve it like a wave. They do 360s on the wall, sliding berts and one-footed nose wheelies. Stacy tic-tacs (unweighting the front wheels and turning the board alternately to the right and left to propel forward) back and forth and says to the camera: "Clay wheels were a drag . . . until the Cadillac wheel came out." He then tells of getting on the Zephyr team. This is a frontline report on the genesis of modern skating.

Following the template laid out in *The Endless Summer*, the skaters go off in search of the best spots. What follows is a who's who of early skating, along with a what's where of spots and a what's what of skating. Tom Sims makes an appearance, riding a four-foot longboard. At the T-Bowl (an early reservoir spot), Stacy and Tom skate with Kenny Means, a cohort of the early skaters who translated skateboard radicalism to roller skates, pioneering the "frog in heat" (toes pointing in opposite directions, legs akimbo) style. Near San Simeon, they break for a surf session and do downhill runs at sunset. In San Francisco, they bomb the hills and attract pedestrian attention. At the celebrated La Costa hill, there's straight slalom and a lot of barefoot riding, talk of "gyrating" and different stances. Bobby Piercy is there with his tight white shorts and Vaurnet sunglasses, swiveling incredibly fast through the cones. At the Escondido Bowl Stacy is ruling the place, carving at speed around the mud at the bottom of the rectangular banked box, saying, "You turn down, you turn up, you get so much speed . . . the sensation is incredible." Then it's to a pool with a foot of blue tile and a lot of slow-motion backside carves. At the Baldy pipe-line, we see Waldo Autry kickturning above vertical while wear-ing lime-green knee-high socks.

Stacy gets a phone call from Australia, inviting him to come down and do paid demonstrations. His guileless response is, "Un-real . . . That's so hot." He quits his job and school, and the audi-ence is subjected to the denouement of his and Camille's maudlin parting (Camille: "My life is rolling with the tides").

It took a year to go from the sincerity and innocence of *Freewheelin'* to Hollywood's version of the skateboard craze. George Gage's *Skateboard: The Movie (That Defies Gravity)* has all the faults, pit-falls, compromises and distortions that low-budget exploitation movies are known for. That skating was hugely popular can be the only explanation for this abomination. But in the strange way that the mass media unconsciously reveal truths about what they are ex-ploiting, *Skateboard*, through its association with real skaters and real skating, got some of skating's concerns right. On one level, it is unintentional postmodern self-analysis. The movie takes an age-old trope (crazy kids face adversity, get a leader to shape them up and triumph in the end) that has been used many times before (*Bad News Bears*, et al) and makes the main character a man who is unabashedly out to exploit the kids without any pangs of conscience. Poststructural-ists could have a field day with the ironies of *Skateboard*'s origins at the bottom of the Hollywood food chain, with some schemers eager to cash in on the fad by making a movie about *exactly that*.

The movie begins with three silhouetted figures kickturning in a full pipe, with the song "Skate-out," written for the movie, playing on the sound track: "We are are children of the new beginning, changing with the times / Breaking through the walls of darkness, soaring high in the sky / Skate-out!" The rest of the movie follows this saccharine mix of idealism and cynicism. It is so *wrong*, but it subtextually, incomprehensibly gets close to a representation of the real soul of skating. Something that was not planned by its makers, surely.

Skateboard's main character, Manny Bloom, is an overweight man with a balding Afro who wears a beige suit and a big necklace. He is a failed movie agent down on his luck and in debt to his bookie Sully, who is putting the pressure on Manny to pay him back. Manny is extremely unlikable from the beginning and sets the pace for the rest of the movie with his recurring habit of engaging in totally unnecessary action and expostulating on what he is doing while he is doing it. The first instance of this is when Manny gets into his jalopy convertible and hits his arm on the car door. The viewer sees it happen, then Manny reaffirms what just happened with, "Dammit, I do that every time." After struggling to start the car on the uphill that it is parked on, Manny asks the car to "just make it one more time." Why he doesn't park the car facing downhill if this is a regular problem isn't addressed.

Skating comes into the story line fairly quickly. Manny's car stalls at the bottom of a hill. In what becomes a predictable response, Manny cries, "Damn thing stalled!" He looks up to see two boys and a girl skating down the hill toward him and yells, "Let me get out of here first!" as though the skaters are a semi that will flatten him. The skaters go by, and one of them high-jumps over the car's hood in slow motion. Manny's mind is blown, and he unsurprisingly exclaims out loud, "Jesus, crazy kids, I've never seen anything like that." Manny's countenance is consistently agitated. At home he suffers through a threatening phone call from Sully. Then the epiphany comes as the skater jumping over the car is seen in a flashback. Manny blurts out, "The youth market . . . skateboards!" to which Sully answers, "You mean those stupid toys all the kids are using?" Manny goes into high gear. "Yeah, skateboards, they're as hot as a pistol. Everybody's doing it . . . it's the biggest thing on wheels." His idea is to start a skateboard team to finance his gambling debts.

Manny rushes back to the scene of his encounter with the skateboarders. Oddly enough, they're still there. The three skaters—Brad, played by pubescent teen heartthrob Leif Garret, a girl named Jenny (Ellen O'Neal) and a guy with unruly hair, a trace of a mustache and giant headphones who exudes attitude, played by Tony Alva—roll up. Manny accosts them, asking if they can "do the stunts, jumping over cars, crazy stuff like that?" In his inimitable way, he proposes starting a skateboard team with them as leading members; he will "make them pros." The notion that they would even talk to this kook in reality is improbable, though in this movie they are skeptical but take him up on his offer. Manny excitedly tells them he is going to get them "flashy" uniforms and that they're going to "tour up and down the coast . . . in full arenas . . . be rich and famous . . . be on TV." Then to a chorus of "Yeah!" and "All right!" he announces his name for the team— the L.A. Wheels.

On the way to their first demo, a Jefferson Starship song is playing too loud for Manny, and when he can't identify the musical group, Alva (whose character's name is Tony Bluetile) utters a line that could be a touchstone for the whole movie: "Don't be such a lame goon, don't you know anything?" The first demo gets off to a shaky start when the riders rebel against Manny's choice of uniforms—shiny yellow-and-green shirts and short shorts. "You expect girls to see us in these?" is the incredulous complaint, along with, "They look gay." The team's career seems to be over before it has started, with Manny ranting bizarrely, "It's all in your mind. If you think gay, you are gay. I got a straight team, and it's going to stay that way." The narrative is saved because one of the main skaters, Jason (played by Paul Van der Wyck), agrees to wear the uniform and the rest of the team follows. The restless audience is unimpressed at first, but then one of the skaters drops off the stage and does a high jump; Tony walks the dog, and Jenny does a two-board nose wheelie before kicking up her board into her hand. The audience roars to life, and the show is a come-from-behind success.

Wacky high jinks are the order of the day. Manny calls Alva "Hot Dog" and at one point screams at the team, "No more skating, no more screwing around," which is an odd thing to say to a bunch of teenage skaters. Randy, one of the girl skaters, gets it on with her boyfriend, Jason. When Manny takes her aside to chastise her, she replies, "Just because you can't get any doesn't mean you can stop other people." In a hotel room, Alva drinks beer, looks at *Playboy* and breaks wind. Manny yells at Jason for not trying hard enough. Alva falls and is told, "You don't have your mind on your work." Work?

Throughout all the silliness, improbability and bad acting, parts of the movie show skating as it really was in 1977. The value of the film is its unintentional documentary aspect. Besides Alva, whose naturalness makes him the best "actor," or at least the most credible human element in the proceedings, there is a contest between the L.A. Wheels and another team called El Tigre at the Reseda

Skatercross park. Tom Inouye flies by, as do Jay Adams, Ellen Berryman, Bob Biniak, Steve Cathey, Paul Constantineau, Dave Hackett, Shogo Kubo, Jim Muir, Layne Oaks, Bobby Piercy, Andy Pryciak, Tom Sims, Laura Thornhill, Chris Yandall and the Logans. An unidentified rider does a barefoot kickflip—a feat that still looks radical.

The movie goes to the limit of cynical self-reflexivity with Jason's inevitable soul searching. A stoner with long blond hair who skates well, he drives a van with "High Roller" painted on the side and is being groomed to be the team star. At the beach after surfing, the problem that the movie exemplifies manifests itself—commercialism vs. soul. Jason's monologue is clichéd but manages to express the conflict of professionalism and money with sport and art: "I just feel like nothing is flowing right, like everything's screwed up . . . I used to be able to skate anywhere . . . I used to be able to skate the spillways, the bowls, the reservoirs, it was all a really mellow thing. Now it's all screwed up." The movie inadvertently touches on something poignant by showing his anguish about trading on the realness of what he loves for money and fame.

Manny takes his dictate as team leader seriously and proclaims, "You people don't realize what I do for you," the complaint of many an opportunist who uses others for his own advancement. That is the reality of the parasite selling and exploiting the "product" without having any connection to the soul of the actual thing, in this case skating itself.

There is a simultaneously hilarious and painful scene of the filming of a television commercial that illustrates this conflict. Jason drinks beer during the taping and is obviously troubled. He intentionally flubs his lines and calls the subpar helmet he is supposed to be endorsing "a piece of shit." Later he drunkenly skates alone down a road with a beer in his hand, almost gets run over and then is arrested by the police, who conveniently cruise by. Manny goes into his usual histrionics on hearing the news, feeling uncharacteristic guilt and moaning, "He wigged out . . . it's all my fault. I'm talking about pressure. Kids shouldn't be put in a box." Pretty humorous, coming from a movie that is by extension doing the same thing. This mercifully leads to the finale; with Jason out, Brad (the Leif Garrett character) has to fill his shoes in the big Burbank Downhill Invitational. To no one's surprise, Brad wins. Manny gets the trophy handed to him—as if he actually did the skating—and thanks "all the kids." They all have champagne in the bus, and Jason arrives for a reconciliation. The L.A. Wheels have a bright future.

Obviously *Skateboard* wasn't representative of skating as a whole at the time it was released. Neither was what was going on in Dogtown and the avant-garde circles of skating. Beyond the movies and the books and the magazines, skating was, without a doubt, huge. A whole population out there was skating without the parks and the good equipment and the latest tricks. Dogtown and certain parts of California had the hardcore innovative skaters who were getting attention for it, but there was a vast demographic of people in the rest of the world who loved skating just as much who didn't know or care about the hype.

Maybe they saw the movies and the magazines, and quite possibly they hungered for a park. But the majority of skaters at the time didn't have one. A lot of them might have been rebelling against the suburban angst and boredom of the seventies, the desolation and meaninglessness of teenage life in residential developments that is trenchantly evoked in the 1979 film *Over the Edge*. In it, Matt Dillon's motorcycle-riding outcast leads the teenage population of one such development to run amok, burning cars and trashing the town after they lock up the cops, teachers and parents inside the local high school. Kids in these places skated wherever they could, whenever, often just for transportation and fun.

It might be going too far to say that all these fun-seekers were socially rebellious. But there may have been something that was inherent to skating that attracted people because it was different and in opposition to the status quo and the standards of competitive sport that children the world over are socialized to accept. Skating isn't football, baseball, basketball or even tennis. Parents didn't encourage their children to skate; usually they did the opposite and actively tried to keep them from it. It has no exclusive positions, no rules, no end goal. It is flexible and informal. Skaters control their own physical activity—there are no coaches telling them what to do, no uniforms. How much that mattered to the average kid who got a skateboard because all his friends had one is unknowable. But certainly the participant control, the resistance that skating embodies, was and is one of its attractions.

These attractions and others held sway on a mass scale for a couple of years. In Southern California, it might be a kid living on the Pacific Beach side of Mount Soledad in San Diego, going to elementary school with Eric Gordon, son of the "G" in Gordon & Smith (G&S). In first grade, he would be butt-riding a wood deck with clay wheels down the driveway. A few years later he might run into Eric Gordon again at the Pacific Beach Recreation Center, and Eric had a new Fibreflex. The kid might have gotten a Stacy Peralta warptail and even made it a couple of times to the El Cajon Skatepark, though he never got that good. At his junior high school, there were older stoners who would ride steep, almost transitionless banks with an insane vengeance, doing barefoot edgers on benches they leaned sideways at the top of the bank. The kid might even have checked out a backyard pool, with a typical tube-top-wearing seventies stoner chick asking for Thai stick in exchange for riding her pool.

Farther afield, out of California, there were countless others riding down hills and taking their boards to school. Every kid wanted a skateboard, and a lot got them. Cheap plastic and dime-store boards were everywhere, all over the country and abroad also. Kids were doing the basics, tic-tacking, doing 360s, jumping over horizontal broomsticks a foot above the ground, going off of curbs, setting up slalom cones with soda cans, riding empty ditches and pools and parks when they were available. There weren't that many people on the level of the California rippers. There was only one Jay Adams. But there were many unheralded skaters whose names are lost to history, who are remembered by friends or maybe no one at all. They ripped whether there were observers and photographers or not. It was a magical couple of years, the real beginnings, the innovators and the fad followers all mixed in together, not that far from one another in terms of what they could do.

It was Free Formers, weighting and unweighting, torqueing it, nose wheelies, 360s, some skaters still espousing the virtues of ball bearings; green, red and yellow wheels, bunnyhops, power slides, handstands, kickflips, twenty-four-inch hot-dog and twenty-seven-inch slalom boards, Olympia beer T-shirts, skating barefoot and getting "hamburger feet"; bombing hills, Road Riders, Bonzai aluminum boards, skateparks and pro shops with Pong games; surfing

and motorcross and bicentennial photo pictorials on the tops of
decks, paved waves, lady skaters, windsail boards, flowing energy,
pot, Grentec, skating demos at Peter Frampton concerts, *Skateboarder*
145 pages long; people riding dirt boards, the dawn of skid plates,
bell-bottoms, long hair, Farrah Fawcett and her hairdo styling on a
little plastic board, smiling at the camera. It was massive.

Chapter Nine
The Death Bowl, Giant Pipes and the End of Skating

Terry grew up in Rancho Palos Verde, just south of Los Angeles but far enough away that he was unaware of the skating renaissance up the coast. It was easy to be isolated in 1975, without the current profusion of magazines and television shows promoting "extreme" sporting activities that were then underground. In the mid-seventies, something could be percolating practically next door and still escape your attention. Terry was fourteen years old and living a sequestered upper-middle-class existence when one day he met his friend Chris at a car dealership. Chris had an aluminum board with urethane wheels, and Terry gave it a try. They began cruising down hills on Chris's board, turning until that point of no return where speed took over and they just went straight, barely keeping it together until the slope leveled off and they could slow down. Soon Terry had his own board and was skating every day, getting towed behind cars and high-jumping over horizontal bars, riding off of ledges and picnic tables, then going to the logical conclusion and attempting to ride off the roof of a van.

Chris took Terry to his first pool at an abandoned YMCA on Ninth Street in San Pedro right by the 110 freeway. It was an area immortalized in all its downtrodden glory by John Fante in *The Road to Los Angeles:* "A man-made land, flat and in disorder, shacks unpainted, piles of lumber, piles of tin cans, oil derricks. . . . Out of the muddy channel bed came the rich stench of oil and scum and strange cargo." Fifty years after these lines were written, the stench remained; the area was strewn with litter, and the only businesses that still existed were liquor stores. The pool had small aquamarine tiles below coping that produced an incredible buzzing noise when someone carved over them; the sound was so distinctive that it remains fresh in Terry's mind to this day. In the beginning, he was pumping only halfway up the walls, but he was immediately hooked. The second time he rode the pool, he fell and broke his arm. Undeterred, he got right back to skating with his cast on. Not long after, he was riding a one-of-a-kind Doug Schneider board, airbrushed with a clown face and fish under the clear grip tape. He swore by Road Rider wheels. They were magical in their unblemished redness under the glass at the Kanoa Surf Shop.

After Ninth Street, they moved on to what became their local spot for the next two years. The First Street pool was nine feet deep with five feet of transition, and the rest was pure vertical flat wall. Terry learned how to fakie, going up the wall forward and coming down backward in a straight line, pumping back and forth. Then he started grinding the coping frontside and backside and edging out at the top of the pool. He and his friends would take the bus there after school, stopping at one of the liquor stores to ogle the naked women and shaved pubis in *Hustler* and buy ten-cent bottles of Smileyflavored water before skating as long as daylight lasted. Local pro Doug Schneider skated there, and sometimes the Dog-towners showed up. Though it was a big deal when Tony Alva came—he was a celebrity of sorts—they weren't in enough awe of him to stop skating. It was their spot.

After two years, First Street was demolished. There was a dry spell, so Terry and his friends stole a bunch of wood from one of the construction sites in the neighborhood and built a half-pipe. They rode that until some Mexicans came by one day and said they "wanted" the ramp. The kid who owned it told them to fuck off, and they drove away. The next day the ramp was covered in tar, destroyed, never to be ridden again. At a session around this time in a drainage ditch, the skaters got busted by the cops. As they were getting in the backseat of a cruiser to be taken home to their parents' punish-ment, one of the cops yelled, "You're stupid for doing this," before directly venting his malice at Terry with, "And you're the stupidest of them all!"

Any empty pool was fair game. They got brazen and usually left some kind of damage, chipped plaster and scuff marks, and sometimes removed the diving board. They stole a pump from a pool-service truck and put it to work in a pool whose owners had gone on vacation, the hose draped over the embankment above houses lower down the hill. Two days later, they saw fire engines and police cars around one of the houses, and realized they had inadvertently caused a massive landslide.

Another pool was at a "haunted" house. They came upon it at night and bailed out the muck at the bottom of the pool without being sure that it was worth it. It turned out to be rippable and they skated it often, but even with repeated visits it never lost its eerie feel. Nobody went inside the house, where family photos still hung on the walls and all the furniture was in place, everything covered with a thick layer of dust. The house also had stables, and the doors to the stalls had ragged holes in them. The story was that the horses had gone insane and bashed the holes out with their heads. Later in life, the tale seemed like a silly legend, but at the time it added credence to the spooky atmosphere. They skated the pool for a while, until more and more people came and it got to be a bust.

There was also an oval-shaped pool at a house high on a ridge at the top of one of the many canyons in the area. The rumor adding to the risk factor there was that a kid had been paralyzed while skating. The skaters' escape routes were planned out much too effectively for the cops, who came for frequent futile visits but never caught them.

Concurrent with their pool escapades, the whole wonderful world of skateparks came into being. Terry had the luck of living near an unprecedented phenomenon of concrete architecture built expressly for skateboarders: skate rinks, man-made bowls and ditches made for skating pleasure. The closest one was Torrance, with a big snake run that ran into the half-pipe. His friend's divorced mother drove them to Concrete Wave in Anaheim; she was cool and hung out in the parking lot while they skated. Terry skated Carson with huge football stadium floodlights illuminating hundreds of kids skating in the hot California night. Paramount had a sixteen-foot-deep bowl that was so big and gnarly it defied logic. It was lit by overhead stadium lights, but even with those on, it was so deep that most of it was in shadow. Terry would pump back and forth and get within a foot of the top, always too scared to one-wheel it. Once he saw a pro—maybe Kevin Anderson—roll into the bowl. Seeing that tore apart his assumptions about what was possible. The rider climbed the wall to the top of the bowl, rode out onto the deck and then rolled back in, plunging down into the abyss. Insanity. Later on they went to the Pipeline in Upland, the height of skatepark design at the time with its full pipe and big bowl. The pro shop also had a great arcade where Terry played Starz and Captain Fantastic, the best pinball games of the era.

When he wasn't at the parks, his routine was going to school and skating during lunch with the large group of kids who shared his passion. They were a normal and accepted part of school society, an offshoot subculture like the surfers but, like them, not really outcasts. They listened to Foghat ("Fool for the City"), Led Zeppelin, UFO, Foreigner and, most of all, Ted Nugent. Energized, loud, driving rock for similarly inclined youth. Nugent was the sound of three summers. At the park, at the pool, at school, "Stranglehold" and "Cat Scratch Fever" were the ubiquitous anthems providing the sound track that pushed them to further extremes.

Andy grew up on the Upper West Side of Manhattan and went to Yeshiva school on Henry Street. The school had only a few students left because of the Jewish diaspora to the outer boroughs. He and his friends would sneak into the gym on the top floor to play Ping-Pong and basketball. Their team was part of that fifties and sixties tradition of a strong Jewish basketball presence in New York. One of their best players was a black kid named Enoch Israel. But Andy had other interests besides basketball.

It had started in the sixties. He had vague memories of being a little kid in Central Park and playing on one of the primitive skateboards of the time. All was forgotten until 1972, when Andy was eleven and found a Mustang 66 model with metal wheels in the basement of his building. He dusted it off and took it to Central Park, where he got towed behind a friend riding a Schwinn Stingray. A couple of years later, Andy saw a kid he knew from sledding in Central Park during the winter. He had something totally new—a Fiberglass "Bunger" board, with Excalibur trucks and Roller Sports Mark Four wheels, much more advanced than anything that Andy had ever seen. Andy was in awe and had to learn. He left behind his old board and got a new one from Grogs Surf Palace in Seaside Heights, New Jersey, for forty-five dollars. They skated the sidewalk, doing 360s and kickturning around a grate. People would stop them and ask where they could buy boards. There were no skate shops then, no magazines, no outside influences.

The wheels had loose ball bearings, seven in each wheel that they would "pour" into the "cone" of the wheel and then spin the wheel down to the truck to tighten it. The boards were temperamental and rickety, and there were always mechanical difficulties and surprises that needed to be fixed. There was a level of upkeep and a close relationship with the board that disappeared in later years with the standardization of skate equipment. Like a bush pilot of a dilapidated single-engine plane, the skaters were always improvising ad-hoc repairs.

Andy became addicted. First the goal was to nose-wheelie or handstand down the hill in Central Park. Then he and his friends found some banks at Eighty-eighth and Madison, and at Seventy-first and Third Avenue, where they learned how to carve and go up inclined surfaces and come back down in one piece. These guys' parents had summer houses on Fire Island, and they actually surfed; they were the first skaters Andy saw get low and do berts on banks. At some point during 1976, they saw *Skateboarder*, which had a major impact. They saw people riding in pools and tricks that they'd never imagined. Unbelievable. But soon they digested this new conceptual and visual information and were ready to apply it. After Andy saw the magazine, California became the Promised Land. All he wanted to do was go there and skate.

Around this time, the only shop that sold skate equipment was the Blacker & Kooby stationery store. Then the wave broke, and overnight skating got huge. Boards were being sold all over, and kids were riding everywhere. Andy would meet his friends at the Alice in Wonderland sculpture in Central Park. Because they were relatively poor and scrappy, a natural animosity blossomed between Andy's friends and the Upper East Side rich kids with their new shiny boards. They would steal the rich kids' boards and throw them in the sailing pond, or force the kids to run laps around the pond before giving the boards back, or sometimes they would just appropriate them. Andy got into a slightly criminal element— just taking boards, nothing serious. Once at Blacker & Kooby he wanted to exchange a board he'd bought and broken that day, but they wouldn't do it, so he ran out of the store with a new board. The owner gave chase and grabbed him, so Andy cracked the guy over the head with the board and ran off with it.

Skateparks were now being built on the East Coast, and soon Andy was localizing the Farmingdale park and the Huntington skateboard arena on Long Island. That wasn't enough, so in 1976 they built a quarter-pipe in Riverside Park with wood stolen from a West Side Highway construction site. The desire for vertical became of supreme importance, and they started searching out pools that could provide better terrain than the parks could offer. They would take the train up to the affluent Riverdale section of the Bronx and skate five pools in one day. Sessions at one called the Death Bowl were great, but they had to worry about the landlord of the building, who would throw bricks at them from the roof. At another pool they were surprised by the sight of a Riverdale housewife walking out onto the deck while they were riding, her shock turning into a wail of "Harry! Harry!" for her husband to come out and put an end to the madness. The skaters scurried away like rats. Pools and more pools, and then bombing the hills of Riverdale.

Andy's heroes were Jay Adams and Tony Alva and the other Z-Boys. He also liked Arthur Lake, a little kid who was in *Skateboarder* backside kickturning at the rock coping in his parents' swimming pool in L.A.; and Gerry Lopez, of course, the coolest surfer of them all. Around this time, Andy's pool expertise was setting him apart. The Kryptonics company had tryouts for their team, and Andy and his pool-riding friends blew away the East Side freestylers. They were way ahead of the competition with their interpretation of the Dogtown style, grinding, doing rock walks and slides, pulling off their first early frontside airs. He skated for Kryptonics and entered contests. At one in Staten Island, the S.I. team would skate together to their song, Queen's "We Will Rock You." Every-body was hyped. Andy was also smoking pot and hanging out with some older guys who were supplying all of New York City with LSD. They looked a little like hippies but were tougher, hardcore rock-and-roll drug guys known as radicals. Andy was friends with the "Rebels" graffiti gang. They wore jeans and Converse high-tops and were much more menacing than the punk rockers starting to appear on the scene.

In 1965, when James was seven years old, his father brought home a skateboard with clay wheels as a present. At first he rode it on his stomach, before moving on to stand up on it, going down hills and riding on the sidewalk. The local school had some banks, and he carved the walls there. He and his family lived a block from the beach in Palos Verdes, California. He was in the water every day, riding early Styrofoam Boogie Boards and rafts on the waves. At eleven or twelve, he started surfing at Torrance and Palos Verdes, learning to ride on a seven-foot-four board, which was considered short at the time. From that time on he was also always skating, using trucks from his sister's roller skates and boards he made in junior high wood-shop class.

In 1973 someone showed up with either Cadillac or Meta-Flex urethane wheels. Within days everyone had them. Cadillacs were deemed the best because they were less slip-pery. Right around this time, he and his friends started get-ting driver's licenses. They heard rumors from their older brothers so they started driving around looking for pools and ditches. This first pool was in Huntington Beach, at an abandoned house where the locals were already hitting tiles. At first, James and his friends weren't that skilled; there was a lot of crashing and backslaps. But they picked it up quickly, and soon they were riding pools every day.

They hooked up with Waldo Autry, who was already known as one of the best new vertical skaters. He made boards out of plywood birch, soaking them in water and using a vise to bend the ends into kicktails. Then he laminated the board with fiberglass, airbrushed it and put clear silica sand on top for traction. This was before grip tape. James and his friends figured out this process from Waldo and started making their own boards—in their opinion, homemade boards were better than storebought. They also bought shaped surfboards from Phil Becker for forty or fifty dollars that they took home and glassed themselves.

Skating was the biggest thing in their lives, bigger than surfing and school. It was automatic, grab your board and go skate. It was unsaid, natural, all-encompassing. And they weren't the only ones. At a ditch there would be four hundred people skating, a playground for teenagers. Sometimes the police would drive up and tell everybody to leave, but nobody would, and the cops would skulk away, defeated.

Driving around, they would see younger kids with boards and ask where the pools were. The kids would say they didn't know, trying to protect their spots. James's friend Nicky Vlaco would jump out and grab them, hold them by their ankles and shake them upside down until they came clean. Things were changing every day; there were new pools, new tricks and new equipment. They first got sealed bearings from a friend who worked at a German bearing company. They took boxes of bearings to all the different spots and sold them, one dollar for one, eight dollars for a set of eight. There wasn't any trouble finding business because they were never skating alone; the entire youth corps of Southern California was out riding skateboards.

James began taking pictures of his friends as a hobby and started bringing his camera every time he went skating. He had a slightly older friend down the street who published a magazine called *Skateboard*. It lasted only three issues, but the friend put some of James's photos in it and gave him some money and once an old motorcycle. This was when Palos Verdes had a lot of open land and you could motocross all over the place. James's other friend Brian Gillogly wrote for *Skateboarder* and started showing the editors James's pictures, which got accepted. Monthly two-hundred-dollar checks began to arrive in the mail. James was in eleventh grade.

Through hearsay they learned about other pools, banks and pipes. There were pools at abandoned houses and kids who had gotten their parents to drain their backyard oases. First Street was a mess when they first found it; half the house was in the pool, so it was a lot of work to clean it up. The Dogtown guys came down. They were more aggressive and dropped in a lot but burned out fast and left after an hour. Their influence was definitely real—after they saw Jay Adams do a bert in a pool, everybody was doing it; things were never the same. Gregg Ayres, Stacy Peralta, Waldo Autry, Doug Schneider, Kevin Anderson and Tony Alva all stood out.

At first it was inherently renegade, because everywhere they rode was illegal. But then the skateparks started opening and they stopped looking for pools as much. The parks had the obvious advantage of no police hassles, and they had lights so you could skate at night. There were certain rituals and migrations, a certain park in the day, a different park at night: roving bands of skaters going from park to park, plus the locals who skated their home spot. There was always a way around paying. James was sure the adults who owned the parks didn't understand skating at all and just looked on it as a money-making venture.

Around this time the mass-media inanity started happening; *Skateboard: The Movie* and everything else. Ellen O'Neal stunt-doubled for Linda Carter on *Wonder Woman*. The ill-fated traveling skateboard stage show, *Skateboardmania*, was representatively hokey. The show used a full pipe with a track that a skateboard was attached to. The skater rode the board down the track while holding on to a handle on the board and went upside down to complete a 360-degree loop. Sometimes they would lose speed at the top of the loop and get stuck there. Duane Peters did it without the track, a stunt that foreshadowed his later reputation as the "Master of Disaster" and wasn't repeated again until twenty years later, when Tony Hawk did it for an Airwalk advertisement. *Skateboardmania* opened at the Long Beach arena, where event organizers had put plywood over the ice that was there for a hockey game. The wood got soaked so the skaters slid all over the place. James's friend Tony Jetton was in it, and everyone made fun of him because of the silly costumes, but it wasn't a big deal to them; they didn't care too much about the mainstream. They were doing what they wanted to do and would skate no matter what.

In the twelfth grade, James was hired as a staff photographer for *Skateboarder*, and a little later he became the photo editor. The guys at *Skateboarder* still skated, though they were of the old school. Brian Gillogly rode long boards barefoot, and Warren Bolster carved down hills; they were more connected to the surfing vibe. James and his gang just liked to go down hills straight and see how fast they could go. That whole flatland-freestyle thing didn't do much for them. James saw a lot of contests and shot copious numbers of photos. The contests were fun, and he could observe the clash between the Dogtown style and the freestyle scene; it was as if they were in two different contests. Jay Adams and the rest were low to the ground, and Brad Logan was doing two-minute nose wheelies. The judging was always locally determined and prejudiced, and that usually led to fights afterward.

James's father worked for the company that supplied the machines for welding the steel rebar on the first Ameron full pipes at the San Onofre nuclear power plant. He got the manager to let James and his friends skate there. They were the only people who had carte blanche to skate there "legally." For a while they also went to the Arizona pipes, where they would camp out in their cars or stay at the closest human habitation, a retirement community called Sun City where they really made an impression.

One trip that stood out was in 1979. A skatepark was opening in Texas, and the owner flew twenty pro skaters out for the event. C. R. Stecyk and James were the only two people in first class who weren't wearing suits. The other skaters were in the back of plane, where they immediately proceeded to smoke pot, do coke and order cocktails. James saw one of the stewardesses go into the cockpit crying and say, "I quit, I can't handle it!" The copilot got on the PA and told the passengers that everything was okay, which of course made the passengers think they were being hijacked. The pilot came to Stecyk and James under the correct assumption that they were somehow connected to the mayhem in the back and told them to get the skaters under control or he would land the plane in Phoenix and have them all arrested. Stecyk went back and while being pelted with ice cubes and peanuts wrote a note detailing what the pilot had said and dropped it on the lap of one of the older skaters. That calmed them down somewhat.

When the group landed in Texas, the three local television stations were waiting. In Texas, Rick Blackhart and Doug Schneider stayed at the park owner's expensive condominium. First Blackhart mangled some modern metal sculpture and then, inspired by Ted Nugent's antics, he got the television and was standing by the window ready to throw it out when the maid came in and screamed. The cops arrived, and Blackhart had to hide in a van at the skatepark all weekend. Hotel rooms were destroyed and rental cars were wrecked.

Watching Blackhart skate was like watching a four-wheel-drive vehicle, since he would go over anything. Probably the craziest thing James ever saw was Blackhart rolling in for the first time in a pool with coping. They psyched him out, telling him that it was possible and that he could do it. He jumped off a dozen times over a few days and then just did it. An insane leap, going from horizontal to vertical in an instant. Then at the Big O skatepark someone said, "Hey, check this out." It was some unknown guy doing rock-and-rolls, the first time James had ever seen that. The skater rode to the top, laid the front part of the board onto the platform until the back trucks hit coping, then turned back into the pool in a sort of seesaw motion. James also saw Darrell Miller doing miller flips for the first time—a frontside handplant that turned into a backflip, landing fakie. Because he was a photographer, he saw these advances early on. One day Stacy Peralta told him, "You've got to take pictures of this kid, he's unbelievable." It was Alan "Ollie" Gelfand doing ollies, a "secret" trick then that was later named after Alan. There was always something completely different.

The Dogtowners and other pro skaters were acting like rock stars. Some of them were living like rock stars. For Tony Alva it was "the best cars, finest food, hottest chicks." He was hanging out with Craig Chaquico of the Jefferson Starship and Bunker Spreckels, the heir to the Spreckels sugar fortune. Alva and others were flown to events and the openings of skateparks, including one visit to a new park in Mexico, where the local police delivered a trash bag full of marijuana and Jay Adams was chased around a bordello by a portly prostitute lactating in his direction.

The Dogtowners were being emulated and imitated, and some of them were prospering, but their cohesion as a group was feeling the strains of greed and excess. An advertisement for the Skateboard City shop in Santa Monica in the March 1978 *Skateboarder* showed the original Z-Boys together for the last time. They had conquered and were now inevitably dividing. The Zephyr team dissolved. Jeff Ho and Skip Engblom went into a partnership with Jay Adams's step-father, Kent Sherwood: that fell apart, and he started Z-Flex without them, taking Jay; Adams's Z-Flex model was hugely popular. Tony Alva went to Logan Earth Ski and then left to start his own company. Peralta left G&S, where his signature warptail model had been selling five thousand boards a month, and went into a partnership with George Powell to form Powell and Peralta. Jim Muir and Wes Humpston formed Dogtown, trademarking the name and using the Dogtown "cross" as their signature graphic. The band had broken up. Some had made a lot of money, some had been exploited. They got fame, they got laid. They made a mark. Changes were around the corner. In a couple of years, Alva would be training to become a dental technician and *Skateboarder* would no longer exist.

The February 1979 issue of *Skateboarder* had Stecyk returning to the subject of Dogtown and its place in the scheme of things. "Death of Dogtown?" was the headline on the cover, and inside was Stecyk's report, "Dead Dogs Never Lie." The first page used a great Robert Frank *Exile on Main Street*-inspired collage, with pictures of Shogo Kubo, Stacy Peralta, El Thumper, Jay Adams, an Ed Roth–style Surfink, a dead shark and Stecyk himself. It was both a visual celebration and a eulogy for an era that was coming to a close: Stecyk wrote, "The 'Death of Dogtown'? Even the concept made me shudder." Having been gone for three months fishing in Mexico, he wasn't up on events. Driving to Santa Monica, he saw a six-foot swell at Malibu Point and then took a left onto the municipal pier in the heart of Dogtown. A new mall was being built, a movie was being filmed and "*Los chingaders de controlla*" types, Eighteenth Street *vatos*, were hanging out. And it was the opening day of the new hometown Marina del Rey Skatepark. "S.M. wasn't dead, it had just mutated into some new evolutionary form." For the first time in at least two years, the Z-Boys were reunited. The sessioning was intense, with Adams, Alva, Peralta, Kubo, Bob Biniak, Wentzle Ruml and Paul Constantineau in attendance. "Dogtown is now trademarked.

The skaters drive imported cars instead of walking. Dogtown has gone uptown; or more precisely, uptown has gone Dogtown." Their "one-time variant style has been adopted by the masses," the perennial syndrome of the avant-garde being co-opted. But had it been neutered? Santa Monica (and, in broader terms, skating) was still vital, and talent was already coming up. The difference was that "the media circus has moved on, looking for new clowns."

Stecyk wrote, "The need for greed has put a lot of people in a bad place. . . . Many who sought the easy buck are out of luck. . . . The doomsayers are calling it curtains for the sport because sales are down and a recession is coming." Too many got into it for the cash instead of the original thrill, bringing the ill effects of commercialization. Nevertheless, Stecyk concluded, skating could go down temporarily, but the hardcore would continue to ride no matter what. "To get rid of skating, you'd have to do away with concrete— in all its various forms."

By 1980 *Skateboarder* magazine was considerably thinner, and sales were plummeting. That aspect aside, skating moves were multiplying and getting harder. A centerfold showed Steve Alba doing an incredibly high (for the time) frontside air over Scott Dunlap's carve in the fifteen-foot bowl at Upland. Darrell Miller was pioneering footplants, in which the skater took one foot off and planted it on the top of the bowl while holding the board to the other foot before jumping back in; and Chris Strople started doing rock-and-roll boardslides, where the bottom of the board was slid across the coping during the seesaw of the rock-and-roll. Inverts, invented by Bobby Valdez, were getting more extended and backside airs were getting higher. Arguably one the best parks of all time had just opened in Cherry Hill, New Jersey. The shoddy manufacturers had mostly died out, and board size had standardized at about thirty by ten inches. Two things in the February 1979 issue could be interpreted as pointing toward skating's downfall in popularity and what unexpected avenues for rebirth might be coming in the future. One is a full-page advertisement for the magazine *Roller Skating*, with the headline "New York City: Advanced Disco Fever Epidemic." The other is a scathingly dismissive review by the Jackson Browne–worshiping Corky Carroll of the Rotters' "Sit on My Face Stevie Nix" single.

The magazine had a wistful quality at this point; the end was nigh whether anybody knew just how drastic the bust would be or not. May's "In Search of Giant Pipes" was one of the last articles Stecyk wrote before the magazine turned into the short-lived, ill-fated *Action Now*. In the article there is a feeling of antihype, the back-to-the-basics ethos of search and destroy. The story starts with Stecyk at a party, where a mystery man with a Texas drawl tells him of secret twenty-four-foot pipes but won't divulge any information except a color snapshot. Contact is made, and Stecyk is awakened by Rick Blackhart blasting Ted Nugent's "Cat Scratch Fever" at 250 decibels outside his house. They're off to Rio Lobo in Texas with Doug Schneider, Steve Alba and James Cassimus to find Hardrock Miller's Last Chance Flying A gas station and the stucco-clad brontosaurus it is in the shadow of. There they rendezvous with their guides who look like "refugees from *Force 10 from Navarrone.*" One of the crew's uncles had worked at an Atlas underground missile base, closed due to the advent of the cruise missile. The pipes were huge—part of the cooling system for the reactors that powered the base—and perfect except that the lack of outside air circulating meant the temperature was 36 degrees Fahrenheit. They found the "Glory Hole," where a cylindrical flume went up to the surface and warm air came in. The structure's cold war associations and massiveness lent it an ominous aura. And in its subterranean aspect, it figuratively foreshadowed where skating was going.

Meanwhile, Terry was going to see Devo at the Santa Monica Civic, the "Duty Now for the Future Tour." These Ohioans made jumpy synthesized rock music with an angle of repressed mutant sexuality and intimations of man's doom and "Devolution." They were the anti-Foghat and everything else of the decade. The Devo "corporate anthem" came on before they took the stage, and an industrial film showed Devo wearing distorted melted face masks and red suits while engaging in unspecified activities at a futuristic toxic-waste site. Then the actual band came out in white chemical lab suits with dark glasses on, an almost hair-raising sight. It was a whole different world. Ted Nugent was left behind. Soon after came Devo's "Freedom of Choice" video, filmed at Marina del Rey with Dave Andrecht, Jay Smith and Eddie Elguera: the meeting of vanguard music and vanguard skating.

The next year, Terry went to see them again, and something was different. In the preshow film Devo's mascot, Booji Boy, was killed off. Symbolically it represented the death of something, the end of the unique artistic quality of the band. There were too many new-wavers, thrill seekers and normal lame people in the audience, fair-weather fans waiting for the hit song "Whip It." Terry and his friends left before the show ended. Like the surfers at Malibu twenty years earlier, Terry had seen his metaphoric beach invaded by the barbarians.

Andy went off to college and majored in "chemistry," so to speak—taking a lot of chemicals. The parks were closing and it was winter, but he continued to skate in the cafeteria. He got kicked out of school on a combination of disciplinary probation, academic probation and police probation. Back in New York nobody seemed to be skating.

James was there to see the fall in California. With amazing swiftness, skate companies started disappearing. The parks closed. The bottom dropped out. There were different theories: that the magazine had killed skating, that skateparks killed it, that there hadn't been enough of an effort to bring in new kids or that vertical riding had become too specialized. James thought it was a natural occurrence, just part of a cycle of death and rebirth. They couldn't do *Skateboarder* in color anymore, so the editors tried to save it and at least have some skating with *Action Now*, which lasted barely over a year. James went back to surfing and got into snowboarding, which came closest to approximating the vertical rush of skating. Skating was almost dead. Again.

Chapter Ten
The Elk and the Skateboarder

Down at the lake on July 4, 1976, after eating hot dogs off the grill and watching the red, white and blue fireworks in that bicentennial summer of overblown patriotism, I borrowed another kid's yellow plastic banana board and rode for the first time in my life. On the nearby tennis courts I pushed and glided and felt the freedom and thrill of rolling. The isolation of the Colorado mountain town I lived in hadn't stopped the intrusion of skateboarding into the collective consciousness. It was a trend and I was as susceptible to the fads of the time as any other nine-year-old. Right after, I made it clear to my parents that I desperately needed a skateboard, and got to pick one out at the local bike shop. It was a seven-inch-wide GT Woody with three strips of grip tape and translucent red wheels. I rode it every chance I got, on the tennis courts and on the streets, learning how to lean and turn, tentatively trying to do a 360.

I had long brown hair, corduroy bell-bottoms and stoner aspirations. Besides trying to act cool, despite my glasses and braces, while navigating the social complexities of middle school, I lived and breathed skiing. In the summer, skating was the closest thing to skiing available. Instead of being a surfer who skated when the waves were flat, I skated when there wasn't any snow. Three thousand souls inhabited Estes Park on the continental divide, surrounded by the Rocky Mountains and the aptly named Never Summer Range. Denver was seventy miles away, but it might as well have been on a different continent. For all intents and purposes, Estes Park existed in a zone far removed from contemporary civilization. News of any kind of excitement got around quickly, and on a dry hot day not long after the Independence Day festivities, I heard there was going to be a skateboard contest at the local Holiday Inn, where my friends and I often sneaked in to play Foosball and carouse in the pool until we got kicked out. The contest was held on the sloped driveway that went from the parking lot down to the road. I sat on the sidelines wearing my oversize Dolomite ski boots T-shirt, habitually tilting my head back to feel my hair's luxuriousness brushing my neck. There was a short slalom course and some freestyling—daffys, nose wheelies and people doing more 360s than I thought possible. An emcee announced; girls with cutoffs and layered hair rode tandem. The guys had even longer layered hair. It was a classic scene of the seventies, one that could never be re-created despite the nostalgic efforts of hindsight aficionados of that decade. I felt like I was witnessing something important that was connected to a world I had only heard rumors about. I knew intuitively that it had something to do with California.

Later that summer, my father took me to visit my grandmother on the peninsula south of San Francisco, where I rode roller coasters at an amusement park and took a tour of the eccentric widow Winchester's Mystery House. I also learned that there was a skatepark nearby. The park was like nothing I'd ever seen, a huge expanse of undulating concrete forms stretching off into the distance. There were snake runs, extremely deep and rough half-pipes that looked terrifying, two pink pools and the "washboard," with three rounded waves leading up to it. I wore smelly, sweaty rented pads over my jeans, and a faded green T-shirt with an iron-on that read "Physical Graffiti" above a picture of a shirtless, barefoot skater. I repeatedly tried to go down the mellowest snake run but kept picking up way too much speed after the first turn. I'd jump off, walk back up to wait my turn and obsessively hurtle myself down again while my father and aunt watched from the spectator walkway overhead. The heat and combination of excitement and culture shock put me into an almost hallucinatory state of mind. I was agog at the sight of hundreds of teenage Californians carving down the snake runs at speed and doing slides and tricks beyond my comprehension. There was an intoxicating odor of sweat, urethane, dust and pot smoke hanging in the air. To me these benighted people were living in a utopia. I went back to Colorado filled with envy and longing and tales to tell of the Promised Land.

But things change, and at ten years old, I was powerfully beholden to the whims of preteen group mentality. A skatepark in Colorado was an impossible dream, and after the visit to Winchester, nothing local really compared. So I put the GT Woody away in the garage and followed the next big fad and got myself a BMX bicycle. On my red Rampar bike with its yellow rims, I rode over rocks and logs, doing an early version of mountain biking and flying off every dirt pile I could find.

My two main pursuits were skiing and swimming, though I was getting tired of the daily three-hour regimen of swim practice. The realization that I was never going to make it to the Olympics had me on the verge of quitting the team after five years of continuous training and getting up at 5 A.M. to carpool to swim meets down in the valley. Skiing was where it was at for me; it had the juice, it was still radical and exciting and not entirely bourgeois. What I was participating in and witnessing at our local ski area was extreme skiing before the term was coined. We were doing backflips off of ten-foot kickers, wearing red, white and blue mirrored I Ski sunglasses, hiking to hidden bowls for virgin powder, skiing close-knit trees at speed, tucking to seventy-five miles an hour on the Columbine run and doing helicopters (a 360-degree aerial spin) into 45-degree-steep couloirs. Also there was the invincible Ingemar Stenmark, the best slalom racer ever, and Steve McKinney, who was breaking the 125-mile-an-hour barrier. It was an experimental and free time, before skiing turned corporate and ceded its outlaw status to snowboarding.

My two sisters were older, and I tagged along with them and was hanging out with skier stoners ten years my senior who were some of the best practitioners of the art I have ever encountered, as well as part of the era's confluence of drugs and rock and roll with freestyle and out-of-bounds skiing. Around them I felt cool smoking pot in vans with teardrop windows listening to "Some Girls" in the parking lot before hitting the slopes for blizzard-condition powder days. I went from the fifth-grade uniform of Toughskins and cheap blue sneakers with the three white stripes to bell-bottom jeans, flannel shirts, hiking boots and the mandatory puffy down jacket. I saw Van Halen and was handed my first joint in the summer after fifth grade at an Eagles concert attended by sixty thousand people. I painfully tried to smoke cigarettes out in the woods, used chew and snuff and sought out any available alcohol. Our town was awash with drugs and boredom, and to alleviate the latter by indulging in the former was something to aspire to, and I did, because everybody around me except my parents was using every mind-altering substance they could get their hands on. Hanging out with the older cool people gave me a certain self-consciousness and distance from my own age group that was to have repercussions later. I was starting to subconsciously register and despair of the inanity and conformity of small-town life. Something was definitely starting to come to the surface by my eighth-grade year, when I started vandalizing school property more than usual, and laughed out loud with glee when our art teacher nervously told us that President Ronald Reagan had just been shot.

I'm sure a rankling disgust and boredom with my town and with my peers' dazed-and-confused mentality had a part in the epiphany that came during my twelfth year. One day my friend Andrew and I were in the bookstore where my mother worked, looking at the magazines. Between the favorites I could look at, *Car and Driver, Cartoons, MAD* and *Cracked*—and to the left of *Playboy*, which I desperately wanted to take down but couldn't—was one forlorn copy of *Skateboarder*. It had a blue cover with a picture of somebody named Brad Bowman flying above a ten-foot-high plywood ramp, somehow attached to his board without the use of his hands. He wore an exotic white Flyaway helmet with blue-and-red pinstriping and a cast on his wrist. The image was immediately and forever seared into my memory. I opened the magazine and entered into an entirely new universe for which I had no frame of reference. The glossy color photos showed people on boards much wider than any I'd ever seen, with different-colored coned wheels, riding in deep pools and doing totally incomprehensible moves above them that looked like one-handed handstands. I was mystified, excited and intrigued. There was something about how the skaters and the graphics on their boards looked that was creepy and slightly subversive. One graphic that made a particular impression was on the Powell Peralta Ray "Bones" Rodriguez board that Alan Gelfand was navigating through an ollie on his ramp in Hollywood, Florida. The board was an unnatural neon yellow, with a serious-looking skull holding a sword in front of itself, looking like an evil cadaverous wizard. Something about this new stimulus, and a latent wish to rebel against Estes Park's constrictions, galvanized Andrew and me. We got religion. We were going to skate again.

Looking back, I can see that my revived fascination with skating had some simmering causes that I could not have articulated at the time. Though I was a devoted skier and swimmer, these two sports are fundamentally different from team athletics and more often than not are about a quest for mental transportation from daily life instead of beating another competitor. In swimming, you race against a clock; and judges or times don't measure real skiing—it's about getting radical beyond quantification. Skiing and swimming are both inherently solitary, and that's why I liked them so much. I was a dreamy child who lived a mile from a paved road and spent a lot of time alone, amusing myself. My predilections for shunning competition and organized activities dovetailed with a growing awareness of how much I despised team sports and their mentality. I had played flag football good-naturedly and enjoyed shooting baskets, but I didn't really like teams and the whole regimented sports scene—at an early age, the institutionalized jock mentality and all its attendant boorishness bothered me. I enjoyed them to some extent, but my bad eyesight and lack of interest were serious limiting factors. In that first look at *Skateboarder*, I saw some glimmerings of a way out through a physical activity that seemed to encourage a diametrically opposed lifestyle.

Deciding to embrace skating went against all the prevailing winds in our town. Skating was passé, and there was nary a skater in sight. But I got the GT Woody out and started pushing around our garage, turning and grinding the back truck on the wooden edge where it ended and the dirt of the driveway began. There wasn't much to skate besides the garage, the flagstone walkway by our house and a shuffleboard court at the closest house to ours, two hundred yards away. That house also had a flagstone patio with ledges to roll off of. Besides that, my immediate surroundings were a beautiful vista of snow-covered peaks, pine trees, rocks and no cement. Our two-man retrograde movement made the big leap beyond Estes Park when we got Andrew's mother to drive us to the skatepark thirty-five miles away in Boulder. The park was in a desolate field across from a bowling alley, next to the highway to Denver, and had a huge key-hole-shaped pool and various bowls. This was the world shown in *Skateboarder* brought to life. People were riding the bowls on ten-inch-wide boards with pink and green wheels, doing the tricks we had seen only in the magazine. That first time we must have looked like religious pilgrims staring in disbelief and wonder at the magnificence of the holy shrine.

The first day, I rolled down the seemingly insanely steep slope of the mellow egg-shaped reservoir without any control over my direction or speed and didn't know what to do when I barely got to the other side. We had to learn how to kickturn. Backside intuitively felt easier and safer than frontside, because at least you faced the direction you were turning. After a few trips to the park, we started getting the hang of it and began to attempt frontside kickturns and berts. We got subscriptions to *Skateboarder* and convinced our parents that we desperately needed new boards. My parents didn't see why, because the GT Woody was in fine working order; they didn't understand the necessity of a wide board. So I "accidentally" broke the GT Woody and there wasn't a choice. I got enough money to-gether to buy a used board from a park local named Jack Lovell, who sold me a Kryptonic "K" sticker-covered nine-inch-wide snub-nosed board outfitted with Gullwing trucks and green Kryptonics wheels. I also got a yellow Pro-Tec helmet and some Rector knee- and elbow pads. I was set. Andrew and I built primitive ramps in his garage, leaning eight-by-four-foot pieces of plywood against saw- horses and practiceing kickturns and minihandplants. I spent an inordinate amount of time on my bed with my board to my feet, pretending to do skate moves.

The park was a magic kingdom away from the boredom and conformity of Estes Park, and whenever we could, we spent the whole day skating there in the summer sun. The pro shop was a ba- zaar of desirable board models and bone-colored Gyros, green Sims Pure Juice and red, green and blue seventy-millimeter Kryptonics wheels in the glass cases. And all the accessories—nose protectors, skid plates, rails made of wood and plastic to facilitate sliding and protect the stickers and graphics on the bottom of the boards. There were also the T-shirts with company logos, and Rector pads with plastic caps to make knee sliding possible, and shiny padded Mad Rats shorts made out of tough synthetic material with their distinctive diamond-shaped logo of a rat on a skateboard. The original cinnamon-colored Vans high-tops had just debuted and were the first shoe made specifically for vertical skating. The smell of the pro shop was the same intoxicating mix of urethane, odor- ous pads and (for lack of a better term) teen spirit that I had first encountered at Winchester.

On the side of the park by the highway was a three-hundred- foot-long asphalt slalom run with wooden start ramps at one end. It was always deserted because nobody was doing slalom anymore. Next to that was a six-foot-deep V-shaped ditch that went into a deeper, rougher snake run at the far end. I never really rode down there, because the few times I did and fell trying to climb out was like scaling a near-vertical rock face. I really learned how to carve and kickturn in the mellow-walled egg-shaped reservoir. There was also a shallow rectangular-shaped reservoir.

The focal point of the park was undoubtedly the keyhole pool. When I first saw the huge concrete pit, eleven feet deep by forty feet across, situated on a rise above the rest of the park and surrounded by bleachers, I was filled with wonder and dread. It took a while before I had the nerve to venture into it. Overcoming my trepidation and making sure nobody was watching, I scurried down into the shallow end, where the walls were over my head and the gaping abyss of the deep end yawned before me. I took a deep breath and rode down the waterfall from shallow to deep, across the wide expanse of flat bottom toward the huge static overhead wave that was blocking out the sky. I slowed down the higher I ascended, and felt weightless at the apex of my trajectory during that first slow-motion backside kickturn, and then down, down, down. The effect was of more adrenaline and excitement than any amusement-park ride had ever provided. After getting used to it, I started rolling in from the top and going much faster. I learned how to grind backside, scraping my truck on the coping while putting the fingers of my leading hand to the board's nose, and then the long drop down the transition to feel the G forces going up the other wall. Gyrating back and forth from wall to wall was a transcendental experience that brought me calm and focus. Like the batter who can discern the seams on the baseball as it flies toward him, I had entered a zone of heightened awareness and concentration bordering on trance.

The park locals were the direct descendants of Terry, Andy and James, and they dressed and acted differently from anybody I knew. They didn't fit into any of the available Colorado teenage

cliques of jocks, stoners or rednecks. They were cultural revolution-
aries for their time and place. Jack Lovell skated extremely smoothly,
doing frontside carves at high speed before blasting super-stylish
tuck-knee frontside airs. He was good-looking, with slightly raffish
blond new-wave hair, and had some local notoriety for skating past
a girl on the sidewalk in a television commerical for a Denver record
store. Vince was tall and wore brightly colored Converse Chuck
Taylor high-tops and, besides doing all the modern tricks, tried five-
foot-high backside airs on the face wall of the keyhole. I don't remember him actually making any, but just seeing him fly that far
out was mind-blowing, considering that a year before the highest
anybody in the world had gone was a little over two feet out. Billy
Fox and Billy Wolfe were both good skaters—Fox had a purple
Protec and did layback airs, a move that was a not quite upside-down
frontside version of the handplant; and I once saw Wolfe drop in
the keyhole barefoot, a feat that astounded me. There was Richard
Condet, whom everybody called Weazer; he had a big nose, and a
white flyaway helmet that I coveted, and did aerial axle stalls. A short
Mexican sixteen-year-old hellion named George was the obnoxious
park jester who would get obscenely drunk and yell profanities at
innocent bystanders. The way he did backside airs confounded and
mystified me, just going up and floating two feet out and barely
touching his board before landing so easily and smoothly. These
skaters had punk and new-wave leanings at a time when such pro-
clivities guaranteed immediate social ostracism and invited frequent
physical intimidation and violence. The mellow hippies and stoner
rednecks who made up Colorado's youth (along with most of the
adult) population were offended and troubled by anything that upset the status quo, and punk rock was more unsettling than anything
they had ever come into contact with.

One slightly older local named Bart made the others seem mellow by comparison. He was a natural insurgent against what was considered normal and sacred at the time. He had short, spiky blond hair, wore leopard-skin-print cutoff T-shirts, was very punk rock, and simultaneously scared and fascinated me. He was one of Colorado's best skateboarders but had decided to concentrate on roller-skating. This might seem like something to disparage, but in fact it was just the opposite. Roller-skating heel to heel, "frog in heat" style, while riding pools doing aerials and inverts is something that demanded respect then and still does. Bart was the progeny of Kenny Means and the contemporary and equal of Duke Rennie and Fred Blood, the two preeminent Californian vertical roller skaters of the era. His black girlfriend lounged by the side of the pool while he skated, and that was more radical to me than any of the moves he did. One incident that really made an impression was when I saw him fall and a large clump of snot flew out of his nose and landed on his arm. He licked it back into his mouth. Years later I heard that he became a Christian youth counselor for troubled teens in Denver. With anybody else, that might appear to be a tragic capitulation, but in light of what Bart had been and done, it seems somehow appropriate.

This was the time of the first flowering of vertical tricks and variations that came with natural progression and the development of bigger boards and better equipment. The basics of grinds, slides, rolling in and out, and frontside and backside airs had been laid down, and the Z-Boys' style had been adapted and taken into the realm of trickery. Eddie Elguera, Doug de Montmorency, Doug "Pineapple" Saladino, Steve Olson, Dennis Martinez, Dennis "Polar Bear" Agnew, Lonnie Hiramoto and Kevin Moore were just a few of the younger skaters starting to go beyond the foundations. The handplant was now a trick almost all pro skaters could do, and layback airs, aerial axle stalls, footplants, rock-and-roll slides and fakie ollies were emerging.

There was an incalculable difference between looking at photographs of these moves in *Skateboarder* magazine and actually seeing them done in real time. To see somebody launch off the coping to catch his board three feet in the air while turning 180 degrees before releasing and floating down to the wall was an amazing thing. It still amazes me after all these years. I was enchanted by the unorthodox ballet and illogical physics at play in vertical skating.

When Andrew's mother begged off, his older brother Sam would drive us down to the park. Sam was a daredevil in the truest sense of the word, and his handling of their father's truck reflected that. Aaron and I would cringe and push ourselves back into the seats as we careered around the curves of Route 36 above five-hundred-foot cliffs on the way to Boulder. I was sure death was imminent. Though his style was somewhat graceless and haphazard, Sam's skiing was awe-inspiring; he was fearless, and his skating was just as balls-out. With him at the park, we were completely free. He didn't care what we were doing.

Something about hearing "Roxanne" by the Police, blasting over the PA system, and watching a guy carve by at speed while singing the lyrics was magical. Later I heard the guy's retort to an older skater who was complaining that he "used to be good." The singing skater snorted, "It's always 'used to be.'" But everything was new then for me. Those idyllic summer days were the first taste of what would become a lifelong obsession and a way of life. I entered the subversive netherworld of skateboarding and reveled in hanging out in the pro shop, ogling boards and wheels, poring over *Skateboarder*, watching people skate the pool and then trying to imitate their moves in the banked slalom run.

That summer of rediscovering skating coincided with my father taking me to the Peninsula again. This time I had only one thing on my mind. I made the three-hour round-trip bus ride through the grimness of pre-silicon San Jose to Winchester every day for two weeks. I had my own board and pads and skate T-shirts now, and instead of being a visiting rube from the provinces, I was an accredited member of a genuine underground. The park was a lot less crowded than it had been during my first visit, and I could make it down the snake run and grind the washboard and the little pink clamshell where people were doing screeching rock-and-roll boardslides around half the pool. Fueled by candy bars and soda, I skated to exhaustion all day before reluctantly heading back to my grandmother's house to arrive late and annoy my father by disrupting the dinner schedule.

Steve Caballero and Scott Foss, the northern cadre of Powell Peralta's Bones Brigade team, were at the park almost as much as I was. I was stoked to the point of distraction to be hanging out near them in the pro shop. They wore flip-flops and Town & Country shorts and smoked clove cigarettes in the afternoon before night-time sessions. There was also a kid up from Los Angeles who had just started riding for Powell. His name was Christian Hosoi, and he had black hair down to his waist and a pot-smoking young kung-fu-master thing going on. He did backside airs a foot out of the keyhole, which wasn't that high, but he would travel eight or nine feet laterally. There was another local whose skating I really liked named Kennedy Brown. He was one of those people who had one picture in *Skateboarder* (a nighttime shot of him doing a very flapped-over Andrecht handplant in the keyhole) and was never heard from again. I saw him skating alone in the clover pool, doing consecutive airs and handplants over the rounded hips protruding between the small bowls, in a way that made difficult tricks in hard spots look easy.

I got to meet kids my own age who were totally immersed in skating despite its fall from grace. We skated together and watched Steve, Scott and Kennedy and the other local rippers. Our admiration wasn't star worship, because we were actually around the "stars," and there wasn't much of a social hierarchy. To ask for an autograph would have been preposterous. One of the things about skating that makes it different from most sports is that it equalizes people, and off-board, there isn't much of a class division between pros and the kids who just started. At the time, skating was so small that nobody really put on airs, and pro skaters were just people who were good, got free equipment and made a little money. As long as somebody wasn't completely onerous, he could be part of the scene just by having the perseverance to skate. Still, at that age, it is hard not to emulate pros, and I certainly did. I remember one kid saying to me, "Maybe Stevie will see me doing my invert on the washboard." One other aspect of my trip that didn't sink in were the conversations I had with the manager in which he talked about problems with paying insurance and not enough skaters coming to the park.

After I got home and regaled Andrew with tales of nirvana, we entered a contest at High Roller. We weren't up to the pool competition, but in the thirteen-and-under beginners' division in the reservoir, I fell a lot and succeeded in doing some slides and carving around. There was something so noncompetitive about the whole thing; nobody seemed that concerned with winning or taking it too seriously, but everybody looked to be genuinely having fun, and all the participants got a board or shirt or some wheels. It was the polar opposite of organized team sports, with their belligerent fathers and screaming coaches and crying kids.

The next year, we went to a pro contest at High Roller and spent the whole weekend at the park, sleeping in the pool after many slides down from the top in our sleeping bags. There were about twenty pro skaters and a hundred spectators. It was incredible to see all the skaters we knew from the magazines—Bert Lamar, Dave Andrecht, Micke Alba, Duane Peters, Brad Bowman, Eddie Elguera and others. I bought some wheels from Andrecht and was a little jealous of my friend Jon Baron, who smoked pot with Duane. Eric Grisham was trying huge backside airs and holding on to slam hard most of the time. Micke won, which cemented my admiration for him, since he was only a year older than I was. Steve Olson was there but spent most of his time skating into the water that had been put in the reservoir. Duane had four different-colored patches accentuating his bleached crew cut, and unveiled the acid drop for the first time in a contest, charging straight into the pool from the platform to drop down five feet to the transition. That was much crazier than normal rolling in where the skater rolls parallel to the edge of the pool before turning over the coping to make direct contact with the vertical. Duane's nickname was "The Master of Disaster," and watching him acid-drop was enough for me to believe.

Back home, we were riding everything we could in spite of the minor problem of skating being illegal in Estes Park. The usual conviction that skaters are a menace to society had us on the constant lookout for the police, and since our town was so small, they knew who we were. There were scattered chases and a few tickets. One night I got chased through the bushes and leaped over what turned out to be a gully with a barbed-wire fence running down its middle. I bounced back as if I had hit some invisible force field, a little bloody but uncaught. I skated the less populated roads and the smooth tennis courts, carving around and doing flatland berts and other slides. The one real spot in town was a rough asphalt bank about five feet high and fifty feet long, next to Woody's Car Wash, behind the Holiday Inn's kitchen and its greasy effluent. I rolled off Dumpsters and loading docks and jumped off them bomb-drop style—holding the board by the tail and leaping onto it before landing on the ground. There was a curb at the bank's drive-up teller and a bump in a parking lot by the bike store. The store's owner, Doug, was a ski patroller, which made him a wintertime enemy, but in the summer I could overlook that and hang out listening to his stories about seeing David Bowie during the "Thin White Duke" tour. I was starting to listen to my sister's records and share her unhealthy obsession with David Bowie. "Scary Monsters" had just come out, and I sat by the record player reading the lyrics and drinking in its spacey post-Berlin decadence. With my estrangement from local society, Led Zeppelin and Blue Oyster Cult were starting to seem stale. Names like the Ramones, the B-52s, the Stranglers, 999, the Clash and the Buzzcocks were becoming familiar to me from *Skateboarder* and its more punk-friendly successor, *Action Now*, even if I hadn't heard the music yet.

We hardly had any spots, the police were on our case and the park was too far away. Anyway, it would be three years before I could drive. Then Andrew and I met Mike, a twenty-two-year-old who still skated, who was much better than we were though his serious skating days were behind him. He had short hair by our town's standards and worked at a turquoise-jewelry shop where the aura of cocaine use was palpable. He had been on a team in the glory days a couple of years before, doing demos on a portable half-pipe that he somehow inherited after the team broke up. He was nice to us because we were the only kids skating, and promised to give us the ramp, causing us to go into shock over this unexpected dream come true. Mike had the ramp assembled at his friend Todd's house, and we went over to this secret location to watch him do edgers and handplants with his hand just below the top. We could only kickturn a foot below the top and do fakies. The ramp was eight feet wide, with no flat bottom and no roll-out decks, very minimal. When Todd was at work, I would skate there, though half the time I was in his unlocked house furiously studying his collection of *Playboy* magazines, alternating between being titillated beyond belief and freaking out and running to the door to see if Todd was coming home. I don't know why I was so scared; I'm sure he would have condoned my browsing.

During the winter, I went to look at the snow-covered ramp a few times and dreamed of what I was going to do on it. The big problem Andrew and I hadn't resolved was that we lived ten miles away from each other, and there wasn't any place in between where we could put the ramp. We both knew that whoever got it would be much, much happier than the loser in the deal. Then my father came home one day after giving Andrew's brother Sam a ride home from skiing, and nonchalantly said, "Did you know the ramp is over there?" I did not. I was dumbstruck that Andrew had tried to clandestinely steal the half-pipe. I called immediately and confronted him, crying with rage. He tried to be apologetic and conciliatory, and said, "I was going to tell you," but the damage was done. Outside of skating, we had been hanging out with different people at school, and our friendship was slipping but now it was definitively over. For the two more years I lived in Estes Park we didn't speak a word, though we saw each other every day in school.

Possession is nine-tenths of the law. I couldn't see a way to get the ramp back, and after this ultimate betrayal, going over there to skate was out of the question. It overshadowed every other problem in my young life. I seriously considered running away from home to live at High Roller. It was a dilemma that combined the abrupt end of a friendship with a huge hurdle to my skating addiction. Mike tried to calm me down and told me it wasn't the end of the world, but I wasn't convinced. Even though I knew that all the pools in town didn't have rounded transitions and were filled with ice, I wandered around snooping at the closed-for-the-winter motels, hoping for a hidden miracle pool that I could skate to resolve my situation and spite my new enemy.

In the spring, Mike and I went over to Andrew's for the showdown. Andrew and I avoided eye contact, arms crossed—after trying backflips off of a kicker we made behind his house, being teammates on the swim team and five years of being inseparable best friends; it all happened so fast.

It seemed Andrew's father had picked a slant behind their house as the only place the ramp could go, and he refused to level the slope to provide a flat plane for the structure. If the spot he deemed appropriate wasn't going to work, he wanted the ramp taken away. I tried to conceal my glee as I saw the loss in Andrew's eyes, not quite believing how my luck had changed in a matter of minutes. His father was a hard and obstinate man, and suddenly I was mentally thanking him, though benefiting from his decision didn't make me like him any better.

Mike and I loaded the parts into our family's red pickup and drove them over to my house while Mike sang, "On the road again, moving half-pipes with my friends" to the tune of the Willie Nelson song. We set it up at the bottom of a sloping meadow not far from our house, next to lichen-covered rocks and ponderosa pine and juniper trees that provided a home for a badger, a skunk and an occasionally prowling mountain lion. We built eight feet of flat bottom and then assembled the two nine-foot-high sides, putting small platforms on top and rounding the ends of four-by-eights to make the coping. The last step was the application of a layer of Masonite, and then it was done. I had my own skating paradise. Todd and Mike skated a couple of times and then lost interest, but before they faded out they goaded me into trying to drop in. Tail-dropping in is how every skater starts a run from the top of a ramp, setting the board perpendicular to the coping with the back truck in front of the coping and the back foot on the tail of the board. Then the skater adds his front foot and weights down to plummet from vertical to the transition. Doing it for the first time is a rite of passage, and I hadn't done it on anything that high yet. I hunkered down over my board and then overanxiously hurled myself into space to land in a heap on the flat bottom, traumatizing myself so much that I didn't get up the courage to try it again until six months later. Andrew rode the ramp a couple of times alone when he thought I wasn't there, then gave up and got into ten-speed bicycle racing before eventually going to France as an exchange student. For the rest of my time in Estes Park, I skated alone on the ramp and the streets.

Chapter Eleven
Revenge Against Boredom

L osing my best friend increased my estrangement from Estes Park
society, and I focused my attentions on a rarified world that
I had only read about, which was happening in London, New
York and Los Angeles. Punk rock and skating were my obsessions,
and they were starting to go hand in hand. In 1981 Ronald Reagan
was in office, there was a recession, unemployment was high and
the cold war was at its height, filling my adolescent mind with
hyperrealistic nightmares of nuclear annihilation. The popular culture of the time was overwhelmingly boring, conservative and un-
willing to address the ugly realities of life. Music was the domain of
overbloated rock bands whose time of innovation was twenty years
past. It was grim. Skating was an outcast activity, and it was becoming increasingly connected to the even more subversive and iconoclastic punk-rock movement, particularly the brutally fast American
offshoot of punk called hardcore. Punk rock then was actually a
movement of substance and importance, not the watered-down ar-
tistically bankrupt genre that it is today. It was new and scary and
against everything establishment. The music was alien—speeded up,
aggressive and genuinely strange. The lyrics dealt with things of real
import that weren't talked about in the culture at large. What the
bands were saying was edifying, and I took them very seriously,

imagining real changes and revolution. A whole world of radical politics and intellectual questioning that was completely absent in the discourse of the day was revealed to me. Skateboarding and punk rock changed my life.

The music was dynamic and against everything sacred. Its ideas forged my rebellion against Estes Park and society at large. I didn't know about punk's debt to Dada and the Situationist International and other precursors; all I knew was that it was really, really different. From the B-52s and David Bowie, I branched out into increasingly inflammatory material. The record store in Boulder had a tiny new-wave section, and I found myself smelling the vinyl and the cardboard and examining the records like they were exotic archaeological finds. My first real punk-rock purchase was the ten-inch EP *Black Market Clash* by the Clash. Right after, I got the Sex Pistols' *Never Mind the Bollocks* and the Dead Kennedys' *Fresh Fruit for Rotting Vegetables,* with the cover photo of police cars on fire. This triad ranged from the dub and punk rock and roll forged from the pre-Thatcher riots of the Clash to the liberating shock and visceral blast of the Sex Pistols to Jello Biafra of the Dead Kennedys "singing" at a hundred miles an hour about Pol Pot, stealing people's mail and lynching the landlord. I listened to these LPs incessantly and was profoundly affected by their engagement with and denunciation of many of the world's ugly truths. It was as if a curtain had been ripped away to reveal the grotesque machinations of a perverted adult world. Then there was *Let Them Eat Jellybeans,* a compilation with D.O.A., Flipper, the Feederz, the Bad Brains and other bands from the extreme margins who illuminated and reveled in the dark side of America. Flipper had a Vietnam-veteran guitarist and played tragically funny dirge music, hardcore punk on quaaludes, the Bad Brains were Rastas from D.C. who played faster than anybody else, and the Feederz did a song about being sodomized by Jesus Christ.

These and the other bands I discovered offered a dizzying variety of opinions, stories, declamations, rants and manifestos, from the existential surf music of Agent Orange and the suburban despair of the Adolescents and Black Flag's rawness in California to the eclectic hardcore bands featured on the *Flex Your Head* compilation from D.C. and the Boston scene's *Unsafe at Any Speed*, some of whom extolled the straight-edge ethic of no drugs, no alcohol and no promiscuous sex. Crass was an anarchist collective from England who made scrappy, beautifully harsh music with lyrics that celebrated collectivism and women's rights. Flux of Pink Indians, Antisect and Amebix were other English squatter bands who were extremely political and exuded apocalyptic bleakness in their heavy, dark music. The spectrum of subjects covered under the general umbrella of punk and hardcore included but was not in the least restricted to antivivisectionism, the joys of cunnilingus, child abuse, the Boer Rebellion, the corporate takeover of the world and many, many fiery indictments of organized religion. It was thrilling to hear these things even mentioned, let alone set to sounds that touched a deep chord.

Along with the change in my musical tastes and nascent political consciousness, my wardrobe went from surf-skate style Town & Country shorts and Ocean Pacific shirts to my uncle's hand-me-down army pants and combat boots and striped work shirts requisitioned from my father, on which I painted band names and logos with house paint. I was really into argyle socks, because they were about as uncool as you could get. I cut the sleeves off a T-shirt and spray-painted the anarchy "A" on it, tied bandanas around my wrist and sometimes around my ankles. The real break came the last day of eighth grade, when I took a copy of *Action Now* to the barber and showed him a picture of Steve Olson staring into the camera with a grown-out crew cut. It took some cajoling to get him to do it; he kept repeating, "Are you sure you want this? I haven't given one of these in twenty years." It was truly unprecedented in Estes Park. My new clothes and hair were a direct provocation to the town, and they really worked. I was looked at as weird at best and, at worst, seriously demented, somebody to be shunned.

I skated alone on the ramp every day the weather permitted and started to really learn tricks. First rock-to-fakies, putting the front trucks over the coping and rocking the board before coming in backward. Learning regular rock-and-rolls was harder; the 180-degree turn after rocking the board led to a lot of sketchy slides down the wall on just my back wheels. I learned fakie ollies below coping, popping the tail off the wall and floating without hands. I did handplants halfway up, grabbing the rail with one hand and going upside down to turn around and land going forward. I aired to fakie and tried miller flips, a frontside handplant where you literally flipped around and landed fakie. I would skate for hours with just the sound of nature and the rhythm of the wheels on the ramp. Often when I fell, I would yell curse words at the great outdoors. Later I suspected that my mother could hear my rantings from inside the house. Other times I would lie there for a long time pondering the sky and the trees. Then I would look over to the meadow and see the bull elk with his harem of cows, calmly eating grass and contemplating my folly. I had only pictures and my own visual record of people doing tricks to go on. I might have been doing things all wrong, but there was no way of knowing; there were no skate videos to study then.

Reflecting the national trend, High Roller was on its last legs. In the three years since 1978, the number of parks in the United States had gone from over two hundred to less than twenty. Steve, the owner of the park, was in his forties and wore the long-suffering mien of someone who had been driven to the brink by unruly teenagers but loved skating, even though he was heading for bankruptcy. The Variflex team did a tour of America's remaining parks, and their appearance at High Roller was like a visitation of messengers from a depleted, embattled tribe. Eric Grisham, Allen Losi, Eddie Elguera, Steve Hirsch and Freddy Desoto skated, and there were at the most thirty people in attendance. The skaters' effort to be there despite dire monetary circumstances, and their exceptional skating, were inspirational. It's hard now to fathom just how forgotten and marginalized skating was in 1981. *Skateboarder* had become *Action Now*, a last-ditch effort that was a mix of skating, BMX, surfing, music and other supposedly alternative activities like people diving into mud pits. Unfortunately, they were ahead of their time as far as an audience went, and they earned skaters' antipathy for their perceived "betrayal of the sport." There were hardly any skate ads in the magazine, and the companies were down to the core—Powell Peralta, Santa Cruz, Variflex, G&S, Tracker, Madrid and Independent. Then *Action Now* folded, and skaters were left in the wilderness.

After the Variflex team came, High Roller shut down but remained intact and unguarded for the rest of the summer. Jack, Vince, George and most of the other locals disappeared. I heard later that Weazer went to the marines and Vince joined the army. There was a feeling of postapocalyptic desolation at the abandoned park, of unsupervised freedom along with the imperative to skate as much as possible before the bulldozers came. Since I was still too young to drive, I would take the bus down to Boulder and basically live at the park until my money ran out. I was starting to carve faster and translate the tricks I had learned on my ramp to the huge pool. I did well in the shallow end with its abrupt transitions because it was like the ramp; and once I did a rock fakie in the shallow end and Billy Wolfe said, "Yeah." That meant a lot to me. One skater who still came was Joe Johnson from Fort Collins. He had become hands-down the best skater in Colorado. He did high consecutive airs, fakie ollies, fakie thrusters and extended layback airs, and he did it all with a silky smoothness and lightness on his feet. His hairstyle made my crew cut look conservative; it was bleached white and shaved in the back with bangs that came down past his chin.

My older sister was in Texas, but her ex-boyfriend lived in Boulder, so when I went down there, I would show up unexpect-edly to stay at his apartment. He didn't seem to mind too much, as I ate the rice he gave me and enthused about my plan to get rich and buy Crass a deserted island where they could put their anarchist ideals to the test. I lived frugally and once found myself at the Interna-tional House of Pancakes with exactly eighty-nine cents, imploring a cashier to sell me a single pancake. The disgrace of how déclassé skating had become was clearly revealed to me one afternoon by the park as I skated by a booming roller-skating rink. A foxy fourteen-year-old girl looked at me and said with utter contempt, "Dude, don't you know four wheels are out, eight are in."

At night, I'd go down to the mall in Boulder and skate the small banks there and hang out at the arcade playing first-generation video games like Asteroids and Galaxian with the young stoner wastrels. One night I was skating back to the ex-boyfriend's and grinded a curb on a dark street until I came to a stop. An instant later something hit me from behind, and I went flying onto the hood of a car. It was a bigger teenager pummeling me with his fists while his friend ran off with my board. I started running after them but gave up after a few blocks. Often I would run out of money and couldn't take the bus home, so I would hitchhike back to Estes Park—this was in the days when hitchhiking wasn't considered totally irresponsible. I would skate along admiring the snow-covered peaks, waiting for the one car that might come every half hour. It would drive right past. Then another half hour. Sometimes it took the whole day to hitch the thirty-five miles back home.

One day at High Roller, right before it closed, somebody said, "There's a new skate mag." I looked over his shoulder at the over-size newsprint cover with an illustration of a skater doing a laid-out grind under the word THRASHER in big block letters. A new maga-zine devoted to skating flew in the face of all odds. After *Action Now* had abruptly ceased publication, *Surfer* (a sister publication) had started appearing in my mailbox. *Thrasher* was an unexpected bea-con that lit up the dreariness of no national skate magazine. I had no idea what a voice and vision *Thrasher* was going to be, and how, in its first few years, it would define and *be* skateboarding. I sub-scribed right away and would repeatedly ride my bike the mile down to the mailbox at the beginning of the month to check in vain. When it finally did arrive, I scrutinized the photographs, read every word and studied each issue with the fervor of a Jewish mystic reading the kabala.

I was driven by the park after it was bulldozed, and forlornly stared at the chunks of concrete and coping bits that were all that was left of that amazing place. There were probably twenty active skaters scattered in the whole state, and I felt lonelier than ever in Estes Park. Besides the ramp and Woody's, I revisited the municipal pool that I knew so well from my days on the swim team. In the winter it was drained, and I would sneak in to skate the banked section in the deep end, watching the snow fall outside through the big windows, the only sound the hollow echoing of my wheels in the pool.

Powell came out with the General Issue board, which bore a graphic of World War II–era bombs. It was narrower than most boards and the first premonition of the back-to-the-streets ethos that would reinvigorate skating five years later. I got one and used it with big, soft red Kryptonics, riding hills and doing vertical tricks like sweepers and backside tail slides on curbs. A freestyler named Steve Rocco was one of the first people shown doing these things (in *Action Now*), and out of necessity, I followed his example. My ramp board was a Madrid Mike Smith model, with a new-wavey trapezoidal design on the bottom. Mike Smith was one of my favorite skaters. He was fifteen and an ambiguous mixture of punk and new wave who oozed style in photographs, doing contorted inverts (the smith-vert) and answered questions in a *Thrasher* interview with "Is a blue-bird blue? Is Elvis king?"

I had purple Bones wheels and Independent 159s with copers—plastic rods that went on trucks to facilitate grinding. I didn't really need them since the coping on the ramp was made of wood, but everybody used copers; it was just the thing to do. I also had a laper, a slanted piece of plastic that covered the bolt on the back truck to make reentering from lipslides and fakie hang-ups easier. That was also unnecessary, but a lot of people had them. The bottoms of boards didn't really get scratched up because of rails—I had Rib Bones—so graphics had a much longer life. The thinking went that you had to have rails to grab for airs, which turned out to be not necessarily so, because nobody uses them today. I had to order skate equipment through the mail, even the nuts and bolts to attach my trucks to the board, since the local store didn't have mounting hardware.

Because there was nowhere to buy the records I had to have, I ordered them through the mail and anxiously awaited the slip from the post office announcing their arrival. Six dollars plus a dollar for handling would get me an LP, an update and a lifeline to the outside world. Most of the records were put out by the bands themselves or through small labels dedicated to the cause; they printed five thousand albums at the most and had no intention of ever making any money. Often these records were accompanied by handwritten notes from band members. One I got was from Ian MacKaye of Minor Threat, apologizing for the delay in sending their *Out of Step* EP. Not being patient enough to wait until I got home, I would take these records directly from the post office to the public library and listen to them on their archaic phonograph with headphones.

There was also an explosion of self-publishing, abetted by advances in cheap photocopying technology, and I started getting small handmade zines from all over the world. *Beyond the Pale; Smashed Hits; Attack!; Phenis; Rip, Shred & Tear* and bigger productions like *Ripper; Maximum Rock and Roll; Flipside* and hundreds of other do-it-yourself manifestos filled with handwritten record reviews, personal tirades against society and poorly reproduced live band photos. Like the music, these zines covered a full range of subjects and opinions, all extremely personal and heartfelt and often truly iconoclastic.

I started making my own zine, *Revenge Against Boredom,* gluing and pasting pictures and doing all the writing myself. The first issue was three photocopied pages that had grown to fourteen by the time I discontinued it after issue number five in 1984. I made five hundred copies of it and sent it to record stores and other zine makers.

My sister was living in Berlin, so I asked her to distribute there; people wrote from Yugoslavia and Australia for it, and I got a letter from Sonic Youth's Thurston Moore that said, "Dear R.A.B., Please send me your zine. I heard it's cool." It was a labor of love without any ulterior motives except to be a part of a community and trade information about the underground. It was fun and creative and something to do instead of getting high and listening to Judas Priest.

The mail was the highlight of my day. I would wait by the mailbox, hoping for something good to arrive. The apotheosis of this was when the January 1982 *Thrasher* arrived in a manila envelope with a circled smudge and "burrito stain" written next to it. I had gotten one of my elder ski cohorts to take pictures of me on the ramp and sent them in to the magazine for their "Photograffiti" section. I ripped the envelope open and found a note from *Thrasher*'s editor, Kevin J. Thatcher, saying thanks and to check out page thirty-three. I was giddy with self-recognition when I saw the full-page picture of myself doing an air-to-fakie. It wasn't about self-aggrandizement or fame; it was about your far-flung tribe recognizing your will to exist and skate under the toughest of circumstances. The funny thing was that Joe Johnson had sent in a picture that they printed small on the adjacent page, even though he was so much better than I was. That says something about skating's egalitarianism and the lack of competitiveness at the time.

Just how important it was to connect with a fellow punk or skater was illustrated by the time a guy in town named Jason who was sympathetic (he didn't really skate but seemed to think I was onto something, so he hung out with me occasionally) called and told me that there was somebody down at the arcade with a Black Flag shirt on. I immediately got on my bike and rode down there to find Richard Waltz, who was on vacation with his parents from

Harrisburg, Pennsylvania. We bonded immediately, and that one afternoon led to a correspondence that lasted for years. I put pictures he sent of his friends on their ramp in *R.A.B.* That was when the brotherhood was at its strongest. The slightest interest in skating was enough to cement a friendship.

My only skater friends were Jon Baron and David Fuller from Boulder, and Joe Johnson in Fort Collins. Making long-distance phone calls was still a big deal, so we talked to each other only when absolutely necessary. I would spend the weekend at Joe's, and we would talk into the night about Joy Division, the Birthday Party, the Fall, Fun Boy Three and especially Public Image Ltd., the most innovative combination of dub and perverse disco dirge that has ever happened, led by Johnny Lydon, née Rotten, of the Sex Pistols. These bands were completely underground in the United States, and sonically unprecedented. They weren't hardcore at all, but their melding of strangeness, noise and art started to really appeal to me. I was also getting into what was called industrial music—SPK, Throbbing Gristle, Nurse with Wound and Non, perverted electronic Grand Guignol—sound experimentation that came from somewhere far beyond the fringe. Joe and I would listen to records and then skate his ramp in the cold, surrounded by flat plains with the mountains in the distance and llamas grazing nearby—his father was an eminent veterinarian who specialized in the South American ruminants. The half-pipe was pink, thirty-two feet wide, with a channel. Joe was doing caballerials, a 360-degree fakie to forward ollie invented by Steve Caballero, and high frontside ollies, skating as good as any pro. The biggest session there was five people. We dreamed of California.

I finally got to see some shows in Denver by finagling rides with some older guys with new-wave inclinations who were working in town for the summer. The Dead Kennedys played at the Mercury Café in Denver, which was a crazy scene. The place was packed to the rafters, and supposedly Jello Biafra's mother (Jello was originally from Boulder) fell through the ceiling during the show. I didn't see that because I was jumping up onstage and running into Jello before diving into the pit and then struggling out on my hands and knees, getting pounded by feet and bodies. It was invigorating. My ears rang for days, and at my job clearing rooms of dirty laundry and trash at the Twin Owls Motor Lodge, I stared at my boss blankly when he spoke to me. There was a great Denver hardcore band called Bum Kon, with a charismatic singer named Bob McDonald who opened for the Dead Kennedys at another show I attended, where the slam pit was more like a riot than anything else—people flying all over the place, fights starting, total craziness.

In Estes Park, I was now a total freak. My peers and skiing idols looked at me askance, like I'd contracted leprosy. I was still totally immersed in skiing, but a lot of the locals didn't seem to be that into it anymore, so I mostly roamed the slopes alone or with my father. My parents talked of moving us away. I had voluntarily cut myself off from society in our town and got a Mohawk, which my mother strenuously objected to, so I shaved it off and started tenth grade as a skinhead. I would take my brown-bag lunch down to Fish Creek, behind the football field where I had smoked pot and done snuff back in middle school. My parents worried about my antisocial leanings and tried to get me to go to dances and other school functions, but I wanted to stay home and work on *Revenge Against Boredom.* They didn't push too hard. Minor Threat and the other D.C. bands inspired me to go straightedge, a reaction to all that was Estes Park. I stopped smoking pot but still hung out with the stoners sometimes, as they weren't that judgmental.

Punk and skating informed everything. They were incredibly exciting and life-affirming, proving that there was something of interest and value out there in the world. Every issue of *Thrasher* had somebody doing a new trick or airing higher, and every record I heard had sounds that had never been made before. It was a call to arms, a call to skate, to ask questions, to rebel, to think. It was an education and an initiation.

Chapter Twelve
Meaningful Photo

Thrasher set out to save skateboarding with an entirely new attitude and aesthetic. *Skateboarder* had been glossy and mainstream; *Thrasher* was black-and-white and scrappy-looking, with a graphic style that made it more like a punk zine than anything with commercial aspirations. The first issue was thirty pages long with only seventeen advertisements. If *Skateboarder* was colorful exoticism, *Thrasher* was urban and raw. It represented the world in a way that the average skater could relate to, and was an accurate mirror of what was really going on in skateboarding. This authenticity embraced the fact that skaters were de facto outcasts, the only editorial stance that would ring true with anybody riding in 1981. *Thrasher*'s cohesive mixture of text and image rang true. "Shut up and skate" was the operating motto, and the magazine instantly began serving as a blueprint for skating and living. The effect of this one magazine on the decimated population of skateboarders who read it in the beginning and skating's subsequent history is immeasurable. It was more than radical and underground—it was indispensable. It was a singular transmission of style, attitude, perseverance and rebellion.

Thrasher took *Skateboarder*'s formula of interviews, letters, music coverage and a dependence on good visuals and turned it into something diametrically opposed in sensibility. While *Skateboarder* took the least offensive route possible, *Thrasher* was tough, confrontational and not pretty, at least in any conventional sense. Its columns, like "Ask Dr. Blackhart," in which Rick Blackhart irreverently answered questions sent in by readers; and "Skarfing Material," with sometimes edible, sometimes disgusting recipes for "skate food," were much more subversive and insouciant than anything in *Skateboarder*. It also had a sense of humor, like a glossary of skate terms for the uninitiated: "Gnarly: a heavy-duty, no-bull attitude, definitely NOT taking the easy way out; as in, watch out, he's a gnarly guy." "Slam: to make full contact with the skate surface; as in, a vicious body slam from coping." One major difference was that it obviously came from people who skateboarded and cared about it, a feeling that was lacking from later issues of *Skateboarder* and *Action Now*. Though *Thrasher* was started by Fausto Vitello of Independent Trucks, in conjunction with a consortium of Northern California skateboard manufacturers, it was a far cry from industry propaganda. These businessmen operated in an industry that was collapsing, and their unconventional response was a wild-card magazine with real skaters at its helm. An Independent Trucks advertisement in the first issue, showing Rick Blackhart breaking a window with his board was emblematic of the aggression and lack of repentance that were the order of the day. This was long before "alternative" graphics and attitude had been co-opted. The editors were way ahead of their time and could not have had any idea that the look and defiant attitude of the magazine would eventually become subsumed and copied by mainstream culture.

"Eastern Front," in the first issue, had pictures from a few of the parks that still existed outside of California—Kona in Florida, Apple in Ohio and Endless Summer in Michigan. That and a letter from Scotland were vital confirmation for far-flung adherents that they weren't alone. Contests still brought people together and helped sustain a feeling of existence against the odds. Money and interest from the outside world were minimal, but as long as the subject had anything to do with skating, it was covered, whether it was the ASPO amateur contests or pro competitions like the Gold Cup in the combi-pool at Upland. The reporting on that contest started with a lesson on the history of skating in the inland empire, and a nod to Tay Hunt, Charlie Ransom, Steve Evans, the Albas, Scott Dunlap and others who had fostered and kept alive the Badlands spirit: "'Rip it, shred it, tear it, thrash it.' There's a full-on pledge to explore the limits, regardless of risk to life and limb." This was the kind of rhetoric *Thrasher* excelled at from the beginning, and it got to the essence of skating. The photographs did the rest. Descriptions of the skating—Duane Peters "showed total disrespect for the terrain and wreckless [*sic*] abandon in his skating"; "Mike McGill . . . who has steadily ripped on the contest circuit, is aggressive and in command of all the modern moves"—might have leaned toward cheerleading, but that was understandable, considering how invisible skating had become. The Gold Cup was the best skating in the world, and it was essential that those out in the metaphorical wilderness saw proof that skating wasn't dead.

Grinding curbs and riding down hills were street skating at the beginning of the decade, and that the magazine treated them like a legitimate aspect of skating was a big leap from *Skateboarder*. "You've got to give the streets their fair due, rolling is way cooler than walking. Don't restrict your boundaries, skate architecture is everywhere." Not by any stretch of the imagination could the editors have predicted how, twenty years later, the street and its environs would become the preferred skating environment. Combined with the appreciation of the street was a return to the exploration of new terrain. The article "Semi-Secret Spots" had pictures of secret full pipes and the admonition "Seek and you shall find, for these places exist everywhere." It was a proactive attitude that practically ordered skaters to stop blubbering and find places to skate. The undercover logistics, the boats, pontoons and other strategic materials "employed by our urban band of terrorists in their assault of this holy ground" and the romance of empty pools where skaters "worshipped daily" gave the prose a quasi-mystical element. Needless to say, the act of trespassing was wholeheartedly promoted.

A typically enticing layout had a file cabinet with a "Secret Spots" folder sticking out, along with three pictures of empty pools without skaters and one of Scott Foss ollieing on a rickety half-pipe. No text, just visual evidence of the potential. The "Exposure" section was the photographic heart of the magazine, full-page photos like ones of John Gibson ollieing in a backyard pool or Duane Peters skating at the Irvine public park with the retro sock-hop-punk look of cuffed jeans and a sweatshirt. Just those two images alone were fodder for hours of fantasizing about being there—California, skating with Duane, living the life. The connection to the past and a holistic view of skating's history were made with a picture of Tony Alva, acknowledging that he was still the most recognizable skater in the world: "From the jungles of Hollywood to the tip of South America, T. A. is known." There was also sixties skater Cliff Coleman styling down a hill in what would be the first of countless "scene reports" on different cities. In the first case, it was Berkeley, with unknowns riding hills, ramps and banks.

From the beginning, the magazine made a concentrated effort to highlight terrain besides parks. This less than reverent attitude didn't exclude a two-part series called "L.A. Skatepark Paradise." L.A. had more parks than any other city in the world, though they were all in financial trouble. Well known and soon to be mourned were Marina's keyhole, Dogbowl and Brown bowls, Whittier's clover pool and full pipe and Big O's capsule pool. Also featured were Colton, Lakewood, Reseda Skatercross and Upland, with its intimidating combi-pool, a square pool and round pool combination with three feet of vertical and huge coping. Nine parks were still open in Los Angeles, down from at least twenty-five two years before.

Advertisements were just as important as the editorial pages for showing tricks and transmitting influential and lasting images. A good example was a Santa Cruz ad, with Duane Peters on his red-and-black-striped signature model, doing a very high and inverted indy air off the three-quarter-pipe at Apple. It was a harbinger of the future—high airs and variations on grabbing the board. Pictorially and graphically, another Independent advertisement was definitive, just a scarred-up board with the tag line "Trucks for sticks." Another one had a graphic of "limits," with a slash through it, accompanied by a C. R. Stecyk photo of David Z. flying off an overpass, a view from below that made it uncertain where he was coming from and what height he was flying at. In retrospect, it looks like contemporary pictures of people doing huge ollies. Santa Cruz had Papo Capiello doing a backside grab off a bank in New York, and another Independent ad showed Bert Lamar in a ditch, the beginnings of advertisements that featured street skating.

At a contest on Kona skatepark's half-pipe in Florida, Steve Caballero won doing fully extended frontside handplants and lein airs. Neil Blender's Andrecht invert was extended and flapped over beyond any precedent, and Monty Nolder made his first appearance doing a high backside air. The first pictures of Tony Hawk, Blender and Lester Kasai appeared, and Christian Hosoi was shown doing a high fakie ollie at Marina. Eddie Elguera invented a fakie to forward 360-degree handplant, called the elguerial, and was doing footplants to fakie, taking an above coping trick in a new direction by going straight up and coming down backward. Soon a lot of tricks would be done to fakie. Going backward was no longer a "trick" to be suspicious of, as it had been in 1976. It was now becoming a normal way to ride.

More people pictured in the magazine weren't wearing pads on vertical, a big change from the skatepark hegemony of full protection and a foreshadowing of a less protected future. There was an article on dropping in, a basic maneuver with many variations. Tail drops, rolling in, acid drops, Blackhart rolling off of an all-night automatic teller machine. The accompanying copy read: "That's what skating is all about—the detachment factor—the split second of not knowing whether one is in control of his or her own destiny." In a slower dimension, the article "Modern Moves" had sequential photos of Rodney Mullen and Per Welinder doing a 360-degree casper disaster and a spinning rococo, respectively. These were not old freestyle tricks; they were much more complex and baroque. The fourth issue's cover introduced the new age: Allen Losi doing a fakie ollie footplant at Colton. This combination of two tricks in one was the model for many variations to come. Losi was an innovator who was also doing ollies to fakie, really mind-blowing and modern. Ollieing was hard enough, but to do it over coping and land backward was taking things to an unprecedented level.

An article about ollies featured the originator of the move, Alan "Ollie" Gelfand, along with Brad Bowman and Steve Caballero, who was pushing the envelope with the caballerial. "The ollie air is a very delicate maneuver that when executed properly looks almost effortless." The ollie was still mostly a vertical trick but the idea of doing it on the street was alluded to, though at that point it was usually executed in a stationary position, just standing there on the board and ollieing up and coming down in the same place. Rodney Mullen was on the cover in October 1982 doing just that, a foot above the ground.

Mike Smith invented smith grinds, reinventing the basic frontside grind by lapping the board over the top to slide it along the coping in an almost sexual coupling. He won a contest in Colton's new pool, which was built (along with a clamshell at Lakewood) just in time for each park to close a few months later. Smith's backside ollie across the channel was also forward-looking. Four other pictures from that contest laid down the state of skating in 1981: Duane Peters's backside air, totally on edge, an expression of complete commitment on his face. Amateur Neil Blender doing a contorted four-foot-high backside air, following the lead of David Andrecht, who had taken airs from just hanging on to contorting the body and pulling the board behind the back in flight. Lance Mountain doing a lein air (a frontside air but grabbing with the lead hand, invented by Neil Blender, who reversed his first name to categorize the trick), and Christian Hosoi, lein air with his long hair flying, his natural style impossible to ignore even in photographs.

The look of skating then was white knee-high socks with stripes or argyles tucked into Rector kneepads; Molly or Mad Rats padded shorts for protection from "hippers"; Pro-Tec or Flyaway helmets; leather Rector gloves with palm padding and wrist guards, sometimes worn at the same time; high-top Vans or Converse

Chuck Taylors in every color imaginable; and short hair, also in every conceivable color. Skaters rode ten-inch-wide boards with Independent 169 or Tracker six-track trucks with rails, noseguards, lappers and copers. A new development in deck manufacture was that they were starting to be made concave to help skaters' feet stay in contact with the board. In the beginning, it was overdone, with Steve Alba's Bevel model from Santa Cruz so hollowed out it could actually hold water. Later, the concave was mellowed and became the norm; no board made in the last twenty years is without it. The designs on the bottom were generally new-wave patterns with an early-eighties Duran Duran album-cover look, a lot of stripes and geometric shapes with the rider's name on the bottom and the company's logo on the top, where a strip of grip tape would be left off so the graphic could be seen. Duane Peters's striped red-and-black board, Steve Olson's checkered flag from Santa Cruz, Brad Bowman's international product-code design and Christian Hosoi's Rising Sun flag from Sims stood out. Powell offered innovative yellow, orange, green and red neon board colors and a distinctive combination of militaristic symbols, like Alan Gelfand's tank or Mike McGill's fighter jet and medieval heavy-metal imagery like Steve Caballero's scorpion, designed by the vastly influential Vernon Court Johnson.

Santa Cruz had Duane Peters, Steve Olson, Steve Alba and Bob Serafin; G&S had Billy Ruff, Chris Miller and Neil Blender. Eddie Elguera, Eric Grisham, Allen Losi and Steve Hirsch were on the Variflex team, and Brad Bowman, David Andrecht and Bert Lamar were on Sims. These were teams in the loosest sense; often the only thing the riders had in common was that they used the same equipment. Skaters skated for themselves, though some teams shared certain characteristics, like the overt punkness at Santa Cruz or the more clean-cut, tech-trick aspect of the Variflex squad. The team that was most held together by a common bond was Powell—the much vaunted Bones Brigade of Mike McGill, Steve Caballero, Tony Hawk, Rodney Mullen and later, Tommy Guerrero and Lance Mountain. Their cohesion came as much from their skating as the company's aesthetic. The Powell ads strongly contributed to the team's ascendancy, with a look that was part military chic and part Dogtown *vato*. Their design was worlds away from the "skater next to a sports car look" that was so prevalent in *Skateboarder*—the team was wearing camouflage shorts and T-shirts with epaulet bombs. A telling example had a background of clip-art dinosaurs, RVs and biplanes. The text read "Specialization" crossed out by "Reality," beside pictures of brigade members skating different types of terrain. The ads were slightly cryptic, funny and self-conscious about what they were doing: "In an era of overspecialization, the Bones Brigade is a diversified force. Specialization breeds stagnation, while functional evolution leads to survival. The future requires creative adaptability."

The letters in the early issues were overwhelmingly positive, evidence that there were skaters out there who were deliriously appreciative of any kind of forum. The optimism was in direct opposition to what was happening at the parks. Pictures from a contest at Apple showed only a few skaters and one or two spectators. To a letter asking about the closing of Cherry Hill in New Jersey (the best park ever built, in many people's opinion), the answer was matter-of-fact: "Yeah, it closed, and so did Apple." Despite (or maybe because of) the setbacks, skating was getting minutely healthier. In October 1981, *Thrasher* changed format, with a smaller size, a glossy cover and expansion to forty-eight pages. The next issue had "100% Aggression" on the cover, and that pretty much summed up the house style and mind-set. The deep underground of the East Coast was shown in pictures of a ramp in Fort Lee, New Jersey, and Puppethead riding a pool in the Bronx. Letters from Indiana, Georgia, Maryland and Canada were all signs of stirrings in the provinces. A typical dispatch: "The skate scene here isn't too good but I am surviving. There's only about six people in my city that still skate."

Photos of abandoned pools and pipes with NO TRESPASSING signs were bountiful; scenes that most people would perceive as dystopian wastelands were cement pornography to skaters. Jeff Newton reported from Texas with "Life Beyond J. R.," offering a description of the local pool that celebrated its perverse persever-ance and decrepitude: "The pool has been thrashed, blasted with shotguns, had coping smashed and tossed into the bottom, and last but not least, survived a tractor being driven into it by local rednecks. Somehow the Rat Hole has endured." The photos in "Top Secret Spots Revealed" had Peter "Kiwi" Gifford sans pads doing a layback rollout over a pool's death box; Tom Inouye at Sanoland (a ditch next to a sewage treatment facility); and an unidentified skater high up in a huge full-pipe, a "spot with such massiveness that it can only be described as 'The Glory Hole.'" A picture that spoke volumes about skating's place as a separate society with strange rituals in-comprehensible to the masses was of Robert "The Fly" Schlaefli carving the shallow end of the Kitty Pool while two guitarists— one wearing surf shorts, the other a sport coat—played on the deck behind him.

"Operation Infiltration" was a phantasmagoric story about the writer skating a pool and being attacked by hooded satanic cultists before waking up from a dream to find his board covered with blood. The story had a certain charm, but it was the photographs that were really evocative: a faraway shot of a pool with a slide, overgrown vegetation and an anonymous skater carving the deep end in the distance, a guy climbing over rocks, another doing a padless backside air, water running through a culvert, a skater pushing down a hill. What was being represented was more than just a trick or action; it was the distinctive aura of a special moment and place, the atmosphere of stealth and danger and covert activities. The philosophy was completely renegade, as in "Pool Mercenaries," which gave advice about looking for pools behind creeks, canals, railroad tracks and in run-down areas, looking through listings of homes for sale and city hall aerial photos and planning possible escape routes. All the information that every devious skateboarder needed to know and put into practice.

Duane Peters embodied the *Thrasher* philosophy and was the successor to Tony Alva's antihero. He won contests and invented tricks but didn't seem to care, got into fights with surfers and always seemed to be on the verge of self-destruction. He definitely wasn't appropriate for parental viewing. An early proponent of Orange County hardcore, he later moved on and got a Haircut 100 hairstyle, wore a headband and started professing allegiance to Echo and the Bunnymen and New Order. Punk was already becoming institutionalized, and he was rebelling against it getting stale. Whatever his musical tastes, he was still the raddest, with no-pads airs at the Punk Pool and extreme backside edgers and his usual unrepentant attitude. Questions in his interview: "Are you naturally hyper?" "Do you care about history?" Answers: "Eat some yogurt, son, maybe you'll find out," and "I don't care, it's boring." He was the dominant figure of the time, the most punk no matter what his hair looked like, and his red-and-black-striped board was everywhere.

An unemployed ironworker named Street Scott was never as well known as Duane, but he was one of the first people recognized for taking a new approach to the terrain of the future, the city itself. He was the prototypical early-eighties street skater bombing the hills of San Francisco, riding off statues and grinding curbs. An unnamed friend was pictured jumping off the roof of a police car. This was the new urban aggression. Another legitimizing aspect of the magazine was that unknowns like Street Scott were not an exception. Photos of regular skaters were coming in from all over and being printed in the "Photograffiti" section.

Back on vertical, "Ramp Raging" was a call to start building "strange-looking wood structure(s)" that "provide the same vertical rush that can be so commonly found in a park or pool type situation, but without the hassle of dealing with irate money-minded park owners or officers of the law. It's free and it's legal. The only rules are your own." That was a clarion call and encapsulated the appeal and necessity of ramps, which would become the main arena for vertical riding over the next fifteen years. In the same issue, "Ramp Building" gave step-by-step instructions and drawings for half-pipe building, everything from cutting the transition templates to painting the ramp to preserve the wood. Debbie Mcaddo's Ramp Ranch, with its channel and thirty-two-foot width, showed the possibility of ramps getting bigger and going beyond the basic U-pipe configuration.

The same possibilities were explored in "Deserted Shapes," by Lowboy (C. R. Stecyk's latest nom de plume), who went out to Palmdale with Stacy Peralta and Tony Hawk to investigate a huge ramp out in the desert. Along with the Ramp Ranch, it was one of the first big ramps with sections of differing heights, built by unheralded skaters who took matters into their own hands.

Builder Keith Stephenson spoke for many future ramp builders: "Everything around here is totally lame, we had no choice but to build the ramp."

Stecyk also sarcastically reported on a freestyle contest at the Magic Mountain amusement park, a wrongheaded attempt to make skating a nice sport for mainstream consumption. The incongruity of real skating at a fascistic amusement park led to Stecyk and Steve Rocco being kicked out . . . for skating. In the parking lot, they found that somebody had drawn a Magic Marker swastika on the contest organizer's truck: "Another critic in amusement land." Most of the article's pictures were of Steve Olson, Steve Caballero and Rodney Mullen doing avant street moves on the streets of Hollywood, nowhere near Magic Mountain.

Less caustic were Kevin J. Thatcher's achingly sincere editorials, which encouraged skating of any kind. In the first issue, he proclaimed, "Thrashing is an attitude, a skate attitude" and repeated the phrase "Grab that board" like a mantra. The editorial extolled skateboards as a mode of transportation, a basis for a valid sporting activity and a vehicle for aggressive expression. Thatcher argued that skating had painted itself into a corner and become overspecialized, that parks were fun but not everything, and that they lacked "the inspiration of a knock-down, drag-out backyard pool session or a skate cruise down the boulevard with the crew. . . . Remember, there are tons of asphalt and concrete being poured every day, so—grab that board!" And more importantly, "You don't have to be a super-talented professional skater—grab that board!" He made it clear that skating could be anytime, anywhere, and shouldn't be constricted by the hierarchies of the past. Such inclusiveness was an explicit call to break down the barriers between pros and the rest of the skating population. It wasn't a message from on high, it was the voice of an equal who felt the same way real skaters did. "If you feel radical when you grind a curb, then, by golly, you are radical. No one is going to prop you up on a board and send you on your way, and no one is going to catch you when you fall either."

Another Thatcher editorial beseeched skaters to send in photos and articles, fostering a collective responsibility for the magazine's survival. He took it further the next month with "How to write, edit, design, photograph, paste up, and print a skateboard magazine," encouraging skaters to get involved in documenting and reporting on their own scene. It was a fairly unorthodox proposition to ask "customers" to make a competing product, and it said a lot about *Thrasher*'s dedication to skating's welfare. The advice was a schematic for making a skate magazine and for the development of magazines and graphics and a fundamental attitude over the next twenty years. It laid out in detail what to do: "First off you must go out and find the action. If you can't find it create your own. . . . There are no skate centrals only separate pockets of energy each having their own history, legends and heroes. . . . Take pen in hand and draw upon this untapped energy and record the action from the source." Other pertinent advice: "If you can't draw, steal artwork from other magazines and books. Use the ransom-note method of cutting and pasting to create one-of-a-kind designs." This was especially germane to skating's future visual style, in which a wholesale and inventive appropriation of imagery from popular culture became commonplace.

A little over a year after the magazine's inception, a graphically striking cover showed Stacy Peralta doing a nose wheelie in a Dogtown setting with the *Thrasher* logo and the background in bright yellow, and two white words highlighted in blue vertical bands on each side of the photo, "Downhill" and "Vertical." Eye-catching, simple, direct. One article listed in the table of contents was called

Ralph Kiewit, Jack Quigg, Dick Reed, and Roger Bohning during California beach culture's halcyon days in Malibu, 1939. (*Don James*)

Children's Aid Society's "Anything on Wheels" derby on the Lower East Side of Manhattan, 1952. The urban beginnings of board-riding with nary a beach in sight. (*Carl Nesensohn/AP Photos*)

Nash Team member performs a high jump at Huntington Beach, 1965. The epitome of 1960s skateboarding: clay wheels, no shoes, and the Pacific Ocean in the background. (*Bill Ray/Time Pix*)

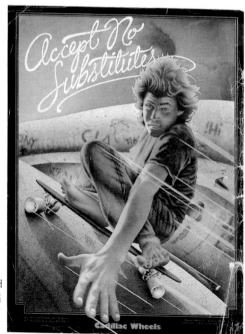

Cadillac Wheels advertisement from the March 1976 issue of *Skateboarder*. The new California ideal at the start of the '70s boom: shoes still aren't required but urethane wheels and graffiti on the ditch's walls are signs of the paradigm shift. (*Jim Evans*)

Tony Alva, the prototypical Z-Boy at Wallos, Oahu, 1976. "I was hanging out with Jay Adams, who is like my younger brother. . . . We both had these superhyperactive personalities, and so we always had to be doing something, and that 'something' was usually causing trouble, being rowdy, surfing and skating." As quoted in *Skateboarder*, February 1977. (*Warren Bolster*)

Bob Biniak at Desert Pipes, Arizona, 1977. In Jay Adams's words, "Biniak's totally rad. Hard to beat in a pool, heavy on the vertical action." (*Warren Bolster*)

Brad Logan at high speed in full arms-forward tuck, 1978. A former '60s Makaha team rider, and part of the skating Logan family of Logan Earth Ski fame, along with his brother Bruce and sister Robin. (*Warren Bolster*)

Jay Adams at the Fruit Bowl, Garden Grove, California, 1977. According to Craig Stecyk, "[Adams] remains one of the most spontaneous, unpredictable persons I've ever encountered. Jay's always been capable of short-circuiting any situation. The man's the stuff legends are made of and everything you've ever heard about him is probably true, or should be anyway." (*Warren Bolster*)

Alan Gelfand does his signature frontside ollie at Lakewood Skatepark in California, 1979. Developing the move in the relative obscurity of Florida, he revolutionized skateboarding with the no-hands aerial. (*James Cassimus*)

Duane Peters, "The Master of Disaster," backside air at The Ranch Skatepark in Colton, California, 1981. Combining a go-for-broke approach, multiple hair colors, and antisocial behavior, Duane ruled. (*Mike Folmer*)

Steve Caballero, one of the smoothest and most influential skaters of all time, brings park-bred moves to the Punk Pool at an abandoned motel in downtown San Jose, 1981. Here he does a sweeper as *Thrasher* editor Kevin Thatcher and Powell & Peralta rider Scott Foss watch from the deck. (*Matt Etheridge*)

Mike Smith doing a frontside invert at Whittier Skatepark in California, 1981. Inventor of the Smith-vert and the Smith grind, he was one of the most stylish skaters of the early '80s park era, and famously asked: "Is a bluebird blue, is Elvis king?" (*Glen E. Friedman*)

Jeff Phillips, boneless one, at the Kona Ramp in Jacksonville, Florida, 1984. Coming out of Texas, he entered contests while tripping on acid, adapted to and destroyed all terrain, and operated his own skatepark in Dallas. (*Jeff Newton*)

Johnee Kop, the undisputed leader of the Hawaiian scene, backside boneless one while wearing his trademark boxer shorts at Off the Walls in Oahu, 1984, with the island of Molokai in the distance. (*photographer unknown*)

Half of the Hawaiian skate population watches Kyle Kiyokane perform a handplant at Tantalus in Oahu, a damp, mosquito-infested concrete pit high above Honolulu, in 1984. Left to right: Mako Sato, Rich Tarantino, Jocko Weyland, Stanford Harris, Danny Barger, Wayne Yata, and Mark Kono. (*Ed Tarantino*)

John Gibson, ollie over the hip, at Pflugerville outside Austin, Texas, 1987. Another non-Californian who made his mark in the early days before skating went international. (*M. Fo*)

Neil Blender, an innovator on both vertical and flat ground, combines both during a bert off a car hood at an anarchic Sacramento street contest in 1986. Note the drunken revelers inside the soon-to-be-demolished car/skate prop. (*M. Fo*)
(*inset*) Neil Blender with a friend, 1984. (*M. Fo*)

Richard Armijo, frontside rock and roll, Los Angeles, 1981. Stecyk wrote: "Richard Armijo was kicked out of Whittier again for the last time. Maybe his hair was too short, maybe it was his attitude, maybe he just doesn't care. Things are different this go around because Richard and his friends say they're not going back. . . . Ever." (*C. R. Stecyk III*)

The crowd at a Los Angeles punk show watches as an inverted aerial by skateboarder Chuck Burke—wearing hightop Vans—illuminates the confluence of skating and hardcore, 1981. (*Edward Colver*)

Christian Hosoi flying as only he could with a backside air at the height of his powers and popularity in Australia, 1987. (*Kevin Thatcher*)

(*left*) Rodney Mullen in San Francisco, 1982. Mullen's intricate freestyle moves, developed during solitary daily workouts on his parents' driveway, had a strong bearing on today's flip-in and flip-out ledge and handrail trickery. (*M. Fo*) (*right*) Tommy Guerrero, ollie tail grab, 1988. Along with Mark Gonzales and Natas Kaupas, a prime mover in adapting the ollie to the sidewalk and ushering in the street revolution of the mid-'80s. (*Luke Ogden*)

Mark Gonzales, artist, poet, tap dancer—and for the last twenty years an unrivaled questioner of accepted possibilities on a skateboard, does an ollie to pivot, in Houston, 1986. "If you can do vert and street and . . . swerve in and out of traffic, ollie up curbs, ollie down curbs, avoid pedestrians, if you can do that, then you've got a good idea of what skating's about." (*C. R. Stecyk III*)

Ray Barbee, heelflip in San Francisco, 1996. Musician, skate-camp counselor, and longtime master of the art, Barbee is credited with originating the ollie blunt and other combinations. (*Luke Ogden*)

Enduring a hardship that often comes with hitting the road, two skaters bed down on the concrete prior to enjoying the satisfactions of new terrain at Tijuana skatepark, 1988. (*Tobin Yelland*)

Thomas Hauser in Yaounde, Cameroon, 1996. Getting back to basics through the elemental act of riding down the road, deep in the heart of Equatorial Africa. (*Jocko Weyland*)

Pat Smith, ollie, Maryland, 2001. The only restrictions are self-imposed. As Larry Bertleman said, "Anything is possible." (*Patrick O'Dell*)

"Kaat'k Fit" (i.e., "Chaotic Fit"), and another was a long interview with Stacy Peralta, who had gone from teenage Z-Boy to selling hundreds of thousands of G&S warptails to joining George Powell in the creation of Powell and Peralta. He spoke about the past and the future and the special breed he knew so well: "Skaters are like, I can't say a counterculture, but they're the culture that doesn't want. It's tired of the same old paralyzing stenchy activities that have been going on the whole time. But what happens, since they're like that, they are viewed as something different, because they're misunderstood. It's like whenever anybody does something different, they're blamed for stepping outside the normal. What else is odd is that many of the kids who thrive on skating are branded as so-called failures of society . . . they're actually pioneers of something new." His accurate analysis of the psychic makeup of the skate population undoubtedly gave many readers affirmation.

A different take on the skater as social pariah was Mofo's (Morizen Foche's) "Wild Riders of Boardz," a *Rumblefish*-like serial about warring skate gangs, whose main character was Eddy Boy. "My name is Eddy Boy. I ride a skate. I'm in a skate gang. We're called Zekes. Blade is our leader. He is mean." Getting ready for a session, a character named Nacho snarls, "We're gonna rip it to shreds—that and any Zekes that show up." The writing was clunky, but it worked with Mofo's drawings of Eddy Boy wearing torn-up jeans and a fedora in an urban wasteland where Black Flag and Circle Jerks graffiti was scrawled on the walls along with "Bow to No Man." It was a *Mad Max* world, with skaters as urban warriors whose closest compatriots were gangs and the homeless. This reflected the real world, where skaters were (and still are) so socially undesirable that they were often thought of as analogous to and as dangerous as those two subsets of humanity.

Besides doing "Wild Riders of Boardz," Mofo began his ascent as the Hunter S. Thompson of skate reportage in his coverage of the Morro Bay slalom competition. "Armed with a briefcase full of firecrackers, various stickers, a truck wrench, toothpaste, toothbrush, a Japanese-made ray gun, half a yo-yo, a computerized screwdriver, a sixth sense in dimes, a pen and a pad of paper, I was on my way to Morro Bay." With digressions like "You know, my grandmother once told me that if you made your eyes crossed and somebody came up and hit you in the back of the head that you'd be cross-eyed forever," his perambulations and search for alcoholic beverages overshadowed the actual contest. Mofo took his gonzo approach to a Del Mar contest, concentrating on his detour to the racetrack, where he won on a horse called Fred before checking out the park. One person he did see was Tony Hawk, who "should apply for a pilot's license for the amount of flying time he logged in this contest."

Mofo was the originator of the irreverent walk-on-the-wildside, everything-besides-the-actual-skating school of skate journalism. It was funny then, though over time it has lost some of its novelty and become a sometimes amusing, often moronic and tedious institutionalized format.

To write about the skating in a contest is practically unheard of now. On a certain level, it's understandable, because written descriptions of tricks and runs are no match for the photographs illustrating the action. Mofo understood this, borrowed the authorial self-centeredness of New Journalism and took it to absurd extremes with a lot of help from the endless supply of off-board antics. That kind of behavior was shocking then, but unfortunately it is less so now, and as the standard binge-drinking, strippergroping, vomit-spewing activities are recorded by Mofo's successors, they have become a lot less funny and more predictable, though skaters still have a propensity for weird behavior that is genuinely beyond the pale.

Mofo's unfettered approach shone through September 1981's "Life and Death": "Now keep in mind that I am writing this while listening to the Germs and watching *The Godfather*." In interviewing Rob Schlaefli, he asked if the skater felt any remorse about the loss of Winchester and Milpitas, both of which he had helped build; he had shaped the famous pink keyhole at Winchester. Schlaefli countered with "Easy come, easy go, after that it'll be just a popular memory," then offered skate koans for all time: "Skating's not nice. You don't grind to be nice." And "Skateboarding should've stayed in the backyard pools, in the streets. . . . It's just a form of expression . . . nothing to be famous about. Nothing to make money off of. . . . What I'm trying to say is that skating was never meant to be a damn circus." His outlaw antiexposure sentiment still runs deep today, although it has lately been overcome by an acceptance from many professional skaters of the circus and its capitulation. Mofo went on to relate a story about Rick Blackhart carving the bowl at the end of a half-pipe . . . on a motorcycle.

On the other end of the spectrum, Lowboy's "Controlled Insanity" was a small slice of prose showing that an era and a magazine had arrived to match his temperament. One of the pictures showed Scott Foss, retired from competition, grinding on a two-foot-high ledge off the sidewalk. It was impossible to tell how he got there, but he looked cool doing it: "The once undisputed conqueror of the AM as PRO approach to the contest circuit now prefers to create in obscurity. He runs his own private contests and he doesn't need prizes." A photo of Richard Armijo doing a frontside rock-and-roll remains iconic. Eddie Elguera had recently invented this move, which combined awkward body placement and gracefulness and was dependent on minute adjustments of the back toe and precise body positioning. Armijo was doing it on a makeshift quarter-pipe with a backdrop of discarded mattresses and low-income suburban blight. He had been kicked out of the Whittier skatepark for the last time, and with his shaved head, jeans, oversize T-shirt and total style, he was a progenitor of the street skate rat to come. I stared at that picture for hours, imagining an existence without parents and with kids who were literally wild in the streets. No rules, just skating and causing havoc.

"Notes from the Underground" was (and still is) the music section, and it was explicitly so. It wasn't a coincidence that the bands written about were overwhelmingly of the punk and hardcore variety. Some of the groups in the first "Notes From the Underground" were the Circle Jerks, Social Distortion, and the Jam. The *Thrasher* World Chart was a wish list of subterranean sounds: The Clash's *Sandinista!*, X, T.S.O.L., the Sex Pistols, the Specials and Adolescents were all mentioned early on.

Vlaadmir Blutonoir's review of Blue Öyster Cult's *Fire of Unknown Origin* LP was indicative of the magazine's sympathies: "It sounds like cheap carnival music played through Marshall amps." At the end, Blutonoir threw the record out of a fifth-story window to smash on the street. He dismissed mainstream rock unequivocally. His subsequent review of a Rolling Stones concert at Candlestick Park went beyond the trashing of *Unknown Origin:* "This form of coliseum rock should better be left alone. It was good when it lasted, but old dead things stink." He spoke for many people disenchanted with reverence of false prophets: "The audience puts a group of human beings on the stage and worships them like new messiahs. Then the group proceeds to control the emotions of the hypno-tized. . . . The motive of all of this is not for your hearts nor your soul, but it is for what man craves most. Slaughter of dignity for financial gain. A businessman trait rarely found in true artists." To drive the point home, he ended with "No false gods, no heroes, just you." Popular music like that of the Stones was pure entertainment stripped of engagement with reality, whereas the music the maga-zine was covering confronted and reveled in the grit and grime of contemporary life. The bands' willingness to look outside of popu-lar culture for subject matter had a strong appeal to skaters who had to deal with being vilified and seeing society at its worst. On the page facing the Stones review was a small ad for the Big Boys' *Where's My Towel* LP, six dollars postpaid, with ransom-note lettering and pictures of the Boys skating. SST records advertised Black Flag's new *Damaged* LP, a landmark hardcore album in its unremitting assault of painfully felt despair and musical fury. Punk was now inextrica-bly linked with skating in the magazine. Readers seemed to be for the most part in agreement, as a P.S. to a letter from Velveeta Boy made clear: "Do something on the Dead Kennedys. Jello is fun."

The connection between hardcore and skating was endorsed by Pushead's "Kaat'k Fit" article, with his skinheads meet Edgar Allan Poe drawings and descriptions of American hardcore bands. Adrenalin O.D., Artificial Peace, Blood Clots, Crucial Truth, Heart Attack, Jodie Foster's Army, Los Olvidados, the Meat Puppets and Shattered Faith were just a few of the groups listed, along with de-scriptions like "Violent Apathy—Brain-blistering hardcore from Michigan." The prose was purple, but the list and the photos by Glen E. Friedman were galvanizing, a map to what was out there and proof that there really was a scene. That Pushead lived in Boise, Idaho, lent credence to that impression. The sound of the music wasn't the only attraction of hardcore; it was just as much about the attitude, the anti-everything lyrics, the disgust with society's hypocrisy, the thrashing and energy and dancing and slamming that skaters (even if they weren't that into the music) could relate to. Around the same time, the magazine ran an article on T.S.O.L. (the True Sounds of Liberty, a name lifted from a church choir), a Southern California band who kept changing, from the political hardcore of their first EP *Property Is Theft* to the spooky dark punk of the *Dance with Me* LP. T.S.O.L. was one of the great bands of the time, with an excitement and violence and thought to their music and live performances. A crucial point was that T.S.O.L. (at least Ron Emory and Mike Roche) and other bands skated, or at least appreciated skating's vibrancy, and their interest facilitated cross-fertilization between punk's energy and skate culture.

The magazine's smorgasbord of skating as sport and renegade activity alongside the link to punk music was expertly explicated in Lowboy's seminal article, "Skate and Destroy, or Multiple Choices (Something to Offend Everyone)," in December 1982. It took up where his tracts in *Skateboarder* had left off, a sardonic style combined with genuine insight into American society and skating's place in it. And the pictures (by Stecyk, Mofo and Friedman) were like anthropological reports from the field. The article was a manifesto of sorts; its words and images made a deep impression. The story's format was multiple choice, allowing the reader to "A) participate, B) nonparticipate, C) discover deep secret messages, D) learn great mystic truths, E) become easily bored." The premise was that Mofo's writing had offended sensibilities and that the "misintentions of this piece were to attempt to convey the essence of skateboarding to the mass populace at large." There was obviously some irony at work and acknowledgment of the futility of the enterprise, along with a disclaimer: "Editor's note: This article in no way reflects the views of this magazine, etc. If you liked it then you probably are the member of an endangered species. Legally we assume no responsibility for its contents or accuracy. . . . We will present more articles like this in the future if this one doesn't get us all fired."

Lester Kasai, five feet out above Del Mar's keyhole, was testimony to "the impulse to skate . . . the only impulse that matters. Choose your own consequences. The modern skater creates his own definition whenever and wherever. Any and all terrains are fair game." Officers of the law are "sometimes called A) pigs, B) Sir, C) The Man, D) in times of emergency, E) only when you're having fun." Cops were said to improve one's skating technique because "they force you into carving the right line at the right time." The age-old authority question was directly related to skaters' place outside of society: "In a culture stuck on cruise control, the . . . skater chooses to operate in a forgotten no-man's-land. In fact, the skater thrives on using the discarded, abandoned and generally disregarded portions and structures of society at large. Skaters create their own fun on the periphery of the mass culture. Sewers, streets, malls, curbs and a million other concrete constructions have been put to new uses." With humor and intelligence, Stecyk pinned down skating's viral ability to evolve and adapt to new situations.

Stecyk traced skating's image in the mass media from Jan & Dean's "Sidewalk Surfin'" through Farrah Fawcett and Erik Estrada to bands like Code of Honor, a San Francisco hardcore outfit with some seriously abused boards (and guitars) on the cover of their *Fight or Die* album. The change was from out-of-touch insipidity to underground authenticity. The article noted that thousands of skaters were forming bands, and that they would infiltrate the "media power structure." It was just the beginning. It has become a cliché, but there is no doubt that large numbers of people with skating backgrounds are now active innovators in music, art, film, graphic design and other creative fields.

"Another question frequently asked is why are you guys so punk?" The obvious answer was that a magazine is a reflection of its readers, but that didn't mean that all skaters were punk. One answer: "The reason *Thrasher* is so punk is: D) contemporary youth is disenchanted with standard traditional viewpoints." That so many skaters were attracted to punk's inherent insurgency was certainly connected to a perception that America was a morass of moral bankruptcy. "So why do I write such shitty articles, anyway? (choose one): A) for the money, B) they are the works of a primitive mutant, C) I don't, they are written by college students, D) you really can't classify this as writing, E) because I care about the future of the sport?" This was someone who really knew his subject and cared enough about it to celebrate its diversity, inspired criminality and gleeful inventiveness.

The memorable photos, a perfect foil to the writing, buttressed a view of skating as a many-splendored thing. Steve Olson, with his rockabilly hair, surrounded by old tires and refuse, skating "amidst the carnage of civilization"; Per Holknekt freestyling on the hood of an abandoned car; Lance Mountain felt-tipping "Wrecking Crew" on a T-shirt; a drawing of a skull surrounded by skate-nazi crosses, Rodney Mullen freestyling while a motorcycle cop looks the other way; a video-still incriminating David Letterman as the epitome of lameness (which was funny, because at the time he was considered "edgy"); Steve Rocco skating in a destroyed house in front of a sign that reads NO SKATES IN OUR HOME PLEASE; Devo; Tony Hawk; and the final irreverence of a fat biker with his crack showing and a huge skull tattoo on his back, getting more ink while a halter-topped hippie chick looks on. No reason. The caption: "Meaningful Photo." The article was complex, erudite and scathingly funny, an unflinching portrait of skating's otherness in a weird America. *Thrasher* was "Search and Destroy" writ large, a serial documentation that was lifeblood to the scattered deviant tribe, a lively secret society at odds with the hypocrisy and staleness of the country.

Chapter Thirteen
Pflugerville Pilgrimage

I t was 1982, two years after the virus took hold, after I suc-
cumbed completely to skateboarding and its handmaiden, punk
rock. Two years after being at Winchester, two years of skating
the ramp daily, even when I had to scrape off a foot of snow and the
temperature was 20 degrees Fahrenheit. Two years after the beginning of my self-imposed exile in a town of three thousand inhabit-
ants, of having a Mohawk and painting band names on my father's
old work shirts, of eating lunch alone down at Fish Creek. Two years
of rolling around on my bed with my board and a year since *Thrasher's*
inception, a year of looking forward to its monthly arrival like a Pitcairn
Islander waiting for the annual supply ship.

I was fifteen years old then, and beyond having any doubts or
qualms. To the contrary, my resolve had been strengthened by isolation and alienation. I was a skater above all else. And I had a plan
to find some like-minded freaks outside of the ten or twenty left in
Colorado. I was going to go south.

Texas was one of the outposts in the heartland. Along with
Michigan and Florida and a few other places, Texas had produced
dispatches from the field—reports of activity and survival. Jeff
Newton of Zorlac skateboards had organized some contests and
written *Thrasher* stories. I had read them assiduously, like everything

else in the magazine, and studied the photos with scientific interest. Texas was significant for two other reasons: John Gibson, one of the three or four skaters outside of California who was in the bigger contests, was from there, and I had identified with his "foreign" status. There was also a band called the Big Boys, incorporated by Mofo as characters in his "Wild Riders of Boardz" stories. I hadn't been able to get any of their records yet, but I knew they skated. They were from Austin.

Austin was special for one other reason. Both of my older sisters were living there after graduating from college. If I could somehow transport myself there, I would be guaranteed a place to stay. My grandmother had died since the Winchester visit, so there wasn't much chance of me going to California anytime soon. Texas wasn't the utopia that California was, but it did have something going on. And anything going on was good enough reason to try to get there.

My parents had accepted and subtly encouraged my immersion in skateboarding. They were slightly pained by my anti-social behavior but, for the most part, were supportive. Their acquiescent attitude bordered on the saintly. They combined being very present with seeming unconcerned, almost to the point of obliviousness. When I was thirteen, I expressed a desire, which seemed rational at the time, to hitchhike around the country for a summer. My father said okay with complete nonchalance. How serious he was I never knew, since the plan fell by the wayside.

My Texas scheme didn't meet with any opposition, either. As soon as my sisters signaled their willingness to put up with me for a couple of weeks, and I had saved enough money from my job at the Twin Owls Motor Lodge, I bought my round-trip bus ticket. In early July, I departed from the little bus depot with boulders demarcating the parking lot, following the familiar descent down Highway 36 from the alpine zone into the foothills, past the Beech Aircraft factory and into Boulder. There I stayed on the bus and continued through the spreading suburban sprawl into Denver and the most impressive station I had ever seen, with multiple berths.

After transferring to a window seat on a Greyhound, I felt the spirit of travel and adventure set in as I turned toward the flowing landscape, staring intently as the featureless plains of eastern Colorado imperceptibly melded into the featureless plains of the Oklahoma panhandle. During the night, the bus stopped at a few desolate farming towns, where I would run out and buy a Coke and a candy bar. I didn't eat anything else over the next twenty-four hours. I had an early metal Walkman my sister had given me, and as the trip went on and the batteries wore down, I listened to one of the few cassettes in my collection, Kraftwerk, over and over. I heard the nascent Germanic techno of "Autobahn" and "Trans Europe Express" as I watched the white lines rush by. Like a frontier trapper coming down to the trading post after a winter in the mountains, I got more excited as I approached the last rise, my imagination and expectations speeding along, my fantasy of connection coming impatiently closer.

There was a short stopover in Dallas, and I disembarked to wander around the huge, dreary station. A black hustler type cornered me and tried to hawk a fake Rolex, extolling its virtues and daring me to pass up such a good deal. I marveled at his attempt to scam a fifteen-year-old kid with no visible signs of income. Was he deluded or truly desperate? I extricated myself and sought the refuge of my bus seat, which was now starting to feel like my own mobile, odorous bedroom. In the late afternoon, the geography changed. Actual hills appeared as we neared Austin, a crispy and yellowish version of Thomas Hart Benton's idyllic America.

My sisters were waiting for me at the Austin station, where the heat and extravagant humidity hit me immediately. They took me home, fed me and showed me the couch that was to be my bed for the stay. I didn't pursue my goals in the first couple days. I had arrived, made it through the gates. The skating and everything else could wait a little. I hung out with my sisters and got acclimated, skating around on the sidewalk as they played hackey sack in the murky heat under drooping trees. I met their friends and, after being introduced as the out-of-town kid brother, usually found a way to ask if they knew where skaters hung out. They didn't know about Pflugerville ditch, my main destination, but they all mentioned Sixth Street as the place where "punkers" congregated, and a record store "near campus" that sold "strange" music. I knew I would be going there.

There was a relaxed, shabbily erudite atmosphere in the house. My sisters and their friends were in their middle twenties, and despite how easygoing my parents were, there was a distinct difference in the lack of parental authority in this house. I saw the huge roaches in the refrigerator, felt the sticky heat, and sat around observing my fairly hip semi-elders. My contribution to the conversation was mostly to enthuse about the unheralded phenomenon called hardcore. How it was aware, straight-edge, political, intelligent, and righteously against everything sacred and lame. I had brought some records and repeatedly played the Dead Kennedys' *Fresh Fruit for Rotting Vegetables* album. My sister Michele generously paid attention; her only negative comment, made with a dose of restraint so as not to dampen my enthusiasm, was, "But you can't understand what they're saying." Of course I had exposed myself innumerable times to the lyrics of "California Über Alles," "Holiday in Cambodia" and "Stealing People's Mail," learning them by heart. Michele's roommate Alan (the son of fifties radio star Alan Freed) took enough interest in my new Big Boys LP to really listen to it and pronounce it "pretty good." He called their music very "staccato." I agreed that it was, before I had to break down and ask just what "staccato" meant.

One of the regulars at the house was Mark, a great raconteur. I was drawn to his warm and funny persona, as everyone else was. I also felt that he treated me as an equal, like I was an adult also. Mark was gay, which I'm not sure I fully comprehended at the time. This was a time when most fifteen-year-olds thought Freddie Mercury dressed that way because he was a rock star and that Queen was just another name for a group; not to mention being oblivious to countless other barely masked clues in popular culture that seem glaringly obvious now. What little contact with gay people I had had up to that point had been unknowing on my part. Mark was somebody who didn't care about putting up a front, while at the same time implicitly acknowledging the inherent risks. I didn't fully understand the nuances except on a subconscious level, in which I felt a connection to him based on sympathy and affinity for his otherness, his unrepentant stance on the fringes of society.

What really mattered to me were his expansive sense of friendship and his amazing stories. They had nothing to do with skateboarding or punk rock, which was fine with me, but they were told with verve that uncurtained a window onto another world.

The one that impressed me the most was a convoluted tale set in the Mayan ruins of southern Mexico. I can only try and do it justice in the retelling and hope to honor the memory of Mark, who died in 1988. He and his friends started off one day by eating large quantities of hallucinogenic mushrooms. After the drugs took effect, they came to the collective realization that they were all dead, and that being dead wasn't that bad, so they should all enjoy it. The first thing to do was divest themselves of the material possessions associated with being alive. They promptly put down their backpacks and cameras on the jungle floor and then took off their clothing, because they didn't need it, either. The afterlife was going pretty well as they wandered through the pyramids naked—until the police showed up and arrested them, covering them with whatever garments were available. In the rural jail, they decided that they had arrived in hell. Hell lasted for at least a day, until they finally came down and got themselves released and retrieved some of their things and returned to being alive and banal reality. This story and others like it weren't the usual fare back home with my parents. My horizons had broadened considerably.

My third day there, I corralled Michele's boyfriend, Kevin, into driving me out to Pflugerville. He liked to ride around on my board and was game to find the drainage ditch I held in such high esteem. We didn't have much to go on except vague directions to an exit off the highway outside of Austin. Somehow we found it, down an embankment from the road, about 120 feet long with fairly mellow sloped walls and ten feet of flat bottom, the concrete brilliantly white under the afternoon sun. At one end was the culvert opening, the one over which I had seen a sequence of Andrew Lopez doing a rock-and-roll slide in *Thrasher*. Near it was one lone tree offering paltry shade. Compared to the banked slalom run at High Roller, it wasn't that great, but it was Pflugerville. It had been in *Thrasher*, and its inclusion in the exclusive history of the time made it better and more exciting than it physically was—and any concrete is for using to the maximum of its potential. The ditch's length made back-to-back frontside to backside carves possible, crouching down and touching the board's rail while edging two wheels over the lip. I did sweepers, fakie 360s, berts and backside one-hand-down slides, just like Duane Peters. No other skaters showed up, but when we left two hours later, I was more than satisfied.

The first place I encountered the people I sought in Austin was at Inner Sanctum, the record store I had been told about. In Boulder, there was a store on the hill that had a small section of punk records, but here was a whole establishment filled with albums by all the bands I'd only read or heard about. I examined and fondled the new Fear record and LPs by Crass, Flux of Pink Indians, Really Red, Flipper, Bad Religion, Black Flag and a multitude of others. In the vinyl-and-plastic-smelling air-conditioned store, I found real punks and assorted new-wavers. They weren't skaters but part of an allied tribe. They were different-looking enough to be exotic and alluring, and I knew they were fellow travelers. It was hard to flip through the records while surreptitiously keeping an eye on my fellow browsers' movements, drinking in their speech and clothing.

I also found two great zines. One was an exquisitely produced ten-page sewn, bound pictorial called *The Western Roundup*, with pictures of local and visiting bands. The other one, *Hymnal (Prayer Ministries and Counseling)*, was much more profane and graphically messy. Its staff was listed as "Billy Shit, Ed Rat, Karl X.V." It offered a Big Boys interview and some very humorous reviews, like one of a Cordell Jackson show in Memphis that ended with "Although Cordell didn't crawl around on the stage or anything she gave a good performance."

There was also a review of a band I hadn't heard of, the Butthole Surfers. It included lines such as "Throughout the set the guitarist stared at his axe in horror as if it were some space junk which had just dropped out of the sky into his arms" and "They are from San Antonio and they don't have mohawks. See them soon if at all possible."

Luck was on my side. At the store, I met a guy named Nathan Gates, who was a skater and whose brother Chris played bass in the Big Boys. He was a couple of years older but immediately took me under his wing as a fellow skater, and told me the disappointing news that I had just missed the Bad Brains. But on the upside, the Big Boys were returning to Austin in a few days for a homecoming show and to judge a small skating contest at Pflugerville. My timing had turned out to be very good.

Nathan was old enough to drive, so we went out to Pflugerville for some sessions. I got used to the abrupt transitions and started going faster and getting some tricks down. The slide-and-roll over the pipe proved to be too scary for me to attempt, though I had been dreaming of doing it since I saw the sequence in *Thrasher*. Nathan was bulky and skated fast and smooth, sliding all over the place. I met some of the other skaters and was already looking forward to regaling my three or four skate friends back in Colorado with stories about the skate paradise down south. That my audience was so small somehow heightened the prospect of the telling—the conspiratorial pleasure of sharing information with a select few.

Cruising through the leafy residential streets in Nathan's truck I felt older and more experienced. Since the Big Boys were out of town, Nathan was taking care of Tim the guitarist's house. We spent an evening there, and I checked out Tim's extensive record collection, spending an hour poring over the cover art, feeling the sleeves and smelling the vinyl. This was when there was a finite number of punk and hardcore albums available—Tim's five hundred or so encompassed just about everything I deemed worthwhile. It was as if the obscure masterpieces of the Louvre and the Metropolitan Museum of Art were collected in one place, all the esoteric and innovative records known to humankind, a trove of the audio rebellion that the masses were ignorant of.

On my own one day, I searched out Austin's abandoned skatepark that had been built during the boom years. From the street it looked like an overgrown lot. I climbed the rampart, descended and found the partially flooded and completely vegetated primitive snake runs and bowls. There was so much debris that the dysfunctional runs were doubly hard to skate. I sweated profusely under the unstinting sun and got burrs in my socks and scratches on my arms and legs from the bushes and branches. I was participating in a pattern that had already begun and would continue, featuring the solitary exploration of apocalyptic, J. G. Ballard–like landscapes of ruined concrete, their former function forgotten. The allure of illicit reconnaissance and maneuvers behind enemy lines. Finding and making use. Search and destroy.

Later, I finally got to see my first punk show. Kevin dropped me off alone on Sixth Street, Austin's main drag. In my high-top Vans, jeans and red-and-white-polka-dot button-down thrift-store shirt with the sleeves cut off, I made my way through the college-age revelers to the Ritz. The band playing was Hüsker Dü, a trio from Minneapolis whom I knew about but hadn't heard. They were supposed to be good and very loud, as befitted a group whose vinyl offering was called *Land Speed Record*. It was an underwhelming experience. The place was practically empty, the audience made up of eight or ten people, a few who were sitting on the stage looking bored. I hung back in the shadows as the band played. They were certainly loud, but the vocals were unintelligible, and they didn't seem very engaged with what they were doing. In later years, I would bad-mouth Hüsker Dü many times without taking into account what they were up against in Austin—being tired from the road with a nonexistent audience and a horrible sound system. Despite not living up to expectations, the show was still new and exciting. I left with my ears ringing.

The day of the contest arrived, which relieved my sisters from hearing me talk about it incessantly. Even though I had been in one contest at High Roller, this was a different scene, and my skating had improved enough that I was a peer, not a little kid who could barely gyrate to the top of the ditch.

To call it a contest was misleading because it wasn't very organized or traditional. It was relaxed; more of a grassroots happening as an excuse for skaters to get together, party and celebrate their existence and survival. Runs were forty-five seconds long; the object, to do as many tricks as possible to the utmost with a dose of style. If somebody fell off, there were only yells of encouragement from the spectators to run back up the wall and continue. The Big Boys were judging in a most unofficial way. The whole thing wasn't too serious, which was what made it so enjoyable. A few cars parked on the grass, a boom box, a couple of girlfriends and a few spectators, a cooler with some beer. But in my head, I was somewhat serious about my runs, having mapped them out mentally hundreds of times since the first day I skated the ditch. My knees were jittery as I dropped in, and I completely forgot my line after doing my second trick. I did some things as good as I wanted, sketched out and lost speed on others and fell once or twice. I can't remember who won or how I placed. It was so fun that it didn't really matter. Everybody was friendly, and I'd met a bunch of cool skaters. I left with promises to see everybody at the upcoming show.

In the preceding week, I had listened repeatedly to the Big Boys record I now recognized as staccato, in preparation for walking up to the Ritz two nights later. Since they hadn't played Austin in a while, there was a big crowd outside, a carnival atmosphere totally unlike the Hüsker Dü show. I saw some people from Pflugerville as the crowd filed in and was thrilled when the band's singer, Biskut, said hello to me in the lobby. It was packed by the time they got onstage, with their horn section including Nathan Gates on trombone. They weren't an overtly political band, more lighthearted and funky than most, a kind of punk Funkadelic. I was in heaven, in sync with my brethren for the second time in three days, singing along and skanking—a skulking ska-derived dance with head down, hands in fists, arms pedaling and elbows up—with a beatific smile emblazoned on my face. The show ended with the crowd onstage, dancing and singing and shouting. I was up there, no wall or distinction between the audience and the band, reveling in the inclusiveness and egalitarianism of punk. I left dazed and flushed, my head buzzing with the knowledge that I had finally found what I had sought, that I was in the right place at the right time. That night, sleep at my sister's was hard to come by.

On successive nights, I got to see two of California's best-known hardcore bands, meaning that about twenty thousand people on the planet were aware of their existence. The Circle Jerks were L.A. pioneers; their lead singer, Keith Morris, had been Black Flag's first vocalist. Their album *Group Sex* (with an Edward Colver cover shot of punks in one of the bowls at Marina del Rey skatepark) had some good adrenaline-charged songs like "Deny Everything" and "World up My Ass." CH3 were from Cerritos and had a song, "Manzanar," that was an indictment of America's Japanese internment program during World War II. An instant veteran, I gleefully flung my 130-pound body into the mayhem on the "dance" floor, running into people, skanking and being knocked around like a pinball. I jumped onstage, dove off onto the heads of the slammers below and incorporated skating by doing one-armed handstands (with the other hand touching my shoe above my head) on the edge of the stage, in imitation of an Andrecht invert, then flipping over into the crowd.

While soaking in as much as possible, I wasn't unaware of time slipping past. I counted down the days to my departure. I had felt the kinship of skating and come face-to-face with the punk music that I loved so much. I felt like a blind man who had miraculously gained his sight only to be told he would lose it in a few days.

As my days in paradise waned, I spent a lot of time at the record store and even more on the sidewalk outside. Street skating at that point wasn't even known; it was just thought of as something to do when there was no vertical available, the same way the first skaters thought of skating as a substitute for surfing between swells. I did a lot of frontside grinds on the sidewalk edge of curbs, rolling off benches and ledges, carving and sliding 180 degrees to fakie, doing adaptations of vertical tricks on the edges of curbs—sweepers, footplants and a combination handplant/footplant called a "hazard." I might have wished for an empty pool, but that didn't detract from the fun of popping off a crack on the sidewalk or grinding a parking block. It was just as radical to do a bomb-drop off a five-foot ledge then as it is now for someone to do a switch-crooked grind 180 out on a bench.

I met Rush and John out on the sidewalk. They were punks about my age, sympathetic skaters who were into punk first and skating second. They identified with skating's rebelliousness and liked to put band stickers on their boards. They weren't diehard skaters, but they weren't poseurs; just to be seen with a skateboard at that time was an act of commitment that took balls. We were united in our hatred for rednecks (and shared experiences of escaping beatings by them) and our tastes for hardcore and straightedge. Punk was much more of an ideology for us than a fashion. We disdained the English punk style of black leather and spiky hair for an almost retrograde look of too-big Bermuda shorts, T-shirts or our father's hand-me-down work shirts and Vans. Rush and John both had shaved heads, which has to be understood as something highly unusual in 1982 in Austin, or anywhere else, for that matter. Even my grown-out crew cut was suspect, eliciting Rush's half-joking comment, "What, are you some kind of hippie? Your hair's long enough."

At John's house, we sat in his darkened room listening to the MDC album that had just come out. The band was at the forefront of the emerging American political thrash, hyperfast and blunt. MDC stood for "Millions of Dead Cops," and their album cover showed a split half-cop, half-Klansman face. It included songs like "Born to Die" and my favorite, "John Wayne Was a Nazi," which had an uncharacteristic country twang and the classic lyrics "John Wayne was a Nazi / He liked to play SS / Kept a picture of Adolph old boy / Tucked away in his cowboy vest." The three of us sat without talking, reading the lyrics and turning the album over and over in our hands, a bulletin of rage and desecration, affirmation for our small antimovement.

I went with Rush and John to the store one last time the day I had to leave, feeling both melancholic and in good spirits. I'd heard about a guy named David Yow from Toxic Shock, an Austin band. Rush had referred to him as a "punk hick." He walked in wearing his hillbilly punk duds, along with the band's singer, Carla. I had seen her picture in *The Western Roundup* and had fallen in love, specifically with her bleached antigravity spiked hair. I had heard it was so spiky because a scar from a childhood head injury caused it to grow that way. Not too plausible, but it made for a good story.

They said hello, and I struck up a conversation with their cute punky friend. When I told her I had to go back to Colorado, she offhandedly said, "Why don't you stay? You could crash out at my place for a while." Her openness and genuine solicitude, along with the hypothetical attraction of staying with her, electrified me. I would never feel the pull of an offer I couldn't accept as strongly as I did that day. I reluctantly declined and said good-bye to my new friends.

Replaying it all in my mind on the long bus ride back, hoping to keep my memories so immediate that they remained present and didn't fade, I tried to ignore the other passengers and plotted how to get back to Austin as soon as possible. A drunk Mexican man got on and sat next to me, engaging me in a one-sided monologue of insinuating, lecherous remarks about teenage girls, accompanied by a lot of winking. After a while, he mercifully fell asleep, and I stared out the window, thinking of the world that I desperately wanted to be in happening out there without me.

In Boulder, I got off and went straight to the closed skatepark. I couldn't go home right away. A few people I knew were there, camping out and skating. It made me feel a little better to tell them about Austin. I had seen the other side, and there was something going on over there. Back in Estes Park, I went out to my ramp and skated listlessly, the despondency of attaining bliss and having to go back to isolation settling in. I hadn't just read about it and seen pictures, I'd seen and experienced it. And now I was back in exile.

Chapter Fourteen
From Tantalus to Wallos

The exile ended after the summer of my sixteenth birthday, when I was transported from the majestic isolated wilderness of the Rocky Mountains to the troubled tropical island that harbored skating's primordial roots. After seven years in Estes Park, my dissatisfaction with its provincial quality of life had combined with a general familial sense that it was time we tried something new. No matter how perfect Estes Park was in many ways, it couldn't tame the habitual wanderlust that had defined our lives as we moved from Bonn to Moscow to Caracas and Colorado. With my father retired and my older sisters away from home, my parents and I were a three-piece unit ready to mobilize.

Like the characters in Chekhov's plays pining for a mythical Moscow, I dreamed of skating city streets and going to shows in D.C. or L.A. Poor business and National Park Service interference had our much beloved local ski area on the brink of bankruptcy, and many of the skiers from the years before had dropped out, leaving the mountain feeling empty and lifeless. On top of that, I was getting into more hassles than usual with our traditional enemy, the ski patrol, over riding an early Burton snowboard that my friend John Baron had lent me after breaking his femur on my ramp. That season at Hidden Valley was diminished because so many of the greats weren't there, and I knew it would be my last. I was obviously restless and ready for a change, pulling fire alarms at school, hanging out with the accepting stoners and delivering pro-euthanasia oral reports in English class. I yearned to be somewhere else, anywhere else.

If we were going to leave, it was going to be a complete break. So the decision was made: we would move to Hawaii. A chance viewing of *The Endless Summer* in Caracas a decade earlier had left my father with a festering curiosity about surfing, and my mother and I were game. My last summer in Estes Park I skated the ramp and visited Joe Johnson in Fort Collins, worked at a gas station/car wash/thrift store and didn't tell many people that I was leaving. I felt like a ghostly bystander anyway, so I wasn't regretful, but I did try to commit the positive aspects of life in Estes Park to memory, because I had a presentiment that in the future, I would look back on that time with fondness. We had a garage sale and sold or gave away the silver, fur coats, books, childhood drawings, rock-and-roll records and *Skateboarder*s and *Action Now*s. In August 1983, my father went to Honolulu to find us a home, and two weeks later my mother and I left to join him.

My knowledge of Hawaii was based on *Hawaii Five-O* and what I had seen in *Surfer* magazine. I was completely unprepared for the real Hawaii, to put it mildly. My father had found a condominium in the Hawaii Kai area east of Honolulu, where the Kuliouou Valley meets the sea across from Koko Head. Getting off the plane, I was taken aback by unknown smells and the sight of Honolulu's high-rises in front of lush mountains disappearing into gray clouds. I was a long way from anything I had known; a new life was presenting itself—and I was ready to live it.

From *Thrasher*, I knew there was something in Honolulu called AALA Park, and I immediately studied the map to plot my route.

The first day after we arrived, I went to the bus stop on Kalanianaole Highway and sat on the bench under a little hut to wait. I heard a growling sound and turned around to see some kind of satanic beast charging toward me, a long leash allowing it to get within a few inches of the fence, where it jerked back, straining and frothing. I had never seen a pit bull before. A dark-skinned teenager wearing Town & Country shorts and flip-flops, carrying an empty McDonald's food tray, came up. The purpose of the tray mystified me, though later I found out that it was used as a directional guide while body surfing. He pointed at my board and conversed in a gibberish that I later found out was pidgin. I nodded and smiled, desperately trying to interpret his gestures. On the bus, I stared out the window in wonder as we passed Kahala, the University of Hawaii campus at Manoa, and downtown Honolulu. At Hotel Street in the red-light district, I got off and walked around with my board, checking out the bums, prostitutes and old Filipino men with braided hair coming out of the moles on their faces. After Estes Park, Honolulu was more than exotic. It was positively alien.

I made my way across the park over to the skate track, where six people were riding, more skaters in one place than I had seen in a long time. The park had been built in the boom years as a flat asphalt track that people skated around while an attendant whistled every few minutes to signal a change in direction. Later, two slightly curved banks about four feet high were built at both ends. The problem was that they were so far apart, you couldn't skate them back and forth. Another drawback was that some genius at city planning had come up with the idea of foot-high oververtical crests on top of the banks, to protect the park's motley crew of loiterers from flying skateboards. That removed the possibility of doing tricks on top, though you could grind the oververtical and do plenty of moves on the banks. I began rolling around, and after doing some tricks and exchanging a few shy "Heys" and "Yeahs," I started talking with the other skaters.

During dinner out on the lanai that night, I excitedly told my parents about my new friends and their tales of other places to skate. The next day I went back to AALA Park and got acquainted with the locals. Mako Sato spoke pidgin with a southern accent because he had grown up in Georgia. He wore long white tube socks that disappeared into his Rector kneepads and had a mellow disposition that belied a sly sense of humor. Mark Kono was a junior high student with a face of androgynous beauty and a really smooth skating style. Stanford Harris had crazy teeth and an equally crazy way of skating. There were two older guys of Japanese descent. Kevin Konishi wore glasses and was a mixture of skate punk and MBA student, sarcastic to the point of cruelty, a tactic that, as I soon learned, many people used to deal with the unpleasant social realities in Hawaii. Wayne Yata was quick-witted and prone to good-natured teasing and wore sweat pants year-round, eschewing pads in favor of running out of bails. I also met Rich and Ed Tarantino or, as they were commonly known, "the punk-rock brothers." They were Caucasian—haoles—and oddly complemented each other, Ed tall and angular, Rich shorter and sinewy. They had lived in Northern California before moving with their parents to Waianae, on the far western side of Oahu, where as haoles they were in a distinct minority. They were totally into hardcore music and skating.

That second day, we went back behind a building and did rock-and-roll boardslides on a curb, ollieing a few inches up onto our rails in an early combination of a vertical trick and the ollie on flat ground. Later Kevin drove us all out to a ditch near Pearl Harbor called Zones, where the students from a nearby high school went to "zone out." It was a fun V-shaped embankment next to a busy high-way, complete with swarms of mosquitoes and a fog of eye-burning red dust. I was in heaven.

On my third day, we drove up past the Punchbowl on hairpin curves with spectacular views of Diamond Head, the sea behind us and thickening vegetation ahead. Our destination was Tantalus, a mountain above Honolulu with almost perpetual cloud cover and air that felt even hotter and more humid than in the city. Down a dirt road was a small clearing where a white-haired kid about my age was sitting on the hood of a mustard-colored Honda, wearing a cast on his wrist and watching a Chinese guy skate. Kevin and Wayne said, "Ehhhh, Johnee," as the guy did fakie ollies and backside airs in the menacing cement pit. I struggled to adapt to the new terrain and managed to do some frontside airs and inverts. Johnee (pro-nounced Jah-*nee*, with the accent on the last syllable) Kop eyed me suspiciously. The only thing he said to me that day was, "You're sweating a lot," in a slightly superior tone.

Tantalus has to go down in history as one of the most unrideable places ever made for skateboarding. It was a rough and pitted con-crete half-pipe without flat bottom, dug out of the ground with cop-ing on one side and a three-foot vertical wooden extension on the other. You had to drop in and kickturn on the extension and then do a trick on the coping side. Added to the difficulty factor was that much of the time it was raining or had just stopped when you got there, so you had to spend time down in the bottom with a bucket getting the water out and then toweling off the surface. Even then, it never seemed totally dry; the air was always damp and the spongy earth couldn't absorb any more moisture. But it was the only struc-ture with vertical on the island, and we rode it out of necessity, as skaters do.

A euphoric week of making friends and skating more spots than I'd ever had access to passed, the brotherhood of skating easily transcending superficial divisions of language and cultural background. Unfortunately, that bond wouldn't be available in my public school, where I was going to be on my own and wouldn't be able to understand half of what was being said to me. The night before the first day of classes, I tossed and turned and sweated, listening to surf pounding in the distance and the insects in close proximity, watching geckos dart here and there on the walls of my bedroom and seeing the encroaching jungle right outside my window.

Kaiser High School pushed me over the edge of culture shock. The whole student body of my old school could have fit into one grade at Kaiser, and the students were a dizzying array of haoles, Asians and other races. Estes Park was so sheltered that to see a black person in the summer was a major novelty, and I was an outcast of my own volition in familiar territory. At Kaiser, I was a fish out of water whether I wanted to be or not, and the exposed female flesh and kaleidoscopic ethnic diversity were discombobulating. Everybody, including the teachers, spoke in at least partial pidgin, a creole language consisting of English and Hawaiian words that was incomprehensible to me for the first two months I lived there. I would listen to people and watch their mouths move without having the faintest idea what they were saying. I felt like a pale mute extraterrestrial trying to make sense of another planet, and after the first day of classes, I came down with a high fever and was delirious in bed for three days. To this day, I'm convinced it was a physical reaction to overwhelming psychological and environmental stimuli.

After recovering, I went back to dazedly wander the vast parklike campus when, in a hallway, I heard a voice say, "Weren't you at Tantalus?" I turned around to see the haole kid who had been sit-

ting on Johnee's car, bemusedly observing my confusion. The relief
I felt in that moment cannot be expressed in words. Davin would
become my best friend, and the knowledge that he imparted to me
about the complexities of life on Oahu was invaluable. He lived in
a nearby high-rise with his mother and younger sister, and we skated
or hung out almost every day. Over time I became good friends with
the punk-rock brothers, Johnee, Mako, Wayne and the rest, but
Davin was the person I spent the most time with. We had the kind
of unconditional friendship that is possible only when you are sixteen. We were opposites in many respects. I had dark hair and increasingly tanned skin and was somewhat socially awkward, with a
passion for anarchist politics; Davin was Aryan blond and classi-
cally good-looking, with a true joie de vivre that contrasted with
my more existential outlook. In many ways, he was worldlier and
had been through a lot more than I had in my sequestered punk
fantasy in Estes Park. He was also a great mimic and a prankster
who could always make me laugh.

At school we ate lunch on a staircase away from the other students, and it was there that Davin explained pidgin and gave me a
long list of tips for survival. Without those talks, I would have been
completely lost. We discussed meanings of words and the byzantine
social and racial interrelationships on the island. He told me that
locals were anyone who claimed some degree of Hawaiian ancestry,
and that when a local said, "What?" or, "What, boder you? ("What,
am I bothering you?"), it was the first step in a confrontation that
would almost certainly end badly. Davin was also the drummer for
the Sharx, one of Hawaii's only punk bands, and he knew pretty
girls and was at ease with them in a way that contrasted with my
awkwardness. We sat around in his room listening to records and
talked about everything under the sun. He was into the Southern

Californian punk of the Adolescents, the Descendents, Bad Religion and Social Distortion, bands that were slightly more "musical" than the less palatable sonic experimentation I was fond of. I fervently liked the same bands, but I tried to get him to expand his horizons to include Flipper, Joy Division and Mr. Epp and the Calculations, a great guitar-meets-noise Seattle group that was the genesis of Mudhoney.

Davin's first order of business was to take me to Off the Walls, a ditch next to the road that went from Hawaii Kai to Sandys Beach and Hanauma Bay on the other side of Koko Head. It was by a golf course, and past that was the brilliant blue ocean where on clear days you could see the island of Molokai. Perpetual sunshine and a cooling sea breeze made it a truly blessed place. The angle from flat bottom to wall was too abrupt to be really skateable, but changes to the original design had turned Off the Walls into a heavenly, long half-pipe with silky-smooth 40-degree walls with grindable lips. Prior to my arrival, Johnee and a posse of amateur engineers had taken matters into their own hands and built a section of transition between the flat and the wall, working at night with rebar and buckets of water they brought from home to mix the cement, ducking every time a car passed. The part of the ditch they altered couldn't have been built better in a skatepark.

You could carve, then ride back and forth, like on a ramp. The steep angle made it possible to do every kind of vertical trick except airs—handplants, footplants, slides and fakie ollie disasters. This was also the heyday of the boneless one, a trick invented by Garry Scott Davis. For days, I studied the *Thrasher* cover with the picture of him doing the frontside version, trying to figure out what the hell was going on. There was even more consternation when a picture of Steve Caballero doing the pretzel-like backside version appeared. It took sequences to clearly convey the secret of the move. To do regular footplants, the back foot was used as a fulcrum to turn on; it felt natural and was in accordance with the laws of physics. During a boneless one, the skater grabbed the board with the back hand while the front foot was used to jump off the bank into the air, where the propelling foot was put back on before landing. The boneless one is a perfect example of skating's evolution into an area that no one thought existed until the day the trick was born. With it, Davis inaugurated an era of doing tricks that initially appeared illogical. Eggplants—a handplant using the leading arm instead of the trailing one—and many other seemingly "unnatural" tricks were to follow.

So in addition to grinds and reverts and laybacks and sweepers (a Duane Peters frontside footplant where you "swept" the tail of the board across the lip), there was a mania for boneless ones. It wasn't long before variations emerged. Besides frontside and backside, there was the iceplant, a boneless to fakie; and the bastard plant, a backside boneless to fakie. There were 360-degree versions and the thread-the-needle, in which you did a backside boneless and passed the board through your legs to jump in frontside. It was complicated. Boneless ones caused a lot of ungainly hopping around on the lip before leaping back in and many stupendous crashes when reentries didn't work out. Everybody was trying them, and the results weren't always pretty. Conversely, anybody who ever saw Chris Miller launch five feet above a pool, with so much speed his foot barely touched the coping, knows what a graceful boost a frontside boneless one can be.

Off the Walls was the nexus in Hawaii Kai, a geographical location and state of mind that was the East Side counterpoint to the AALA Park scene. Stacey Gibo was a big, burly half-Japanese guy whom I first saw in the parking lot of the Hawaii Kai mall, riding a tattered Duane Peters board with insanely loose trucks and blue wheels worn down almost to the bearings. I think he had that same setup the whole year I lived in Hawaii. He was jumping off a retaining wall bomb-drop style, with greasy hair and a contemptuous snarl on his greasy face. In art class, he sat next to me and was a source of mischief and entertainment from day one, a born troublemaker who constantly tested the patience of our mild-mannered teacher and the other students. Sacrificing his body to his skating led to scabs and scars all over, all the time. When he did a grind whatever he was skating shook, and when he slammed, it was even more intense. He was one of the most go-for-broke skaters I have ever seen. There are hardly any skaters like that anymore—he was pure gnarl.

Besides Stacey, Davin and Johnee Kop, there was Jon Silberstein, a surfer and lifeguard who drove a VW bus and had a sarcastic outlook that might have been related to his premature baldness. He would carp like a Catskills funnyman, sighing, "Everybody wants to be a comedian" in response to our lame attempts at humor. Doug Guthrie was a rakishly good-looking carve-and-grind style monger. A memorable occasional visitor was a tough, fetching tomboy named Erica who rarely skated, but when she did, it was with an astonishing combination of aggression and finesse, doing backside grinds lapped over the top like a female Duane Peters. I was completely entranced but could never get past my intimidation and the fact that her family were reputed to be speed dealers.

Johnee Kop was the absolute master. From the first time I saw him at Tantalus, I was convinced that overall he was the best skater in Hawaii. It wasn't only that he could do the current tricks and learn new ones, it was the way he whipped his compact body and arms around in a style that was all his own. He had an extraordinary amount of determination and would practice a trick all day to get it right. He had also been to California and learned a lot from the experience, inviting himself into the Hoffmans' home and localizing Upland. Skating with Micke and Steve Alba and the then- twelve-year-old Chris Miller pushed him to another level. He had seen the words "Sex Pistols" on Steve Alba's board and thought, "That's a cool name," without having any idea who they were. From then on, it was dying his hair, wearing locked chains around his neck and getting kicked out of school. He brought punk to the Hawaiian scene, in concert with his skating and personal style, and had an incalculable influence. He bomb-dropped off the fence into Off the Walls, one of the craziest things I'd ever seen—until Stacey did it. The whole time I lived there, I dreamed of trying it, but I just couldn't get up the nerve to stand on that thin pipe atop the fence and dive onto the cement five feet below.

Beyond being the best skater on Oahu, Johnee was a truly amazing character. He was short, with naturally spiked black hair and hairless muscular legs, and he drove around with his skateboard strapped to his car's surf racks. When he developed pimples, he refused to leave the house, eventually emerging with Band-Aids on his face—as if that didn't draw even more attention. He played tennis well and often beat my father, who was at the courts when he wasn't surfing. According to Johnee, I was a "robotic" skater who lacked style, but that was compensated for by my "features." At my house he would make sly comments about my mother's yoga leotard while winning her over with his impish charm. An irrepressible rascal with intellectual curiosity, he was always asking about the meanings of words and their pronunciation and engaging my parents in intellectual inquiry. What was really astounding was his way of dealing with locals and their attempts to intimidate him. His skating reputation helped in this regard, but it was more the way he used his slightly malicious intelligence to verbally annihilate people much bigger than he was, finding their weaknesses and belittling them and getting away with it. One of his favorite put-downs that always caught aggressors off guard was "Yeah, but can you skate?"

Off the Walls was a paradisiacal after-school hangout. Not only the ditch itself: across the road, there was a soccer field where we would screw around and Silberstein would insist on playing barefoot. Sandys was a two-minute drive away, and we would go down there after skating to bodysurf and skimboard. The waves could get double overhead on big days, and they broke in the shallow water right by the beach. This caused more than a few broken necks among ignorant jarheads and sometimes led to unsuspecting women getting their bikinis ripped off. We would cleanse ourselves in the salt water there as darkness descended. It was sublime.

Hawaii Kai was more middle-class, more white and Asian than the rest of the island, a safe haven and a less threatening zone than other parts of Oahu. The Hawaii Kai vibe was different from AALA Park's; they were more into "style" and the connection to surfing. I got made fun of for being a trick-oriented robot and was nicknamed "Spock." Luckily I had features. They were into melodic California punk, while Rich and Ed Tarantino's sympathies lay with fast political hardcore like the Neos and Rudimentary Peni. Same interests, just slightly different sensibilities. Hawaii Kai–dwellers tended to be more socially adept and connected to the outside world. There was a joking rivalry, but I hung out equally with both camps, and skating was so underground that there were about two dozen active skaters on the whole island, so the smallness of the tribe led to everybody accepting one another. It was the same with the punk scene—the hardcore people, the death rockers, and the new-wavers might have made fun of one another, but everyone hung out together. At a nearly riotous screening of Penelope Spheeris's seminal L.A. punk documentary, *The Decline of Western Civilization*, the fifty or so people in the audience made up the whole eclectic scene on the island.

My clothes changed to reflect the climate and began to prefigure skating's sometimes unfortunate hold over fashion in general. I wore the same army pants and Converse high-tops but started going to thrift stores to buy truly atrocious Hawaiian-print polyester shirts. I made Bermuda shorts out of my father's old suit pants, and their bagginess was the forerunner of the looseness in clothing that later became omnipresent. Many claim that such sartorial lack of fit comes from rap music through oversize prison uniforms, but it can be argued that skating contributed just as much to the preponderance of baggy clothes in today's hip-hop nation. Besides T-shirts and shoes, there was no such thing as "skate wear" yet, so we improvised and put a premium on freedom of movement, endurance and utility. This led to a lot of good-natured lamentation on my father's part about the "youth of today" and their inability to find clothes that fit.

One Hawaii Kai fashion that I followed was the boxer short as outerwear, long before Madonna began to appear publicly in brassieres. Johnee Kop began the trend of wearing oversize boxers over another pair, a very comfortable option in Hawaii's soupy-hot climate. Christian Hosoi's stylistic excesses fostered a fad of neon plastic bracelets and shoelaces and other odds and ends around wrists. My hair progressed to the long-in-front-cropped-in-back look that I had first seen on Joe Johnson. With my bangs hanging down to the bridge of my nose, I was constantly blowing upward to see, a habit that aggravated my mother to no end. My new hairstyle created a need for headbands, and the one I used the most was a cloth rice bag that I carried around with me at all the times because you weren't supposed to bring skateboards on the bus. The way to get around this was to put your board in the bag. The drivers would usually look the other way, and upon exiting, I would tie the bag around my head like a turban and proceed to skate.

Unsurprisingly, water permeated my life in Hawaii. My father started surfing right away, riding a ten-foot longboard that he locked up in a cage on the beach at Waikiki where lifeguards, tourists and drug dealers congregated. In the beginning, I went with him and had some fun, maneuvering a rented ocean-liner-size log and getting to the point where I could stand up and turn. I tried serious short-board surfing with Jon Silberstein a few times in Hawaii Kai, in particular at a reef break called Toes. The waves were half a mile out over coral that was an arm's length below the surface at low tide. You paddled with your board backward and upside down, the fin in your face, moving your arms horizontally so you didn't cut your hands on the reef. The biggest day I ever surfed there was probably three or four feet, which translates into waves with six-foot faces. That's nothing compared to big surf, but the waves were big enough for me to feel the ocean's unmistakable power. I got caught inside and held under for uncomfortably long washing-machine cycles before coming up gasping in the foam just as another wave was about to break. I could drop in and turn frontside and backside and actually do a few cutbacks, the surfing equivalent to a frontside grind on a skateboard.

The sensation of surfing is incredible and difficult to describe. William Finnegan, in the story "Playing Doc's Games," has come as close as anybody: "A sudden sense of height fusing with a deep surge of speed. I hop to my feet and drive to the bottom, drawing out the turn and sensing, more than seeing, what the wave plans to do ahead." It was an intoxicating challenge, but it couldn't win out over skating in my life. Localism was one of the reasons. Being a haole teenager, I had enough problems avoiding confrontation on land, and out in the water there were even fewer societal constraints. Fights over waves were common. I also knew that I would never ride the four-story-tall waves at Waimea and Pipeline unless I devoted my life to surfing, and if I wasn't going to do the real thing, it didn't seem worth it. No matter how good it felt and how undeniably radical it was, surfing had a sell-out mainstream aspect that made it anathema to me. It was no longer the sacred ritual it had been at Malibu in the golden era. Surfers were wearing neon wetsuits, had glossy magazines and girls in bikinis handing out trophies. The difference was glaring.

Surfing or not, I was in the water every day, bodysurfing at Sandys or skimboarding. In skimming, you run and throw down an oval-shaped board to jump on it and skim over the thin layer of water left by a receding wave. You hit the next wave coming in to do cutbacks or launch off it to flip into the air. One of my favorite activities was walking across the lagoon behind our house to an unpopulated peninsula where the carcass of a rowboat lay slowly disintegrating. The water in the lagoon would be knee-to-thigh-deep depending on the tide, and the bottom was viscous mud that squeezed deliciously between my toes. I spent a lot of time wandering around there on the beach and out onto the coral, contemplating the thin white line of surf pounding in the distance. Then I would go back and take a swim in our complex's swimming pool. The pool was always deserted, and Davin and I would throw Boogie Boards in the water and run and jump on them to "surf." We also employed skateboard decks to do handplants in from the coping and pose fantasy tricks underwater.

Hawaii's most famous drainage ditch, Wallos, had been featured in *Skateboarder*, ridden since at least 1975 and was a place of primeval mystery that wasn't for the weak at heart. It was also a ten-minute skate from my house. Like Los Angeles with its debris basins, Oahu's valley neighborhoods were safeguarded from washing into the sea by a massive system of public-works projects that diverted excess water from the rain-soaked mountains to the ocean. A metal ladder from an overpass at the end of Niu Valley took you down to the bottom. The ditch's environs were a vision of nature run amok, with vines and creeping plants spreading down the walls onto the flat. Convicts from a work-release program would clear the voracious vegetation every few months, and a week later, it would be right back. Houses were hidden behind the flora on either side, and if not for the contemporary graffiti, it would have been easy to imagine myself in the ruins of a fallen civilization, made even more eerie by an unsettling stillness interrupted by birdcalls and the buzzing of insects. Walking toward the mountains, you ascended three-foot-high sloped "steps," as if approaching an ancient temple lost in the jungle.

In the ditch, rough reddish cement with a small curve at the bottom transitioned to 50-degree-steep flat walls about six feet high. At every "step" was a concave pocket between high and low. After you looked down at the houses of Niu Valley and the Pacific beyond, you pushed off and carved the first bowl, then skated diagonally across the flat bottom to the next bowl, each drop dramatically increasing your speed. By the time you got to the last wall, it felt like you were going fifty miles an hour. There was a bowl with "Air Bowl" spray-painted on it, and that's where frontside airs and boneless ones were done from high to low. There was also a pipe in one of the walls discharging slimy water that you had to carve over. The thing to do there was cess-slide, coming up frontside and sliding 180 degrees to travel backward for a few feet before going back down forward. Skating Wallos was akin to surfing consecutive big waves, a downhill run and a half-pipe combined. It was insane. Once I made the mistake of trying to knee-slide, which instantly pulled off my pads and scraped a huge hole in my kneecap that turned into an oozing scab. It stuck to my pants for a month and left a faint purple circle that remains to this day. When I skated there alone, I felt like a modern- day Aguirre far from society's rules. I would push off and start flying, worrying about cracks, water, weeds, and irate neighbors who sometimes threw rocks during my run. It was an experience.

Along with Zones, Off the Walls and Wallos, there were many other places to skate. Pipeline Bowls and Uluwatus were two of my favorites, even though they weren't that good. Pipeline Bowls, above Hawaii Kai, was just one big wall that you could barely get to the top of, but it had an amazing view of Koko Bay and a *Land of the Lost* ambience. Uluwatus was a huge place with gradual thirty-foot-high walls next to the murky end of a lagoon. There was something almost prehistoric about it, and locals hung out there, getting high and skating barefoot. Hahaieones was right by Davin's apartment building; from the sidewalk, you went down through some overgrowth into a malarial gorge to the ditch. There was a half-pipe part that you could skate back and forth, and then it sloped down and got bigger and steeper, with a lot of pipe holes and cracks to make it exciting. Down at the bottom, the jungle got thicker, and there was always some slimy water that occasioned many desperate chases in pursuit of runaway boards. It was a mellow after-school scene. One regular was an inscrutable kid named Bo Ikeda, who was always quietly improving and later became a pro rider for Hosoi Skates. Jon and James Kroll lived in the adjacent condominium complex. They were two social misfits and sometime skaters who became good friends of mine and went on to form the nucleus of the band Chokebore. At that time Jon, James and I collaborated on our musical project, Nok Mub. I wanted it to be a funk-dub experimental cross between the Birthday Party and Public Image. I'm not sure what Jon and James had in mind. We never played in public, but we did make some good noise in their living room when their parents were gone in the afternoon. There was a nearby convenience store called the Pantry where we would hang out and drink sodas on the curb. That was where I heard Stacey Gibo loudly utter one of his immortal lines as we went up to the cashier behind a woman in her thirties: "Whoa, check it out, that lady has toilet paper hanging out of her shorts."

Across the street from Hahaieones was a high-rise apartment building called the Mauna Loa, where there were two incredibly smooth eight-foot-high brick banks that formed a half-pipe on either side of the guardhouse in the driveway. They were so well watched that trying to skate them was like infiltrating a military base. Everybody who had done it had been apprehended immediately. I was obsessed with skating them; they were a screen on which I could project my most fantastical skate dreams.

So one day Johnee Kop, Doug Guthrie and I decided to take a chance. Our plan was to skate down the sidewalk toward the banks, kickturn once and get out of there before the guards could catch us. They went first, and I followed. The sound of our wheels clacking across the bricks added to the adrenaline rush. I saw them go up and frontside kickturn near the top. I hit the abrupt angle at speed and shot up the wall. Just as I was looking over my shoulder to start turning, I peripherally caught sight of a guard running up the bank toward me.

In that split second, I decided that instead of staying on my board and turning right into him, I would jump off and try to evade his oncoming body. I jumped off and caught my board in my right hand and began running down the wall and across the driveway with the pounding of the guard's feet right behind me. Scurrying up the other side, I tripped over the bank's sharp edge and pitched forward into a swan dive onto the sidewalk six feet below, lying there dazed as the two-hundred-plus pounds of the guard landed on top of my skinny frame. I squirmed and tried to slither away, but he had me pinned down. I became vaguely aware of my friends taunting and then kicking the guard, and got a glimpse of one of them brandishing his board above his head with the intention of bringing it down on my wrestling partner. Wriggling free, I staggered to my feet and skated up the sidewalk at full speed, only to realize after going a block that I was alone. In saving me, Doug and Johnee had sacrificed themselves. Another guard had come out and, along with my torment or, cornered the two of them. I went back to face the music with my comrades.

I found Doug and Johnee nonchalantly standing by the two security guards, one of whom Doug had just tried to brain with his board. The cops came, but they ended up letting us go. How Doug and especially Johnee handled the situation was directly responsible for the cops' lenience. What transpired then and many other times was a masterful display of Johnee's unique brand of psychological warfare. He made fun of the guards, saying things like "I have a brand-new car and surfboard, what do you have?" and "I'm taking classes at UH, and I'm going to be rich in two years. What are you going to be doing in two years?" intermixed with derogatory comments about their clothes and mustaches. The guards' consternation and befuddlement was palpable. They were no match for Johnee, who walked away with his trademark coup de grâce, "And you don't even skate."

Another time I wasn't so fortunate. It was another sunny beatific day at Off the Walls, with a big session in progress. You had to be on the lookout for the police, who would swoop down and try to interfere, though usually by the time they got over the fence between the road and the ditch the skaters had dispersed. The cops drove by a few times, but whenever they came near, we ran up the ditch to wait it out and then walked back to skate again. A few people left, and then two police cruisers appeared out of nowhere. Everybody ran for it, but we weren't that worried until two cops suddenly came down toward us—they had driven around on a back road through the golf course to cut us off. We had no choice but to go back down to where the other cops were waiting. Trapped and busted. Jon Silberstein, a twelve-year-old named Chumley and I got put in the backseat of the car and driven downtown, where Silberstein went to the adult division and Chumley and I went to juvenile.

I was interrogated at length. I had to provide even my mother's maiden name. In the cell next to mine, a husky Samoan girl yelled abuse at the cops, demanding to be taken to the hospital, then informing me that she had to go *shi-shi* (piss). Then she did, the liquid slowly flowing under the door into my compartment. I started really worrying after two hours, but then I heard my father's voice.

Johnee had driven him down to the station. When I got home, my mother was more upset than usual, saying that we had moved to Hawaii for my sake and now I was thanking them by getting arrested. I felt bad for my parents, but tempers cooled. I think they secretly agreed that the cops were in the wrong.

On weekend nights, my friends and I would pile into someone's car to head down to Waikiki and park by the Ala Wai Canal. The slightest chill in the tropical night air added to our anticipation before we set out to rampage through the streets, scattering tourists in our wake. Our main rendezvous point was the 3-D Club, where local new-wave bands played and they spun punk records, engendering intense slam dancing that often escalated into violence as jock and local interlopers, attracted by the pushing and shoving of slamming, would join in and start punching people. 3-D was a microcosm of Hawaii's potential mayhem at every turn. Agent Orange and the Circle Jerks both came for one-week engagements, and everybody went to see them more than once, since bands from the mainland were a far-off dream.

Waikiki had an abundance of parking garages, mostly square-shaped. Sneaking by the security guards into the elevators was easier then because video surveillance hadn't yet become a national obsession. On the top floor, we would push off en masse and get into tuck stance, jockeying for position in close formation, zigging and zagging, trailing behind one another to cut down on drag, sliding low around the curves with palms skimming the cement, watching for oncoming cars and other surprises. The rolling din of skaters' wheels reverberated through the bunkerlike structures. We would fly out onto the street past the security guard, who would come running after us for a block or two as we rolled into the night to some other garage or to session the curb in front of 3-D.

Amfac was the best garage in Honolulu, a six-story spiral wonderland near the red-light district that was fast and smooth and unguarded. On the roof under the equatorial night sky, we would look down and smell the rot and tawdriness wafting up from Hotel Street. It was a smell of complete freedom. We had the place to ourselves and would skate down and go up over and over again, a pack of skaters racing without much concern to who "won." It was more about pure speed and enjoying something in a way its builders never intended. I did get satisfaction from coming out ahead, but really it was the camaraderie that mattered. In the garages, I saw the paradox of skating—a highly individualistic activity that often depended on a group dynamic for cohesion.

The violence that manifested itself on the dance floor at 3-D was just the tip of the iceberg. Security guards and bouncers were usually Samoan, locals or haoles who acted like locals. There was always the chance that the most innocent encounter would turn into a conflagration at the drop of a hat. Though it didn't start in an innocuous fashion, an incident at 3-D was indicative of the animosity in the air. The bouncer was a huge Samoan guy who already didn't like us. Samoans mostly kept to themselves, with whole families overflowing out of pickup trucks like South Sea Joads. They picked coconuts and had raucous barbecues on the beach, and every few months, there would be a horrible rape or murder perpetuated by a marauding gang of drunken Samoan men. One time my parents were riding home on the bus from a party, and two drunk Samoans got on and terrorized the passengers and assaulted the bus driver. They were the wild card in Hawaii's racial sweepstakes, and if you gave them a wide berth, everything was usually fine.

But one night Doug Guthrie's long-simmering beef with the bouncer came to a head. Doug spit on or hit him; in the ensuing chaos, I never found out exactly what had happened. Davin and I hastily followed Doug down the stairs into a dark alley where we stopped and waited for the inevitable, shaking with fear. At least I know I was. The bouncer came after us like an understandably enraged bull, and then we heard a crash and a shout of pain and Doug ran by us at full speed. He had hit the guy over the head with a bottle—very punk. With Doug in the lead, we literally ran for our lives, the bleeding Samoan right behind us. I could practically feel his breath on my neck and could definitely hear his shouted threats. It wasn't much of an exaggeration on my part to think that, if caught, I would be killed. Things like that happened in Hawaii. Adrenaline pumping, sweating, the three of us split up and went in different directions, running for blocks. Then we reconvened and laughed and laughed, giddily exhilarated. We didn't go back to 3-D for a while after that.

In Estes Park the police and rednecks had given me grief, but that was nothing compared to Hawaii. The police were low on the scale of enemies; the locals were the real problem. Being a sixteen-year-old haole guaranteed a wide range of antagonists. On that island thirty miles long and twenty wide, with a population of eight hundred thousand, was a volatile mixture of every ethnic group imaginable—Chinese, Japanese, Portuguese, Fijian, Samoan, black, white, local and every possible genetic combination thereof. Behind the rainbow-coalition facade fabricated for tourists were a lot of ugly thoughts and actions. The haoles owned the most; the Japanese controlled the government and were buying a lot of property; and the locals were the understandably disgruntled underclass. I have never heard so many ethnic slurs and jokes in my life, a daily barrage from all sides directed at all the other sides. Everybody had something against other races: a state of minor differences blown way out of proportion.

The natural teenage tendency toward confrontation made the locals vs. haoles situation worse. You always had to be careful. Hawaii Kai was a haole and Asian enclave, which made it relatively safe for people like us, but on other parts of the island, we felt viscerally unwanted. We had to be prepared at all times for an impromptu threat or attack, ready to fight or to take flight, and fleeing was definitely the sanest course of action.

Because I could skate well, locals gave me a modicum of respect that normally wouldn't have been forthcoming. My skating ability negated my whiteness and elicited an approving "Brah can skate." Other times, there was a resentment that implied my skating was just another example of haole oppression. More common were locals surrounding you and saying, "Ho brah, you get one nice board, I like check 'em out real fast." You knew if you let one of the guys ride it, he would probably steal it, but if you didn't, he would beat you up and take it anyway. A no-win situation. The best thing to do was to smile like everything was okay and then, if the opportunity arose, skate away as fast as possible. Away from skating, as Davin had first told me, the traditional local provocation was "What?" if you looked at someone the wrong way: that would be any way. I learned early on not to study anybody too closely. You would be staring into space and some local would cross your field of vision, and then the "What fucka, you like beef?" or "What, haole, I owe you money?" would come out and you were screwed. Whatever you said would provoke a negative response, since they just wanted to fuck with you. And it wasn't directed just at kids. Teenage girls would accuse my fifty-year-old mother of giving them stink-eye on the bus all the time.

It was like being in a hostile country. The tribulations of moving were compounded by the incredibly arcane and complicated social and racial rules that I had to pick up on immediately. One thing I had going for me was that with prolonged exposure to the sun, I got very tan, and my hair was dark so I could pass for some kind of haole-other mixture. Davin wasn't so lucky; he had the whitest hair imaginable and his last name was the comically Teutonic Neubacher. He had to endure some really bad times, like the almost officially sanctioned "Kill Haole" day in middle school, when local kids were given free rein to chase and beat up white kids—not that they didn't do that regardless of what day it was.

I acclimated well, though, and despite the dangers, living in Hawaii was one of the greatest experiences in my life. The racial skirmishes added spice; it was a real education. In summer school, I had to take a required class in Hawaiian history, and every day I was bombarded with allusions to how "we" had "stolen" Hawaii from the Hawaiians. That might have been so, but I had nothing to do with it. The lyrics to Minor Threat's "Guilty of Being White" came to mind daily. Though the song was about growing up white in D.C. and dealing with black resentment, it hit home: "I'm sorry for something that I didn't do / I killed somebody and I don't know who / You blame me for slavery, a hundred years before I was born / Guilty of being white."

Shockingly, that year I lived in Hawaii, I escaped serious injury at the hands of others. I turned my face away a lot, ran a bunch of times and used diplomacy as often as possible. The one time I wasn't so lucky was at a big backyard graduation party. Hawaii's premier hardcore group, S.R.O., played along with a local rock-and-roll cover band. That made for a majority of local and haole "rock" people tensely predominating over the punks and skaters. Of course

I found the cover band contemptible, and I couldn't help snickering and making jokes to my friends. During one particularly excruciating guitar solo, I said, "When are they going to play 'Freebird'?" a little louder than I should have, and immediately a wide, muscular haole friend of the band turned around and gave me a look. He was a haole who had gone local, full-on pidgin-talking and everything. He said, "What?" and I replied, "Nothing." I'm sure my bright red-and-white aloha shirt didn't help matters. To my attempt to get out of it, he said, "No, I heard you say something stink about the band." As I was demurring again, he stepped toward me and said, "You like me falsecrack [sucker-punch] you?" As he spoke, he falsecracked me in the face. I toppled over, he was restrained and we got out of there before things got worse.

Notwithstanding such escapades, life was good. I spent many hours on the bus going to AALA Park and other places to meet up with the crew. On the ride down the Kaneohoe Highway, I repeatedly encountered a pretty Japanese mental patient wearing an orange summer dress who would rub her crotch and look at me suggestively and then announce to everybody that her "*chi-chi* itched." The Cobra skate shop across the street from AALA Park was our default hangout. It was owned by an overweight New York Jew by the name of Cobra (hence the name of the shop), whose relationship with the skaters was far from one of mutual appreciation, but everybody congregated there for lack of someplace better. Cobra's claim to fame was that he "invented" puka-shell necklaces, contributing in no small way to the sordid history of questionable seventies jewelry. The shop was cramped and dark, with an assortment of skate equipment and a Pong video game. Cobra bore an uncanny resemblance to the Manny character in *Skateboard: The Movie*, always annoyed with the skaters and habitu-

ally banning them from his shop. We tolerated him in part because his wrath paled in comparison to that of Mrs. Cobra, his
Korean mail-order dragon-lady bride, who really hated skaters and
was constantly getting into screaming matches with anyone who
crossed her path. Goading her into one of her frenzies was the
house sport.

Six months after I arrived, a sixteen-foot-wide half-pipe was
built at the Red Hill Coast Guard base, a big improvement over
Tantalus that fostered a lot of progression. The level of tricks was
getting higher. Mako was ripping with one-foot backside airs, and
Stanford was doing high frontside ollies, and everybody was trying
all kinds of bonelesses and other tricks. Comparing myself to the
pictures in *Thrasher* and what Johnee told me about the mainland, I
began to think I was getting good enough to get sponsored. Soon a
North Shore character called "Dinosaur" Dean built a ramp at
Waialua. He was in his thirties and totally into skating. He encouraged us to drive out past Schofield Barracks and the sugarcane fields
to skate at the ramp and stay overnight on the beach, where we got
attacked by mosquitoes and sand ants. Something else worth noting happened at Red Hill. As I stood next to Wayne's car, he played
the first tape I ever heard of Grandmaster Flash. "The Message"
was so fresh and exciting, an exotic transmission from the Bronx
that had almost as much impact on me at the first listening as the
Sex Pistols had.

The punk-rock brothers and the other East Side hardcore crew
were compatriots and good friends. They would venture to Hawaii
Kai to skate Off the Walls and visit my house, where my mother
would supply us with juice and cookies before we went carousing
in the pool. It was a twisted punk version of *Leave It to Beaver*, good
kids into anarchy who got along with their parents. Rich and Ed

were straight-edge, so we had the evils of drugs to agree about, along with our anticapitalist, antisystem politics. Their zine was called *Thrash N'Tool*, and it was a fierce samizdat of skating pictures and snapshots of their mom in front of the Tower of London, along with their sister Rosetta's attacks on Adam Smith's "invisible hand" theory in *The Wealth of Nations*. With Rich at the helm, six sweaty teenagers would squeeze into a beat-up brown Toyota Corolla to go on skating expeditions all over the island. When we pulled up to a gas station, Rich would invariably declaim, "Okay, guys, bust out your wallets." Their band was Scarred for Life, with Danny Barger as the first lead singer, but he moved to San Diego, so I became the frontman for a few months. I was always off-tempo, but I did scream with ardor. The drummer, Kerry Iwamuro, was a good musician, and my lack of respect for melodious proprieties drove him to distraction, as did my penchant for grabbing Rich's guitar and torturing the band with extended feedback interludes. My one gig as singer was at a party near Dean's house, where we played D.Y.S. and Rudimentary Peni covers, along with originals like "Fast Gas" (about running out of gas in the Corolla), to an appreciative crowd of fifteen. Since we knew only eight songs, we played them all twice.

Rich and Ed were committed. Back in the Bay Area, they had stolen instruments from their neighbor Steve Perry (of Journey) to get a band going before moving to Hawaii and starting S.F.L. Thrash N'Tool records was an offshoot of the zine, a record store in the trunk of the Corolla. There were no record stores in Hawaii that had punk stuff, so other than mail order, the shop in the trunk was it for a very small, elite demographic. Sometimes the records would get warped from the heat, but those that survived were sold practically at cost. Rich and Ed were do-it-yourself, antihero, antiestablishment, smart and engaged. They also had a sense of humor about their seriousness—and we were very serious, about politics, about punk, about skating. They defined hardcore as a way of life, ready to drive anywhere to skate, Xs on their hands, hand-lettering *Thrash N'Tool.* They had real conviction and were real friends.

Rich and Ed, Jon and James, Davin, the AALA Park and Hawaii Kai crews, the Oahu punks, all were part of something that no longer exists, and that's sad. Nostalgia about inevitabilities aside, it was a great year. I had my own *ohana* (pidgin for "family") of like-minded miscreants and visionaries and got to skate to my heart's content, was allowed by my amazingly tolerant parents to run wild and associate with whomever I wanted, to experiment and learn and taste unknown metaphoric fruits. By the end of the year, the pit bull and I had made friends. I tentatively put out my hand and patted his head before saying good-bye to Oahu. Then it was time to finally stop dreaming about California.

Chapter Fifteen
The Future Is Yesterday's
Point of Departure

Who cares if the rest of the world knows what we're doing . . . the big media moguls only cover events when they've reached their final stage . . . it's at its hippest when it's underground. Let it run its natural course." Stacy Peralta's article "Skate of the Art '85," in the August 1985 *Thrasher*, revealed his usual insight. Through the eighties, skateboarding was undergoing a metamorphosis. Freestyle and downhill gradually got subsumed into skating as a whole, while in the street, a strange mix of old-fashioned and radical moves was receiving equal attention. Skating was about to reach a plateau of progress and mainstream acceptance. It was approaching the end of its own history. Stacy's questions and predictions addressed what had been and what was to come: "Is skateboarding a culture? A happening? An event? A lifestyle which sets itself apart from other sports? . . . Some feel it can be the next Little League with international status, but no way! Maybe in fifteen years when worldwide saturation sets in, but not until."

The same year, Scott Smiley's letter to *Thrasher* gave voice to the apprehensions that recognition aroused. "I totally disagree (about wanting skating on TV, etc.). Skaters will be skaters and not jocks. Skate for fun or not at all." Jesse Davis was more emphatic: "AAAHHH! Stop it! Stop it! What are these people talking about?! Who wants skating on Wide World of Sports? Never! Doesn't anyone learn from mistakes?" Their concerns were well founded. For better or worse, fifteen years down the line, saturation has set in.

But in 1985 the parks were mostly reduced to rubble. Some, like Colton and Reseda Skatercross, became off-limits territory like backyard pools, ridden illegally after they went out of business and before the bulldozers arrived. Parks had been important and fun, but their erasure meant they could no longer be relied on, and the street and ramps took precedence. A flurry of untrained construction meant scores of bigger customized half-pipes. Mile High Ramp, the Fresno Ark and Joe Lopes's ramp were just a few in California. Cambodia III in Florida, Annandale and Cedar Crest in Virginia, the Keystone Ramp in Pennsylvania, the Clown Ramp in Dallas, painted blue with yellow stripes. Things got official in Virginia Beach when Mount Trashmore, built on a garbage dump, opened with a ribbon-cutting ceremony attended by the mayor. Henry Guiterrez, Mike Crescini, Rob Mertz, Jimmy Murphy and Dan Tag all came out of an East Coast scene that revolved exclusively around wooden half-pipes. Ramps went up all over continental Europe. In London, there was Crystal Palace, with Danny Webster, Bod Boyle, Rodga Harvey and Lucian Hendricks, the British Christian Hosoi. Anywhere there were skaters with initiative and access to land and wood, some form of skatepark substitute was brought into being.

Contests were held in backyards almost every weekend, some big, some small, some with pros, most without. For one at Eagle Rock, near L.A., first place earned five dollars. Fun was the operative principle. Owner Jay B. Moore explained the rationale in *Thrasher:* "Doug,

Mark and I decided to throw a contest when we went to Jim's Burgers for a lunch break." Tony Magnusson and Eddie Reatigui tied for first, with Eddie doing extremely stylish smith stops by the channel. These affairs were often "jams," which meant contestants rode for as long as they wanted (or could stay on) before the next person went, a format that was less exhausting and more in tune with a session's rhythm than the quarter/semi/final system borrowed from other sports. The Midwest Melees in Lincoln, Nebraska, were representative of the jam format. Organizer Rich Flowerday's older brother's reflections could have been about any number of teenage sculptors with a purpose: "My perspective is unique in that, since 1978, I had watched a homemade halfpipe grow out of a 4' ∞ 8' piece of plywood set up against a picnic bench at the bottom of my folks' driveway, into a ramp termed 'state-of-the-art' by Melee coordinator Fausto Vitello." Vertical skating's progression was incubated and refined on these undecorated, profoundly functional objects. Tricks got more complicated with variations, fakie moves and the beginning of switch. Airs got higher. During this unfolding there was a borrowing from vertical combined with simultaneous developments on flat land that became the new street riding.

But it was not an overnight process. What transpired first was on and above the curved plane between flat and vertical. Eddie Reatigui jumped from an adjoining roof onto the Hunter's Point ramp, a death-defying act that was a direct precursor to the brazen stunts of today in which skaters literally ollie off buildings. Channels—an opening with a rounded entry onto the transition—were incorporated into half-pipes, making airs and other maneuvers over them the next logical step; and "bridges of death" were put across channels to grind over. Christian Hosoi did airs to fakie over the channel at Joe Lopes's ramp, traveling sideways instead of just straight up and down before landing backward. Lance Mountain was one of the first to do frontside inverts over channels, flying upside down with his back to the flat before landing on his leading hand at the other side. The amazingly gifted and humble Steve Caballero won contests left and right and is still at it twenty years later. His 360-degree caballerial survives on vertical and in a version of the ollie on street. Frontside inverts with his hair in braids at the Jew Drop pool in San Jose were just one of the countless iconic moments in his oeuvre.

Airs went from two feet out in 1978 to eleven feet above the coping (Caballero at the Raging Waters ramp) by the end of 1987. People didn't just fly out anymore, they boned (extended the back leg straight) or meloned (front leg straight), contorting and twisting their bodies in space. The board became a pliable tool to move closer or farther away from the body during flight, instead of something that had to be held on to for dear life and kept directly in position. Christian Hosoi was doing backside airs in which his body was completely over his flattened board. Stalefish, indy grab (a Duane Peters contribution), lein, mute (and its more gymnastic variant, the Japan air), roast beef and tail grabs were all different ways of holding the board while hurtling through the air. At Lance's ramp, Kevin Staab did indy airs face-high while Lester Kasai, on his Sims green-and-blue "splotch" board with yellow magnesium six-tracks and four different-colored wheels, wore argyle socks pulled up under his duct-taped kneepads and did mute airs in the upper stratosphere. Jeff Grosso was caught by a fish-eye lens at Del Mar, dive-bombing in from five feet during a backside air with his back leg stretched rigid. Tony Hawk started finger-flipping backside airs, spinning the board 360 degrees and catching it at the apex of his trajectory. Then he went beyond that with the 720, not as breathtaking as the McTwist because he didn't go upside down, but it did pave the way to other multiple spins. In Sweden, where Mike McGill had secretly made his breakthrough, skate campers ignored topless women sunbathing and instead keenly observed Tony perfecting the double revolution. Tony did the "circus" tricks that were derided by many as styleless and fake, tricks where, as he said, "you twist your body, your hands, your board in the air, you get so flamboyant that you can't even tell what it is." But he persevered and was vindicated, and today his tricks are the backbone of vertical riding at its highest level.

Today's moves are complicated, and the nomenclature is accurate, but not as colorful as the popular-culture references and humorous wordplay that went into affixing names to maneuvers back then. The gay twist was a caballerio with the skater grabbing the inside rail; catching it like a backside air made it a les twist. A frontside air grabbed on the inside rail was a stalefish. Lein-to-tails got one-footed and were called Madonnas; the backside version was a Sean Penn. People started taking the front foot off during backside airs—a frigid was when the rider kicked back a foot; when it went the other direction, it was a judo air. Then Tony Hawk took both feet off in flight, and that was the air walk. Christian Hosoi did rocket airs by putting both of his feet on the tail during a backside air and then made the air walk his own by holding the board in one hand and assuming a crucifixion pose while sailing through space. The Christ air.

Jeff Phillips came out of Texas and started blowing minds with huge bonelesses, alley-oop ollies and an idiosyncratic way of skating and living life. At the Clown Ramp, he was reported to ride for half an hour without missing a trick before hopping on someone's board and inventing ten street moves on the spot. His Lone Star State compatriot, Craig Johnson, was, in Mofo's words, "a MAD-

MAN and he skated to that effect. That's all I can say." Rob Roskopp was called "The Barn" because he was big and came from Ohio. Huge fakie thrusters (a footplant where the rider jumped out from fakie and came back in forward) and sadplants (an invert with the front leg straightened) were his stock-in-trade. Gator, with his tousled hair and mischievous grin, did things only he could do, like 360-degree footplants and, in one video, spinning consecutive McTwists while wearing a camera helmet and blithely narrating his whole run into an attached microphone. Unbelievable. His board was everywhere, and he was almost as big a star as Christian Hosoi.

Neil Blender said, "Take handplants; you can do handplants like a lot of people and you can just get the trick over with. . . . Or, you can do a handplant, and try to get so much out of a handplant." He consistently backed up his words by taking tricks into unknown territory. His miller flips were over the coping and stalled to become jolly mambas. Handplant variations proliferated: invert reverts by Duane Peters, one-footed, no-footed (Jeff Hedges), switcheroos in which the skater moved his hand from one rail to the other (Billy Ruff) and the reverse elguerial Phillips 66, by Jeff Phillips. Billy Beauregard gratuitously flapped over his andrechts, and Steve Caballero did tuck-knee inverts that were so contorted, his heels almost touched his back. Tom Groholski fully extended one-footed inverts while transferring from low to high on his Plexiglass ramp in New Jersey. Tony Hawk and Billy Beauregard twisted themselves into pretzel shapes before coming back in fakie. The invert to fakie was a result of the Eddie Elguera influence that opened doors to landing backward. And Micke Alba did varial inverts in the combipool. That took guts.

Monty Nolder, a deaf skater from Florida, did high gay twists and everything else. When I first saw him do a backside smith grind in Del Mar's keyhole, I let out an incredulous "Fuck!" because he had such power, raw speed and flow. The father type watching next to me asked why I had gotten so excited by a trick that looked so ostensibly simple. It's hard to explain how locking in the rail with pinpoint back-toe balancing while sliding on the coping can require much more finesse than an aerial. Backside smiths and frontside rock-and-rolls—an Elguera innovation that can also be credited to his coach, Dale "Sausage Man" Smith, who came up with the idea—are tricks that have survived the transition to the street. Wherever the frontside rock-and-roll is done, the focus on pivoting the back toe at a small corner of the board's tail during the difficult turn frontside adds up to a moment of physical grace. Along with Mike Smith's eponymous grind, the frontside rock-and-roll is a timeless move that is just as good today as it was then. Toward the end of the eighties and through to the present, lip tricks flourished on vertical, and there has been a wholesale adaptation of them to handrails and ledges—smiths, fifty-fifties and feebles are all vertical grinding variations. Conversely, the give-and-take has gone the other way as people take flip tricks from the street to ramps. What comes around goes around.

Street skating in the summer of 1983 was everything from Andy Kessler's one-footed nose wheelie in New York, on the cover of *Thrasher*, to Paul Hoffman sliding into garbage cans, Jay Adams's sidewalk bert, Lance Mountain skating off a roof and Steve Caballero running up a wall to jump onto his board. Those pictures accompanied Lowboy's "Don't Tell Us How to Live and We Won't Tell You How to Die, Or New Etiquette for a Street Society" in the same issue. He was as conspiratorially incisive as always: "Can't anybody accept the fact that the activity of riding a skate is as valid a reason for existence on this planet as any other. . . . Are [they] shocked that skaters constantly reinterpret the urban planners' rigidly one-dimensional theories?" Pavement had always been ridden; the difference was the explosion of tricks on the street, born out of the scarcity of vertical skate areas. "The only rule was the basic axiom that there are no rules. . . . Why read when you can be rad? Why theorize when you can terrorize? Why socialize when you can radicalize? . . . Oh yes and just one last thing . . . kindly disregard the maneuvers on these pages and go out and invent your own. The future is yesterday's point of departure."

The first modern street contest was held on Conservatory Road in Golden Gate State Park, not long after Stecyk's polemic appeared. He was there with a stuffed opossum art piece that got him into trouble with the police, who also had some issues with organizer Fausto Vitello's lack of a permit. There was a little pyramid ramp and bigger wedge ramps and the asphalt road. The virtually unknown Tommy Guerrero became the first person to ever win a pro contest as an amateur, a symbolic victory on par with the Z-Boys' emergence at the Del Mar Nationals ten years before. Tommy's fastplants at the Fort Miley banks came a little later, along with bizarre varial hazards and early ollies. The flatland ollie was so incipient that a little while later, at Huntington, they were described as "hops." Tommy was already consistently ripping down the streets of San Francisco ollieing over shrubs, doing fifteen-foot curb grinds and whatever else came into his mind with a nonchalance that made it all look easy.

What Tommy and a host of experimentalists did was adapt vertical tricks to the urban landscape, including hazards in which the rider went up to the curb and did a footplant-handplant combination move, or boneless ones with a hand down on a ledge. Neil Blender's 360-degree eggplant off a picnic-table ramp was this kind of hybridization at its best, as was Lance Mountain's wall-walk-to-handplant. Another early mutation was substituting 90-degree angles for curved transitions. Third-generation Dogtowners Natas Kaupas, Tim Jackson and Jesse Martinez were routinely doing it by the middle of the decade. In Mofo's assessment, "The sacerdotal sanctuary of the wall has been assaulted, challenged, abused, violated and conquered by a select and creative personnel." Natas said Dan McClure did it first; Jesse ran up to a wall and jumped onto his board on the vertical surface to ride back down; and Eric Dressen took the next step, forcing his board through the unforgiving angle where the sidewalk meets the wall: wall rides. Dressen first appeared in *Skateboarder* at age ten before going on to three decades of underappreciated all-around ripping. Another early wall rider was a very young Julien Stranger. Dressen and Stranger are just two of the hardcore who have been out there through the good and the bad, regardless of whether anybody was paying attention or not.

More street than vertical was Neil Blender's no comply, manipulating the board over a curb with his feet instead of his hands to land on the other side. For posterity, Neil also nollied into a pogo rock-and-roll on a ramp, bouncing his front wheels off the coping and effectively inventing the other version of the ollie that is so prevalent today, in which the rider pops off the front of the board instead of the tail. In Neil's view, street was a place for being "rambunctious, a way of expressing yourself without having to look good, looking like a dork—who cares?" Natas Kaupas, with his spiky white hair and cutaway Santa Monica Airlines board, doing a layback air on a wall, was pure vertical as street; but then he went into unknown territory with ollies up to a car's bumper. To ollie that high and turn it into a trick on an edge above the ground was just amazing. Maybe the most prescient and primal move (photographed in a *Thrasher* sequence by Craig Stecyk) was Christian Hosoi's incredible running leap off a roof over a wall onto a bank, the kind of leap of faith that Jaime Thomas and other like-minded daredevils now do in the guise of massive ollies across distances of twenty feet. Unlike Yves Klein's leap of faith, these are real.

Not long after Golden Gate Park, Mark Gonzales was riding for Alva and bonelessing off a ramp at the Capitola contest, tweaking the nose of his board so much it was pointing away from where he was headed. Then he ollied over Sasha Steinhorst's head at the Fort Miley banks. After quitting Alva ("'cuz Tony cut off his dreads, man. It just disappointed me"), he was on Vision with a very popular "face" graphic. He started the trend with Lance Mountain and Neil Blender of Magic Marker art on grip tape. This doodling led to an effusion of painting, sculpture, embroidery and writing that has garnered him much renown among skaters and art mavens alike. Before all that, he was just a hyper kid who was light-years ahead of everybody except Tommy Guerrero and Natas Kaupas. The three of them make up street's holy triumvirate, with Rodney Mullen as an oddball fourth partner. Mark said in 1985: "The street is neat . . . street skating is a great sport, invented by a guy named Natas Kaupas, ollie master of the 80s, he's insane." His next comment is the Rosetta Stone of the upcoming historical shift: "Well me and my good friend Natas have been practicing ollie flips. See, it's like a freestyle trick, but we do it on the street." Mark also skates vertical incredibly well, doing airs, bean plants, frontside inverts and eggplants in his own unique style. Early on, he ollied as if the board were magically attached to his feet, setting the stage for the effortless pop-and-glide of hundreds of thousands of skaters to follow. At an Oregon contest in 1986, insanity ensued in the rain as Mark did a rock-and-roll boardslide on a vintage Cadillac's fin and landed it. It was an epoch-defining moment. To see Mark Gonzales skate is to observe musical improvisation turned physical; it's like watching Mikhail Baryshnikov dancing alone for fun.

Meanwhile, Rodney Mullen was appearing in almost every issue of *Thrasher*. The impossible was a trick that seemed literally that: from a standing position, he kicked the board 360 degrees below him before landing. The ollieflip was basically the modern kickflip, ollieing before flipping the board with the feet along its longitudinal axis. The lollypop, the fifty-fifty switchfoot, the sidewinder: his mind-boggling maneuvers were so esoteric that they were like a higher form of math that hardly anybody understood, complex freestyle equations that are a lost science never to be replicated; though his obscure realizations did live on in modern flip-in, flip-out ledge tricks.

Skaters were making a sea change from rolling off a loading dock to defying gravity by popping ollies up and over, making for height and length as well as the ability to get up on the coping simulacrum. Instead of riding up to the coping, as happens on vertical, the skater ollies up to a bench or handrail. What brought the revolution home to me was watching Johnee Kop at a school in Point Loma in 1988. He had his own model on Vision by that point and was living the pro-skater lifestyle. We were by a sixteen-step staircase with a big drop that seemed impossibly long. He tried it three or four times, bailing and flying through the air before tumbling on the ground. Then he made it, a long, lengthy flight that showed me things would never be the same.

There was also the whole "dork" session phenomenon, which was just fooling around but provided a hotbed of progress. One case of life following art was a ludicrous OJs ad with Christian Hosoi, Tony Magnusson and Johnee Kop. Johnee was posing a backside smith grind on a ledge. It was completely fake, but reality comes out of imagining, so now you have people doing fifteen-stair backside smiths. Screwing around in Dallas during a Clown Ramp contest, Lance and Steve Steadham did intentionally stupid-looking "tricks" while playfully, unconsciously advancing the art. Mofo's reporting captures the flavor of inadvertent invention and outré skater behavior: "We laugh at people taking stupid tourist family photos with the book depository in the background. Lance and Caballero do curb grinds in front of where Kennedy was shot." The "posing with a wino who thought Steadham was Michael Jackson" was part of a long tradition of unbridled skater mayhem as performance art and social confrontation. In 1976 people heard about Jay Adams's shenanigans; in 1985 Lance and Steve were photographed doing them; and by 2000, *Big Brother* had made some very amusing videos incorporating such frolics, as did Bam Magera in his "Camp Kill Yourself" tapes. They are funny as hell, but saturation sets in with neutered television shows trying to capitalize on a kind of humor that is best when it's unplanned and unrecorded.

In the formative years, a lot of vertical riders won street contests—Billy Ruff, Neil Blender, Steve Caballero and Christian Hosoi all adapted and emerged victorious. By 1990 that was over, and a crop of street-only skaters was being noticed before going on to deserved legendary status. Ray Barbee, with his smooth and jazzy presence, a master of footwork and fluidity; Guy Mariano and future actor Jason Lee. Watching Jason, Guy and Mark Gonzales in the defining *Video Days*, directed by Spike Jonze and Karol Winthrop, is to see the DNA of all that would come afterward. The frontside boardslides Mark had done on flat ledges had been taken by him and Julien Stranger and others to slanted handrails, a big change from sliding horizontally to traveling downhill that meant increased speed and danger.

These are people whose names will survive, but not everything came from them. Hail the unknown innovators, like Paul Hoffman on the cover of *Skateboarder* in 1978, grinding his front truck on a curb while doing a nose wheelie, predating the ollie nosegrind by twenty years. Or the kid named Chris whom I skated with in Waikiki, right before I left Hawaii, who was doing street plants and proto-ollies before their time. At the time of Tommy Guerrero's arrival, Keith Butterfield was shown in an OJs advertisement doing a fifty-fifty grind off a ledge, riding toward the edge that met the pavement to grind off. He didn't ollie onto it, but the idea was there. In a similar instance, Street Scott was pictured setting his board up on a rail before stepping on it to slide down, giving premonitions of the handrail madness to come. Somebody out there might have done it first or at least thought of it before there was official photographic validation. One aspect of skating's liberating appeal is that any skater can be the first one to take a leap of imagination that leaves the past behind.

In his 1985 "Skate of the Art" article, Stacy Peralta wrote about skating's relationship to architecture: "Years ago light posts, cars and buildings were purposely avoided while skating streets. . . . Now they are the way, the ride. . . . There are no more white lines to stay within, sidewalks to conform to or bases to tag. It's all an open highway with hydrants, curbs, bumpers, shopping carts, door handles and pedestrians. It's the total-attack approach where the skater is not a separate entity from his terrain. . . . Now he is the terrain with all of its intricate pieces." Skaters have always looked at architecture more appreciatively than most—in a wholly unorthodox way—and they were starting to view walls and stairs and everything else with a revised set of standards. The ignored and unremarkable aspects of buildings and the urban infrastructure are all game, and as long as the runway to the ledge or stairs is smooth enough, it can be approached and ollied onto. The marble plazas of Mies van der Rohe and his imitators are the perfect playgrounds for contemporary trick science. It isn't just the corporate environs but all the cracks, sidewalk bumps, simple curbs, abandoned shopping carts, bent signposts to grind up and over, the handrails and handicapped ramps that lead up to them. The developed world is a vast man-made skatepark, waiting for a worldwide population of astute urban surveyors. Street skating can happen anywhere.

Two individuals who had a lasting influence and highlight skating's ability to bring disparate personalities together are Neil Blender and Christian Hosoi. Neil's skating was innovative, and so was his off-kilter view of the world. With his short, no-nonsense hair and a facial expression hovering between intense concentration and mild amusement, he was a self-invented Dadaist who wasn't really that into punk—he liked the Jam. At over six feet tall, he made his his board look tiny under him while he did the strangest things on it, like no complys, and then just pushed around sliding on the tail. Nobody knew what to think at first of his creative attempts to exceed the limits of what had been established. Garry Scott Davis asked him, "Do you ever skate without copers?" "Yeah." "What's it like?" "It's like hot-dog stands. No big deal." Neil did backflips off of walls without his board and said, "Jeff Grosso looks like a moth." Pictured on the cover of *Thrasher* seriously contemplating a hand puppet, he wrote the introduction to his interview with a nod to the past and his own idiosyncrasies: "I hate cold conditions, snow, wind, rain. I like animals, squirrels, monkeys, you name it. Skateboarding was an obsession with me, now it's just an art expression." He listed the parks he rode and the people there: Skip Disney, Tony Howlett, Brad Jackman and Huggy Bear. "I guess you'd call me a park rider. I still talk to some of these people. But it's never the same." There was a wistful quality to his remembrances, how he would "sneak off with my skateboard to Sadlands" in junior high. At the Concrete Wave Skatepark, Neil recalled, "My first day, I had long pants on, I rented equipment, I overheated and vomited." That innocence contrasted with his view of skating's overcommercialization and why Duane Peters had bailed out: "Duane's an anarchist . . . Duane Peters was rad, o.k.? He saw badhood coming out of skating and he said 'shine.'"

Accompanying the article were pictures of Neil's toes, ears, mouth, worse-for-the-wear knees and his drawings. One was of a pained-looking man with a glass, a hammer, a bird, an insect and a baseball flying at him, with the caption "Bombardment of all surroundings, but not really wishing for anything in particular." Neil's musings got at skating's appeal as a physical and mental challenge and a sphere apart from the rest of society: "To error means you're trying, how much effort you put in is your measurement. . . . You earn quality when you skate. . . . In yourself, you like what you do. You keep skating because you keep getting higher feelings, and then you try to go higher." His six-foot-high fastplants at Lance's ramp were definitely higher.

Christian Hosoi was on the other side of the sensibility spectrum, with star potential and street smarts. Holmes was also just plain Christ. The Christ air and the slow-motion 540s were exhibit number one for Scott Foss's definition of virtuoso riding: "Style and radicalness are not necessarily two separate aspects of the art and are, in fact, one and the same when a true master works the brush." Christian did backside ollies off the oververtical at AALA Park, something nobody had even thought of when I lived in Honolulu. He was seventeen in 1985 and unabashed about his ambitions as a kid riding Marina del Rey: "I wanted to . . . become the best skater in the world." He had reached that point, and somehow his assimilationist attitude and his affection for Sheila E., Prince and Madonna; silly highlights in his hair; and pink pants and shirts unbuttoned to the waist weren't offensive at all. Even in those hardcore correct times, he was hard to dislike. Saving money didn't seem to be one of his priorities. He bought W. C. Fields's old house in Echo Park, installing a big half-pipe behind it with all of L.A. as the backdrop. A typical item in "Trash" reported, "Is it true that Christian Hosoi lost a wallet with six hundred bucks in it and didn't even know it till a week later? Is it true Christ rolls so heavily that the funds were never missed?" The way he glided through life without rancor toward anyone would make his incarceration on drug charges in 2000 seem even sadder.

Less well known but just as crucial was Allen Losi, not a "star" like Christian or as bizarrely ingenious as Neil, but he and Mike Smith and Eric Grisham were the kind of maverick skateboarders who rode hard and contributed much. Some of the moves Losi pioneered were attributed to others, but no matter—whoever did what, he ripped. He did stand-up grinds in the combi pool, a primal move done with authority, akin to the surfer Drew Harmon in Kem Nunn's *The Dogs of Winter*, who carves a bottom turn that is "a thing of beauty, perfectly timed and executed. . . . It was too pure and too clean for the admittance of cheap theatrics." Losi embodied balls-out vertical riding and had insight into the intricacies of Mike Smith: "Smith shreds and he's from my age. . . . He'll throw a mean little lapover hang-up grind and has to grab the tail to get in, and people don't understand." Grisham was older and not winning contests anymore, but he continued to defy expectations and screw with the status quo through nonsensical moves like the el rollo neckplant in Del Mar's reservoir and the aptly named fakie body slam. He was one of the first higher aerialists and consistently pushed tricks past the fringe.

Eddie Elguera had quit skating and moved to Mexico before reappearing in California, where I saw him at the University of California at San Diego ramp in 1988. Nobody recognized him, and I wasn't even sure when I asked him, "Aren't you Eddie Elguera?" He smiled demurely. How quickly people forget. In *Thrasher* around that time, he said, "I feel that it was harder back in the 70s; we had to think up a majority of tricks off the top of our heads. Many of the tricks today are variations of tricks that we established back then."

It's true, people today don't know who these skaters were and what they did; their reward is their own memories. When Drew Harmon in *The Dogs of Winter* sees a young surfer who won the masters, he asks a burned-out surf photographer his own age, "What's the payoff on that little item now?"

"I'm not sure. I think he made thirty, forty grand."

"You know what I got the year I won that thing?"

"A trophy?"

"A fish dinner at Ahi's."

Santa Cruz, Independent, G&S, Variflex, Powell Peralta, Tracker, Rector, Madrid and Walker had all survived the skating downturn and, along with some new entries in the field, were starting to thrive by the late eighties. Brad Dorfman bought out Tom Sims to put together his Vision behemoth. The whole operation was pretty cheesy, with many heinous new-wave graphics, though they did produce the Gator and Mark Gonzales models and had great riders like Lee Ralph and Tom Groholski. (Applicable Dorfman quote: "It doesn't matter if you are a dork if you have money.") Santa Monica Airlines was a partnership between Skip Engblom and Steve Rocco, who had been working as a used-car salesman—more than ironic, considering how big a player he would become in the business. Lance Mountain's assertion that "every circus needs a clown, that's why we have Rocco" was belied by Rocco's genius for turning provocation into profit.

Zorlac used gory Pushead artwork and violent imagery in their advertisements, such as a Santa doll lanced by pins with a caption that read, "Dear Santa: bring me a Zorlac or else." Jeff Newton jokingly blamed aliens from the planet Zorlac for his rash decision to set up shop in the lean years. Brand-X was a smaller Santa Barbara company whose boards overlaid a skull and crossbones on geometric patterns; John Dettman rode for them and produced an exceptional zine called *Galloping Giraffe*. Rick and Peter Ducommun's company, Skull, summed up their image in one advertisement that showed a white cat lurking by their boards next to freshly filled-in graves and the tongue-in-cheek admonition "Skate Safe!"

Tony Alva's reconstituted venture had some truly weird advertisements, with Tony, Mark Gonzales and Mondo made up like jesters. Another one was a Chokey Boy picture of Tony mock-crucified, with his decks at his feet between two surfboards. One of his interviews started with the proclamation "Skating is not for sissies." Hosoi had Johnee Kop (before he defected to Vision), Monty Nolder and mini-Christian Sergie Ventura. Hosoi's Hammerhead model was so popular it was counterfeited. At the time, hammerhead, fish and toe-notch shapes were all the rage, prompting Rick Blackhart to say, "Some make you look like you're riding a bulbous dildo with wheels." The belief that they were functional was genuine, but they were also a way for manufacturers to differentiate product in an increasingly crowded marketplace. John Lucero's board on Madrid had an evil clown holding a voodoo doll, and along with the progressively horrific "flexing arm" Rob Roskopp series, designed by Jim Phillips at Santa Cruz, it marked a turn toward sensationalistic imagery. Walker's Mark Lake model had somebody's head being ripped off from the top. Offensive imagery was becoming the norm, like the OJs "Slime Balls" ads that showed Roskopp upchucking and said, "*&^%$#% Fast!" One for Thunder trucks had a woman in a bra with a truck for a head and the tag line "Socially incorrect." Outraged parents wrote letters, and of course that made kids want the things more. Hysterical incidents, like the attempted Orange County boycott of Natas's boards because his name spelled backward was "Satan," undoubtedly helped sales.

Arty approaches cropped up. A Salvador Dalí quote, "I cannot guarantee that this fragment of a dream will be well received," was used in a Vision ad above Mark Gonzales mute-grabbing off a ramp wearing long johns under his shorts. Designs became bolder and more graphic, like Vision's Hippie Stick psychedelic paisley scheme. Old Ghosts, John Grigley's Vision offshoot, used grainy photos with a lot of black-and-white reversal imagery. Skulls were the major motif in graphics throughout the decade, going back to V. C. Johnson's trailblazing Ray "Bones" Rodriguez "skull and sword" that had so titillated me in Estes Park. Powell Peralta's Steve Steadham board had a dreadlocked skull over sergeant's stripes. Later, the reliance on skulls began to fade, and Blockhead came out of Sacramento with cool eight-ball graphics and the motto "Skater made, made to skate," a harbinger of growing defiance against companies run by businessmen who didn't ride.

Powell Peralta was dominant, with a cohesive team of ac-
claimed riders and the most inspired marketing campaign. Lance
Mountain holding a stuffed German shepherd with the caption
"Choose your dinner": what did it have to do with skateboarding?
Absolutely nothing, but it was funny and compelling; as was an ar-
chival Miss U.S.A. pageant photo with riders' heads superimposed
on the contestants' bodies. The company made light of their image
as a slick conglomerate in an ad with a burning car and text that read,
"What they are saying about our new '86 line," paired with a Corey
O'Brien put-down from *Skate Fate* zine: "The Bones Brigade are the
Bee Gees of skateboarding." Then they introduced the character of
a peasant-hat-wearing old Chinese man, a mythological über-skater
gone into hiding and the unseen star of *The Search for Animal Chin. The
Bones Brigade Video* featured the original Brigade—Mike McGill, Steve
Caballero, Tony Hawk, Lance Mountain, Steve Steadham, Rodney
Mullen, Per Welinder, Kevin Staab, Eddie Reatigui and Adrian
Demain—and was thirty-one dollars postpaid with a choice of VHS
or Beta. Lowboy's "The Making of a Skate Video," about the creation of the follow-up, *Future Primitive,* appeared in *Thrasher:* "On a
side street in Alhambra, California, a professional Hollywood video
cameraman lay in a gutter bleeding. Standing next to him laughing
were the ever-so-guilty-looking Lance Mountain, Steve Caballero
and Mike McGill . . . the professional resigned from the crew moments after Stacy Peralta fired him." The lads "simply begged, borrowed, rented and otherwise procured the necessary equipment." The
result was avidly studied at home and abroad.

Everyone was initially afraid to say skating was back, but it
was, and street was the thing. The thicker and more colorful magazines were full of people launching off jump ramps and grinding
curbs. Boards got lighter and smaller, and the greater abuse they

suffered on the street meant they expired quickly, bolstering sales in the post-park age. Established manufacturers who had been living on the edge for years saw their original designs appropriated by sleazy Johnny-come-latelies. Nash and Action Sports were two of the biggest offenders who sold shoddy goods with rip-off graphics; Nash's "Go Home—Locals Only," with a palm-tree background, was particularly insipid. That these inferior sleds had a detrimental effect on the industry is without question, though it can certainly be argued that many kids got their start on them—they did roll. In 1984, Lowboy wrote "Why They Don't Sell Polyester Leisure Suits in American Samoa" about the Action Sports Retailer Show, an annual trade show of legitimate skate and surf manufacturers rubbing elbows with shameless opportunists. "'Skating is hot' is the call of the day and non-skate stores are calling for low-cost assemblies, i.e. poor-quality complete boards. Skating the business is warming up. . . . In other words after a couple more shows like this watch for bikini-clad skate wenches hawking their assorted roller wares from crushed velvet pedestals."

Tracker Trucks' Larry Balma started *Transworld* magazine in 1983 as a rebuttal to *Thrasher*'s "skate and destroy" ethos. The first issue included their "Skate and Create" manifesto, and from that point, they have been much more mainstream-friendly and positive, with an emphasis on striking photography. *Poweredge*, a good magazine that fell somewhere in the middle on the ideological battlefield, debuted and lasted a few years. *Body Slam, Lapper, Yakk, Death Skate, Skater of Fortune, Down Syndrome* and *Apathetic Injection* were just a few of the homegrown zines floating around that "cost" a stamp and were circulated through the grapevine with the help of the postal service. *Spontaneous Human Combustion* had a great name. *Thrasher* reviewed *Bung* and had this to say: "You can't get this bad without trying very hard or possessing a truly perverted soul. Hardcore adolescent cartoon porno capable of offending just about everyone." *Bung* and other transgressive efforts were the models for a formula that, in its neutered version, would later prove extremely lucrative. The three magazines and the zines were it until 1992, when Steve Rocco used his World Industries financial muscle to unveil the hilarious and juvenile travesty *Big Brother*, taking the *Bung* template to a national audience with a mix of soft-core porn, skating, fecal fixations and articles such as "How to Kill Yourself." It was brazen incitement, fulfilling Rocco's desire to turn up the heat and expose the hypocrisy of what has come to be called "The Industry." Just like the Natas/Satan to-do, it worked like a charm.

The letters in the magazines throughout the decade were mostly of the "your mag is the greatest" variety, with a minimum of carping. Now that skating is commonplace, there isn't as much of a fight for survival, but at the time there was a unity that came from battling common enemies, a shared sense of persecution and purpose. "My friends and I had our ramp burnt down by an old man." "Me and the other skaters from the neighborhood built a halfpipe. While we were having a session, a bunch of Klanners pulled up in a pickup and threw a Molotov cocktail on the ramp. No one was hurt but the ramp burnt to the ground. The cops won't do anything because half of them are in the Klan." "The other day me and a few fellow skaters got our boards taken away by a cop—when he was taking my friend's board away I told him to fuck off! I had to go to court and I had to pay a $75 fine." "Stop skate harassment" and "Skateboarding is not a crime" were cries heard (and stickers seen) across the land. The eternal conflict with the police and sticks-in-the-mud who find skating distasteful continues unabated. Today it is even worse on the streets, with people constantly getting kicked out of public places or being arrested. There is also a plague of antiskating devices installed to render spots unskateable. It's a huge pain, but at least it keeps skaters searching and prevents them from going completely soft.

Another development that would eventually dwarf sales of "hard" goods—i.e., boards, trucks and wheels—was the move toward "soft" products—clothes and shoes. Life's a Beach, Ocean Pacific, Jimmy Z and Gotcha all came over from the surf camp to cash in. Vision offered ghastly "streetwear" and shoes. Along with Airwalk, they challenged the Vans monopoly on shoes expressly made for skating. Now there are countless purveyors of "skate" clothing, and the profits of the twenty or so manufacturers making signature model shoes have been high enough to attract big fish like Nike and Adidas. Curiously, in that primordial era many people followed Mark Gonzales's lead and began wearing the decidedly nonskate Nike Air Jordan. They were good shoes but also an explicit attempt to avoid the scene's internal commercialism by using a product that had no connection to it. The wider problem was that with all these accoutrements captivating the general public's attention and buying power, it became harder to tell who actually skated—anybody could dress the part. Like the high-minded surfers at Malibu in the early times, skaters saw their insular universe corrupted and overrun. Even disenfranchisement's Eden couldn't last.

Accompanying all the filthy lucre was much hand-wringing about the "future of the sport" and another round of predictable mass-media attention. Articles appeared, bad movies were made. *Thrashin'* was released in 1986 to be instantly forgotten, except for the historical interest of the skating by Hosoi, Staab, Kasai and Steve Olson. A revenge-seeking brother played by Christian Slater and a scene where Tony Hawk rides into a Pizza Hut truck figured into 1989's *Gleaming the Cube,* a title so absurd it still elicits chuckles. Both movies capitalized on skating's resurgence in exploitative *Skateboard: The Movie* fashion. The "skating" in the enormously popular *Back to the Future* led some to confusedly think that the movie was responsible for the upswing. And, as usual, the articles didn't come close to reflecting the reality of what they were about.

The second end of innocence was helped along by the extravaganzas put on by the National Skateboard Association. On one hand, there was the California Associated Skateboard League and all the grassroots shop events that were (and are) low on seriousness and competitiveness and high on camaraderie. On the other hand were the NSA's overly orchestrated pro contests that were great showcases for the "sport." They also elicited a lot of understandable complaining, much of it directed at the autocratic methods of grand pooh-bah Frank Hawk, Tony's father. At one contest, Mike Vallely was ollieing to fifty-fifties down rails and turning heads while Frank called him a "padless punk" and told him he'd never make it in the NSA. The proponents of the "Let's promote skating as all-American fun and expand our customer base while we're at it" school that the elder Hawk represented had their hearts in the right place and did a lot of good, but their organizational impulses made for a perverse, watered-down dilution. Great skating but too much sterility.

Lowboy opined, "The crime of fun is often punished by the minions of commerce," and the NSA was doling out beatings. Scott Foss covered an NSA production at Del Mar in *Thrasher* and bemoaned the security guards with headsets and the spectator fee. Brad "Don't Call Me Disco" Dorfman's RV out in the parking lot was indicative of the new ostentation. There were "numerous confrontations with the hierarchy and their enforcers. . . . Skaters and figureheads from the past, who really helped elevate skating, are totally disregarded in exchange for an attempt to establish a sleek, big-bucks approach towards skating 'promotion.'" Mile High ramp owner Mike Chantry was kicked out for videotaping; original vertical-contest coordinator Henry Hester was denied entry, and so were Skip Engblom, Doug Saladino, David Andrecht and Danny Bearer. "One thing is for sure; if the present attitude of the promoters does not change, then street skating will become more than the latest trendy catch word; it will be the only word . . . those who forget the past are condemned to be forgotten." A contest in Arizona took place in a drained wave pool with a blue chlorine cloud hovering in the air, jock security, a slippery ramp and a seven-dollar charge to get in. Thankfully, one thing never changes, as Foss observed at another fiasco held at a bike track in Carson: "The pre-contest jam was a typical exhibit of skate anarchy at its best, or worst, depending on what side of the rule book you're on. The initial twenty-five entrants, the only ones who were supposed to be skating, were instantly joined by at least forty others."

These lollapaloozas helped spread the word and make skating accessible, but they existed in a sort of parallel universe that in many ways has nothing to do with skateboarding except to highlight it as a purely athletic pursuit. What had been a community without much caste difference between levels of ability began to turn into a commodity with performers and fans. The unusual thing is that many skaters don't ever enter these games; they let their skills and image do the talking and can still do very well for themselves. Chad Muska is just one example of an immensely popular and financially successful skater who hasn't entered a contest in at least ten years. The spectacles and the atmosphere they brought into a formerly hermetic scene made it possible for gifted athletes, who lay it on the line in ways most citizens can't even imagine, to make a living and sometimes even get rich from doing what they love. The downside was a diminution of what skateboarding was all about.

In a reaction against the NSA and all it stood for, Steve Rocco started taking his "Hell" tours around the country, causing havoc and attracting ire for throwing stickers and disrupting contests. One nonbeliever sniffed, "As far as Rocco [goes], being a pop star to a bunch of kids puts you in the same league as Simon Le Bon and Madonna," but it can't be denied that Rocco's genius for mayhem provided a much-needed alternative to the sanitization the other side was offering. With his merry band, he crossed the land skating shitty jump ramps and getting yelled at by kids to "Do a rocket air!" and "Do a McTwist!" The Hell tours were down and dirty, an extension of the road trips skaters had been doing forever, and they weren't very glamorous. They often didn't get paid at all, and this scenario was common: "Rocco calls the next shop in Albuquerque, and they tell us not to bother coming." These kinds of demo tours live on as antidotes to the big spectaculars, an ongoing ritual of motley crews in stinky vans hitting the road to ride local spots and forge ties with their admirers—that is, skaters just like them.

As reported in "Trash," someone anonymously suggested that "this sport will never make it, these professional competitors look like animals. If you're going to take skateboarding to the masses then these guys must look presentable." Looking presentable was going to be out of style soon enough, with dreads and tattoos and everything else becoming accepted and desirable and easily worked into marketing plans. Fred Smith was a hard-boiled Alva team member with spiky blond hair, tattoos and the ability to pull a chain through his nose and cough it out of his mouth. Today that's par for the course, and his conceptual progeny are on MTV's *Jackass*. Skateboarding was not quite at that point in the eighties, but it was spreading its subversive gene in a plethora of ways that inevitably led it to co-optation. Jodie Foster's Army toured the country, playing "Cokes and Snickers (Is All I Need, Health Sucks)" and meeting skaters. At one Oakland pool, a dispute with heckling kids ended in a truce, with the band riding the deep end and the antagonists break-dancing in the shallow. Sticker and product tosses got out of control; I witnessed one at Del Mar with Christian Hosoi on the deck, winging boards to a roiling mass in the pool below. At the same gathering, somebody from Sacramento hosted a barfing contest on the lawn. At Mount Trashmore, there were big crowds and a huge sticker toss, with Mofo reporting that "skaters began signing autographs more than they wanted to skate. It was cool. It was wonderful. It was curious." At the second Midwest Melee, Mark "Gator" Rogowski unveiled his tattoo; aficionados surrounded Christian and he "played" his board like a guitar; cheerleaders loitered and Craig Johnson did barefoot handplants. A thrown dead cat won the "highest air" award at a Mile High ramp in Tahoe, and Keith Haring, Kenny Scharf and Jean-Michel Basquiat all released limited-edition "art" boards.

Bands of the punk persuasion with skater members were "skate rock," and Sin 34's lead singer, Julie, was shown doing a bert in *Flipside*. Los Olvidados, the Faction, Agression, the Big Boys, Youth Brigade, Society/System Decontrol, Christ on Parade and the immortal Bad Brains were just a few of the groups that skaters were listening to. Pushead wrote about the expanding international hardcore scene in his turgid prose and rhapsodized over Finland's Terveet Kadet and Japan's Laughing Nose. The punk tour movie, *Another State of Mind*, came out, as did the seminal book, *Hardcore California*, and Glen E. Friedman's photo zine, *My Rules*, furthering the spread of information. Black Flag headed in a different direction that wasn't metal, but it sure was heavy. Henry Rollins grew out his hair, got a bunch of tattoos and began to write in a style embarrassingly indebted to Charles Bukowski. He was also featured in an Independent Trucks advertisement. A Suicidal Tendencies video with skaters in it got shown on MTV late at night, and their Venice couture hats and shirts sold well to teenagers in the heartland whose closest brush with gangs was watching the movie *Colors*. Hank Williams and Sonic Youth shared coverage in *Thrasher* with Slayer and Motörhead, and Canada's metal mathematicians Voivod. The punk versus metal battle raged in the letters section: "Take another bong hit before you read this, you'll need it . . . my head is out of my ass and yours needs to be kicked. Heavy Metal is sheet metal; it sucks and always will."

In 1985 everybody still had rails, but they would soon be deemed obsolete; and after Steve Caballero was pictured grinding a backyard pool without copers, they were on their way out, too. Now nobody can fathom using either device. The daunting aspect of the combi-pool and big half-pipes was countered by a blooming of six-foot-high mini-ramps that were a less dangerous proving ground for a batch of hybrid tricks. The worldwide appeal of skating begat Lee Ralph from New Zealand, with his gnarly skating and barefoot grinds. Brazil began to percolate, thanks to concrete parks and a kid named Bob Burnquist. Back in California, a youngster named Danny Way was making some noise. Lip tricks progressed and took from street, with lipslides becoming disasters and being slid backside. Kevin Staab was grinding backward, and Ben Schroeder did lein-to-tails to revert as fakie became part of everything and the idea of switch was born, skating counter to a person's regular footing for ambidextrous riding. It is so hard to do that it defies explanation. Imagine the Wimbledon champion serving right- or left-handed at will, then multiply the difficulty factor by ten. In the next decade switch would be taken to ridiculous heights on street, and on vertical Bob Burnquist can basically do everything both ways. That was still a long way off at the end of the eighties, but the building blocks were there. The future had begun, and skating was poised to be massive again.

As skateboarding was becoming mainstream, snowboarding was rising from an unexamined secret to a huge "sport" that is now an event in the Olympics, a story smartly and succinctly told in Susanna Howe's book (*sick*) *A Cultural History of Snowboarding*. People had always dreamed of simulating surfing on snow, and at some unknowable point in the mists of time, somebody stood up on a sled, and that was snowboarding. The first manufactured incarnation was Sherman Poppen's rudimentary Snurfer in the sixties. Then Jake Burton handmade boards and started a company in the late seventies that catered to a tiny group of similarly obsessed enthusiasts. There was also Dimitrije Milovich's visionary Winterstick. At the start, snowboarding was underground and not allowed on ski slopes. Snowboarders borrowed their stance and tricks from skateboarders and, in the beginning, were just as vilified.

It was a foregone conclusion that, as a skier and skateboarder, I would be eager to try my friend's Burton Performer board with its metal edges and primitive bindings at Hidden Valley. It didn't work on any snow that wasn't powder, but I could fly off a log and do a pretend method air. It was a lot easier, since the board was attached to my feet, and falling on snow is a lot less painful than slamming on concrete. For these reasons, many looked down on it as too easy, a kind of skateboard fantasy camp. The link to skating was immediate, with Lonnie Toft, Chuck Barfoot and Tom Sims riding and making boards. Lake Tahoe's Terry Kidwell was an originator of the snow-as-skate-style, soaring backside airs in backwoods gullies that looked just like their equivalent on ramps. Shaun Palmer and Damian Sanders, two of the biggest names in the history of snowboarding, were first seen in *Thrasher* doing skate-derived aerials. Almost everything in snowboarding came from skating, and as snowboarding attracted more followers, the culture mutated into its own but never lost a dependence on skating as a model for tricks, graphic sense and attitude. It is a somewhat unhappy testament to skating's influence that the culture at large, along with snowboarding and the other so-called extreme sports that are rampant today—BMX, the unspeakably contempible eight-wheeled scourge of in-line skating, even surfing—continually look to skateboarding for inspiration.

Chapter Sixteen
Mecca and Beyond

California was the shrine I worshiped at, and strangely enough, it was higher education that got me there. In the middle of the school year at Kaiser, my father asked me if there were any skateparks left. I answered that one of the few still standing was in Del Mar, California. He knew how obsessed I was with skateboarding and did some research before coming back to me with a proposal: if I applied and was accepted to the University of California in La Jolla, we would move to San Diego. I had serious doubts about the concept of college, but I couldn't pass up the opportunity. With all the ambivalence it entailed, I made the necessary steps to continue my education. The prospect of leaving Hawaii made me melancholy; my friendships there were extraordinary and the life experience without parallel. But my sadness was tempered by the prospect of finally reaching the end of the hajj's winding path to Mecca. San Diego had the park, the best skaters in the world, bands, everything I had been searching for. A year to the day after we moved to Hawaii, we left for the Golden State.

Driving through the balmy August night to the wealthy seaside enclave of La Jolla, we stopped and ate outside at Taco Bell, smelling the salty air coming off the ocean a block away, not far from Windansea, where Bob Simmons had tested his groundbreaking early foam surfboards. An apartment near downtown La Jolla became our new home. I wandered around getting the lay of the land and experiencing a peculiar sensation of reverse culture shock, since white people were everywhere. The very apparent wealth and aura of safety were unsettling after Hawaii, as if I'd come back from combat to be surrounded by coddled, provincial namby-pambies. Blond preppy girls driving convertible Volkswagen Rabbits, and expatriate Iranians dripping with gold and cologne posturing next to their Mercedeses, were amusing caricatures I could stare at with impudence. That freedom was unsettling at first.

Finally, I was *there*. The Del Mar Skate Ranch was five miles away. Our arrival was fortuitous: the week leading up to the 1984 National Skateboard Association finals. Skaters from all over the United States and Europe were in attendance. There was no corporate sponsorship then, and the first-place purse was only a thousand dollars, but nobody really cared about the humble nature of the whole enterprise. Contests were few and far between, and what mattered was that the best skaters were there doing new tricks, and old ones better and higher. The mainstream media didn't pay attention at this point because skating wasn't definably salable. Skateboarders were looked down upon and misunderstood as noisy, property-damaging punks who dressed weird. They couldn't have cared less. No one was going to get rich or famous; at most they might get their photo in *Thrasher*, where twenty thousand people would see it.

I spent the days before the contest skating for free without pads, because security was even more lax than usual. Away from the keyhole pool, heavy sessions were going down in the square pool, the banked slalom run and the half-pipe. The end of the half-pipe was a sloped ditch with a grindable edge, a perfect acclimatizer for me after Oahu. That week I went back and forth from inspiring viewings of the pros skating the keyhole, to the slightly illicit gatherings at the back of the park.

Tony Hawk was as skinny as a famine victim, a contortionist who was one of the top pro skaters of the day. Many people, me included, didn't like his gawky skating form, but that can be attributed mostly to simple jealousy. He could do anything, period. He ollied his airs, touching the board with a few fingers as more of a gesture than anything else. He did backside ollies four feet out, and backside varials—an aerial where the skater grabs the board and turns it 180 degrees to land on it backward, a trick Eric Grisham first did frontside over the channel in the Big O's capsule. Mike McGill skated tautly and with control. Mark "Gator" Rogowski did incredibly hard combinations of tricks, like 360-degree lein airs, with a wiry physicality. He also destroyed the rest of the park. A Grim Reaper tattoo adorning one of his biceps was disturbingly prophetic—a few years later he would rape and kill his girlfriend's best friend and bury her body in the desert before turning himself in and getting thirty years to life. Billy Ruff flew around smoothly and incongruously drove a Porsche. No longer a Variflex trick robot, Allen Losi, who was over six feet tall, did huge airs and powerfully punished the coping. Along with Mike Smith, he was the first person I ever saw do a frontside lipslide on vertical, sliding five or more coping blocks. The lipslide (now called a disaster) was a trick that had been done since the early days on banks, but to do it in on vertical brought edge play to another level.

There was Christian Hosoi, the closest thing skating has ever had to a sex symbol, the antithesis to the prevailing down-and-dirty ethos, with Asian-haole good looks countered by impeccable Dogtown credentials. Hands down, he is the most natural and flowing skater of all time. Jeff Grosso competed as an amateur but was as good as the pros. When he did a lein-to-tail, the thwacking of his tail on the coping reverberated across the park. Joe Johnson had come out a few months before for an upset amateur win with tricks like the reverse ice plant, a boneless variant. He was sponsored by Powell at the time, and I was proud to see a Colorado boy making good. John Gibson, Neil Blender, Eric Grisham and Kevin Staab were there—basically everybody. I finally got to see Mike Smith and was not disappointed. Even the way he held his hands out with his fingers together while riding was classy. One of the most beautiful things I have ever seen was when he ollied over the hip where the half-pipe turned into a ditch, an effortless fusion of form (his style) and content (a hard trick) done with what can only be called élan.

Something happened that week that is hard to find an analogy to. Dick Fosbury's introduction of the Fosbury flop, which revolutionized high jumping at the Mexico City Olympics, provides one. Maybe Captain Cook's arrival at Botany Bay in 1770 is a better comparison. *The Endeavour* was the first vessel of its kind to be seen in that part of Australia. Despite its alien nature, a group of natives on the shore ignored the ship when it anchored—the speculation is that it was too bizarre to be understood, so they perceived it as a collective hallucination. What I saw at Del Mar was like that ship, something so unfathomable that it appeared unreal. There was no gradual build-up, just a violent progression into the future, causing the unparalleled exhilaration that comes from contact with the unknown.

As part of the universal brotherhood program, I befriended a local named Pete Finlan who told me he had seen Mike McGill do an astounding backside air turned one and a half times and upside down. I questioned him and tried to figure it out. People were doing aerials six feet out—six feet above the coping and fifteen feet from the bottom of the pool—and there were plenty of handplant variations that put the skater upside down for a second, but what Pete was describing didn't compute. I was curious, but there was so much else going on that I soon forgot about his seemingly exaggerated account.

The day before the contest, I was sitting in the bleachers watching the pros along with about fifty other people, enjoying the skater paradise, feeling like a character in a book that I had heard about for years. McGill pushed along the top of the pool deck and rolled into a high backside air, landing and gliding up the other wall. And then it happened. Grabbing like a mute air (backside hand around the knees, clutching the board near the front foot) and strangely torquing his body as he launched, McGill flew five feet out and went upside down. He spun and spun until he had turned 540 degrees, completely inverted at the 360-degree point. It transpired quickly, then he landed and continued his run.

As he came down, a collective gasp turned into a wail of astonishment. People lost it. There was a shared and unifying hysteria. Everybody howled. I howled along with them. In those hoarse yells was the agony and delirium of a severe cognitive break. The animalistic cheer was equal parts confusion and comprehension's bliss, a tearing of the mental fabric. A new dimension had opened up. The McTwist, as it was first called, was a quantum leap out of the imagination into the real. McGill went on to place second in the contest (Tony Hawk won), which struck me as more than a little ungenerous on the judges' part, considering how dramatically he had expanded the boundaries of skateboarding with one unfathomable trick. He would be cheered wildly every time he did the McTwist, but never with as much abandon as that first unhinging of our collective consciousness. To see it firsthand was to experience an epiphany.

Del Mar was the focal point of my existence, and as soon as I got a used Datsun B210 and the chaos of the contest faded, I settled in as a local. The Ranch was a moonscape of concrete confections bigger than a city block, located near the beach between the freeway and a horse track, where "the surf meets the turf." It was a second-generation park with all the expected faults. Some of it was good, a lot was all right and some parts were totally useless, but we didn't even think of complaining, since it was the only park left in the state besides Upland. To the left of the pro shop was the keyhole, with bleachers on one side, where contests were held and people did their serious skating. It was hard to get used to, with its mellow transitions and the shallow end that wasn't rideable at all. Soon I was rolling in—a sensation not unlike riding off of a building—to do backside airs and handplants and producing that sonorous whirring by carving on the blue and orange tile. On the left side, behind the spot most people tail-dropped in from, was an Astroturf-covered wooden platform with a couple of chairs where you sat to put on your pads while checking out the action. There was a miniature golf course next door, and some trampoline basketball contraptions that never really caught on but were fun to bounce around in. I knew I had reached nirvana when I walked from the sunlight into the dimness of the pro shop, looked behind the counter at the skate equipment and around at the abused pinball machines, video games and Foosball tables, and filled my nostrils with that indelible scent I remembered from Winchester and High Roller.

Next to the pool was a banked rectangular reservoir where everybody warmed up before skating the pool, as was the custom of the time. You carved around and did footplant variations and slides for a few minutes before moving on to the keyhole. Later, curbs and extensions were added, and the reservoir got recognition as a place to skate in and of itself. Tod Swank even put on a down-home "bank jam" there.

The Kona Bowl was modeled on a backyard pool, with tight transitions and a lot of vertical. Most people just carved and grinded, boomeranging from deep to shallow and back at speed, but a few like Steve Steadham and Gator managed airs. Acid-dropping into the deep end was a rite of passage. There was a deep onion-shaped cavity without coping that hardly anybody rode, a useless snake run and another reservoir, and the square bowl that was screwed up except for corner carving. Gator could do things in there that boggled the mind. Two parts of the park that provided enjoyment were the long, banked slalom ditch that you could carve forever, and the half-pipe, which was two hundred feet long, had no flat and no coping but was easy to air out of and had a hip where it made a 90-degree turn into the shallow end. I liked it because it reminded me of Off the Walls.

Along with local and visiting pros, there was a diverse crew who practically lived at the park. Bruno Herzog refuted the laid-back Californian cliché by being a constant source of hell-bent anarchy ready to acid-drop into anything. Chip Morton was a surf-skater and bad-influence older-brother figure who worked there. Their coconspirator Reese Simpson was insanely good but never got much coverage, an example of how riders of real merit are often those whom many people have never heard of. Trench-coat-wearing, acoustic-guitar-playing Filipino Adrian Demain rode for Powell and skated with extreme precision, doing numerous airs in a row and hardly ever falling. Owen Neider wore a Mohawk, rings on all his fingers and a good-natured snarl. One night when it was just the two of us, I saw him roll in and do the longest rock-and-roll boardslide I've ever seen. Steve Claar did frontside grinds and rock-

and-rolls and would repeatedly try and bail stalled inverts. Randy Janson was a cutup who would later become the Gullwing team manager and be videotaped publicly defecating. His brother Pete had the coolest bleached-out long blond hair, an early reaction against the increasing number of kooks who had gotten into punk and cut their hair short. Appropriately enough, Pete is now a much sought-after hairdresser.

A large-framed humorist named Dave Swift worked at the park, smoking light cigarettes and throwing his bulk around nicely on vertical before going on to be a father and the editor of *Transworld*. Tod Swank skated with his head down, had a beaklike nose, rode for Sims and made the standout zine *Swank*, featuring sparse handwritten text tending toward the facetious, mingled with full-bleed black-and-white photos by Tod and *Transworld*'s J. Grant Brittain. Later incarnations included *Scrap*, "The Most Famous Magazine," and *Big Blue Hair*, "A Piece of Shit Production." I liked *Swank* so much that I sent Tod a letter typed on a barf bag taken off the flight over from Hawaii to precipitate a meeting. *Swank*'s interesting faux-naïve graphic sense and Tod's elongated drawings contributed to the subsequent rise of his Tum Yeto skateboard empire.

Vagabonds from all over made the park their home. Steve Douglas came from England, along with Smeg and Deacon, two Brighton chaps who provided a caustic dose of English humor that clashed nicely with the sunny beach vibe. They made me jealous with their stories about seeing Killing Joke, one of my favorite groups, who came out of England and never really fit in: they went through the audience to the stage wearing kilts and playing bagpipes and had the heaviest tribal sound. Garry Scott Davis made his way south and rolled around the reservoir wearing a full-body skull-and-bones suit and witch's forelock inspired by his favorite New Jersey horror band, the Misfits. Nomadic, tattooed, footplant specialist Bill Danforth, who relocated from Michigan, also had an unhealthy Misfits obsession. Daniel Harold Sturt came from the Midwest and began shooting what would become some of the most arresting images in skateboard photography over the next ten years. His penchant for pranks was amply demonstrated at a ramp contest in Los Angeles when he dropped in and purposely slammed with fake-blood packs under his pads. The resulting medic-attended commotion made for a comical photo by the young Matt Hensley.

Everybody congregated at the Denny's restaurant next to the park. Pity the waitresses; it was amazing that any skaters were served at all. Ten hyped-up miscreants in a booth causing havoc, betting Owen couldn't drink whatever effluvia fit into one glass. At one point, my hair got set on fire. It was a true melting pot, from mustached, jacked-up Chevy Blazer–driving Pete Finlan to Owen Neider to Paul Votolva, who did backflips in the keyhole on roller skates and made his living breeding snakes. Skating, hanging out, screwing around, going to Denny's, heading to the beach or a ramp somewhere and coming back. The Skate Ranch was open late, and somebody you knew would always be there to session with. Nights were particularly good, wearing sweatpants and a flannel shirt to ward off the chill as the fog rolled in, riding the pool with Randy, John and Steve; then maybe Owen would show up, or Gator. As Tod Swank said, "Del Mar skatepark was the best. . . . Skateboarders from all over the world would come there. I skated with so many of the best skateboarders. I was very lucky . . . I practically lived there. I met everyone I know there." It couldn't have been better.

Danny Barger from Oahu had been living in San Diego for a year and done reconnaissance, so he was my main guide to the smorgasbord of terrain the Southland had to offer. Sanoland was not far from Del Mar, near a sanitation-treatment facility, which made the aroma there unpleasantly fruity. You walked up the ditch from the road about a half a mile to where there was a steep section with a sharp lip. It was dirty, dusty, smelly and a little rough but had a certain appeal. Sanoland reminded me of Hawaii and eased my homesickness somewhat. Imperial was way down El Cajon Boulevard, east of San Diego, near a giant replica of a lemon with a sign proclaiming THE LEMON CAPITAL OF THE WORLD. The ditch was four feet deep, with tight transitions and the obligatory curbs on top. Farther up, where the walls were higher, a crass graffito never failed to make me laugh: "I fucked a mod chick in the ass. P.S. It was great." The neighborhood could be threatening, and a few times at one nearby gas station, the brothers refused to sell me gas, the sole reason apparently being that I was white.

We made periodic nocturnal raids on a dark and forbidding place that was a far cry from the sanitized urban theme park it is now—downtown San Diego. Gangs, bums, hookers and rampaging drunken sailors lurked, but the streets were a postapocalyptic landscape of wide-open marble plazas, ledges and benches. The biggest attraction for us was the eleven-story Concourse parking garage, which was even better than Amfac. Many late-night races with multiple skaters tucking down to hit high speeds would end with cop cars popping up around the next corner, forcing everybody to scatter into the night.

One of my first pilgrimages out of San Diego was to the Pipeline in Upland, the heart and soul of the Badlands. It was two hours northeast into the Inland Empire, and of course we got a speeding ticket on the way. The park had a full pipe inspired by the Baldy pipeline, and the infamous combi-pool—separate square and round pools linked by a common shallow end—that was steep and deep, with three feet of vertical and coping that stuck out at least two inches. It was a proving ground that made Tantalus look easy. To this day, I am in awe of anybody who could really ride it. I got to see Micke and Steve Alba and Chris Miller and was blown away by their speed and facility. One atypical local was a sixty-year-old man named Bill Dohr, who had a little dog that barked and ran in after him every time he dropped into the combi to skate. It was in the square pool a couple of years later that Chris Miller took one of the most sickening slams ever recorded on video. His long backside air into the corner of the square terminated with him hanging up on the coping and being shot headfirst to the flat eleven feet below. The resulting crunch and unconscious convulsions are hard to write about, let alone watch.

Early street contests were held around this time. Then as now, they might have been on a street, but they didn't resemble any actual city environment. Dave Swift, Danny and I drove to one in Huntington Beach that was held in an asphalt parking lot that had picnic tables with slanted ramps and a couple of portable steel curbs. Skaters were doing boneless ones and airs off the ramp. Neil Blender did 360-degree eggplants. A feral kid riding a pink Alva Fishtail skated exceedingly well and won sponsored amateur, doing ollies in a way that I had never seen before, effortlessly soaring by popping the tail of his board. That was Mark Gonzales.

Street was evolving at a phenomenal rate, although it still revolved around the adaptation of vertical tricks to flat ground. Ollies would allow street to break away entirely, but it didn't happen overnight. One example of the awkward stage before the ollie ascension was the rage for street plants. You popped the board into your hand and did a handstand and put the board to your feet. It was static, but everybody was doing it. Flowing tricks together and not touching the board via ollies wasn't being done by anybody except for a few iconoclasts like Gonzales, Tommy Guerrero and Natas Kaupas. A kid out of New Jersey named Mike Vallely was at the forefront of street plants, but Rocco and Blender were the early pioneers. Vallely was a street originator who is known for his burly skating and physical attacks on meddling security guards. A unique stylist covered in tattoos and muscles, he now does spoken-word performances heavily indebted to his hero Henry Rollins, dabbles in professional wrestling and engages in questionable macho confrontations with photographers and others in his way.

Around 1986, this early phase of street exhibited traits of its straight freestyle roots and what was to come. Freestyle was still slow and boring, too similar to gymnastic floor routines, and no matter how complicated the tricks were, there wasn't much rolling going on. It didn't have aggression and continuity. Freestylers were thought of as kind of lame, but their tricks were respected, and many vert skaters still entered freestyle contests. I had a freestyle board (a symmetrical deck seven inches wide) and diligently practiced in our parking space on Summer Street in Honolulu. By mid-decade, the moves had gotten increasingly complex, a development which can be traced entirely to Florida's singular prodigy, Rodney Mullen. The debt skating owes to this mop-topped genius who invented and perfected nearly impossible moves in his parents' driveway is enormous. Swedes Per Welinder and Per Holknekt and Frenchman Pierre Andre were also responsible, as was the face-mask-wearing Tim Scroggs from Florida. Whatever their former ignominy, freestylers have certainly gotten the last laugh, because modern street skating is heavily indebted to the kickflips, shove-its and other board manipulations and footplay that Mullen and the others took from the seventies and made more technical. To add to their stealth victory, a frightening number of ex-freestylers have become millionaires as major players in the skateboard industry.

In La Jolla, I was completely alienated. The people I felt strongly about were either in Hawaii or at the park, and the chances of finding confidants appeared nil among the predominantly entitled La Jolla High School students. When I wasn't at the park or doing homework, I explored La Jolla at night, observing the recently exiled Persians and other exemplars of moneyed tackiness. My wheels echoed in the silence of the empty streets away from the strip as I skated the Saks bank behind the store of the same name, and a few other bumps and small banks, or bombed the hills on Mount Soledad. There were no skaters at school except a couple of retrograde longboarders living some kind of tired Pump House Gang dream twenty years too late. They were right out of *Fast Times at Ridgemont High*, but they lacked the wicked charm of Sean Penn's Jeff Spicoli character. I didn't initiate contact, as there was obviously no common bond.

I floated around the campus like a ghost. With time, I did meet a few other displaced souls, beginning with a bewitching girl in my English class who had spotted me at a Social Distortion show. Caitlin had been to England, dressed in black, wore a lot of makeup and was much more experienced than I was. Along with her beautiful red-haired friend Shawn, we got into a ritual of going to Shawn's boyfriend's house at lunch to watch the television soap opera *All My Children*. I met a guy named Matt Wagner, who had been a breakdancer and was an interesting anomaly. David Railey, a pale, thin death rocker with long dyed-black or cyclamen hair covering his face and an effeminate manner, sat in front of me in Spanish class and introduced me to the lush dreaminess of the Cocteau Twins and This Mortal Coil. Androgyny and bisexuality were very au courant, and The Smiths' "How Soon Is Now" had just come out and gave achingly longing voice to all the confusion that David was part of. What might have seemed like a trope wasn't really, since David cultivated some entertainingly perverse notions and liked to borrow my Metallica tapes.

Two suit-wearing students with buzz cuts were noticeable, and I was surprised to see them skating in town one day, wearing Bermuda shorts, square-bottomed button-down shirts and checkered high-top Vans. Their names were David King and Peter Busse, admittedly recreational practitioners who didn't care about the park and were into it just for fun. They were La Jolla natives who disdained everything about the place and had an unwavering allegiance to ska, an up-tempo multiracial hybrid of punk attitude and dancehall exemplified by the Specials, the Selecter, Madness and the English Beat. As far as they were concerned, no other bands mattered, though the Jam and the Clash were acceptable, and they did have a thing for Smokey Robinson. I liked ska, but while I admired Pete and Dave's conviction, their monomania struck me as a little strange. That wasn't an impediment, since Pete hilariously made fun of everybody, and we became fast friends. Since the ska scene in San Diego was marginal at best, they compromised by going to mod shows and trying to pick up mod girls. I went to a few parties with them and was alerted to the news that mods weren't a historical footnote who had died out before the making of *Quadrophenia*. These slavish adherents to a music and style that came out of the early-sixties English working-class were alive and well and driving their Vespas in droves around Southern California. It was strange to see young people so obsessively clothes-conscious and propagating such an ossified form of youth rebellion.

During the transitional summer after graduation, I went back to Hawaii and stayed with Davin. Rich and Ed weren't so straight-edge anymore; Ed had a girlfriend, and Rich wore his hair bleached and down to his shoulders, and was now into sex. Times change. There were more kids skating, more punks than before, and Bo Ikeda was better than I ever would be. We went to a tiny ramp in the jungle that was five feet high with a foot of vertical, and rode Grant's ramp on the North Shore. Baroque shapes like Hosoi's Hammerhead model, with its square nose and a shape that sloped in by the back wheel wells, then went out again at the tail, were popular. So were Alva's fishtails and Santa Cruz's Rob Roskopp boards with toe notches by the back trucks. Neon was prevalent. I had a pair of lime-green Vans. We jumped off the rocks at Waimea Bay, where Dick Noll and others had first ridden really big waves in the sixties. In the winter, waves the size of buildings shook the ground and scattered people on the beach, but in the summer, the water was as placid as a New England pond. Red Hill was gone, and Off the Walls had been rendered a total bust and the transitions were ruined.

Christian Hosoi was there in all his glory and going out with a friend of mine from Hawaii Kai. At that preposterously tight ramp in the overgrowth, I saw him do one-foot backside airs high enough to scrape the overhanging branches, flying out as far as the ramp was high. His backside ollies were smoother than silk, and his McTwists were like nobody else's, spun with leisurely slow motion and other-worldly grace. Christian had style. He was an exceptional phenomenon, charming, smoking pot constantly, attracting besotted females left and right and wearing atrocious ensembles of pink and white

Jimmy Z clothes, shirts with the neck and sleeves cut off, silly head-bands and numerous trinkets and bracelets. Occasionally he wore spandex or fishnet stockings. The thing was, he could pull it off. On any other person, it would have been ridiculous, but Christian inhabited his special place on earth with such panache that he could have worn anything without diminishing his stature. Part of his appeal was in being a genuinely nice guy. I never saw a hint of atti-tude directed at the fans who thronged around him, and he always said hello and was friendly—an unusual personality trait in some-one who got so much attention.

Back home just prior to my induction into the ivory tower, I went on a road trip. Skating's inherently nomadic lifestyle makes for mandatory traveling to places heard about through the grape-vine, and riding whatever comes up along the way. Tod Swank, Dave Swift, Davin, my friend Greg Lipman and I set out for San Fran-cisco. In Oxnard, we fell asleep in the parking lot of a bank after making jokes about watching out for satanically inclined serial killer Richard Ramirez, the Nightstalker, who was still at large. After get-ting ejected by security guards, we rode a mini-ramp in Santa Bar-bara before resuming our drive up Highway 1 to San Jose, where our merry band made for the storied Montague banks. At ten at night, there were at least a hundred skaters and girls hanging out, the situation completely unsanctioned and out of control. Chris-tian, Lance Mountain, Steve Caballero were there, as well as the O'Brien brothers and other San Jose luminaries. We hooked up with Johnee Kop, who had also come for the Capitola contest we would be attending the next day. Davin met a blond Dumpster diver named Tanya, and we slept at her xenophobic skinhead friend Brandy's house while Johnee slumbered sitting up in the car's front seat be-cause of his bad back.

Capitola was on the hill near Santa Cruz where many down-hill contests had been held in the past. It had been only a year since Tommy Guerrero came out of nowhere at the Golden Gate Park contest to win as an amateur and usher in the second modern age of skateboarding. Street contests were different then. There were no ledges or handrails, just some jump ramps spaced down the hill, and at the end, a large ramp faced an old graffiti-covered car. It was a weird hybrid, a lot of vert skaters who couldn't ollie pregrabbing off the ramps, and only a few like Tommy and Mark Gonzales who really had pop. The usual authority problems arose when Mark ollied over Lance Mountain, rolling onto the course coffin-style at Mark's instigation, and a security goon attacked Lance for interfering. Johnee and Christian aired over the car while Steve Olson styled nose wheelies and did lipslides on the roof.

Kurt Carlson's article in *Thrasher* got to the heart of street's appeal and potential: "Every style is included in the Capitola Classic . . . speed, freestyle, vertical style, old style, circus style, nut style . . . STREETSTYLE. Every kid can watch a pro street skater and say, No way, that's too much, but at the same time see the possibility for learning that trick or their own variation. Radical skating in the most simplistic terrain is easy to envision and act out. Sure, every skater craves vertical, every skater plans on building a ramp . . . but street skating is adapting to unfamiliar terrain. A kink in a ramp can ruin a session . . . but a crack in the sidewalk, or a hole in the street is seen as a challenge to the streetskater."

After the contest, everybody went to Derby Park, one of the earliest examples of public skating architecture that is still being ridden. Thirty skaters at a time invaded the pit and ran into one another, and a car was backed up over the lip so tricks could be attempted off the trunk. Alcohol was consumed, and a general sense of anarchy prevailed. Stacy Peralta was taping and, unbeknownst to me, starting the video revolution. Respect for legends wasn't really on my mind, so I thought, "Oh, there's Stacy Peralta," and went about my business. With advances in technology, video was becoming practical and cost-effective. Stacy and his Powell Peralta collaborators (most notably Craig Stecyk) did the *Bones Brigade Video* and went on to make *Public Domain* and the influential and classic *The Search for Animal Chin.* They pioneered video as an indispensable promotional tool, and now every company puts out videos, some of them being shot on film with several-hundred-thousand-dollar budgets. Videos spread the word far and wide and make it much easier for people in far-off places to see how tricks are done. Slow motion, in particular, is a visual mnemonic aid that has improved countless people's skating in a way that was inconceivable before the advent of the VCR. It has gotten to the point where video cameras are always out, and it is rare to see a still photo in a magazine where you don't see a video "creeper" off to the side.

At another mid-seventies relic of a mellow bowl called the Dish, in San Francisco's gnarly Hunter's Point ghetto, we were unwanted visitors but deemed it safe as long as it was light out. A cute young girl watching us slyly said, "I like your hair," which made me feel good. Following Pete Jansen's lead, I had bleached it numerous times until my scalp burned and my hair attained an unnatural strawlike consistency and color that made it look a little bit like an Andy Warhol wig. Before heading south, we skated the nearby Hunter's Point ramp, which had a lot of vertical and one rollout deck on the edge of a cliff with a stunning view of the bay and the Marin headlands in the distance. When we got back to San Diego, we were tired, worked and satiated.

Chapter Seventeen
"We Just Want to Have Some Fun Before We Die"

What X referred to as "The Unheard Music"—"There's nothing outside / We're locked out of the public eye / Some smooth chords on the car radio / No hard chords on the car radio"—was becoming much less so by the mid-eighties. As the music I listened to gained a wider audience, it altered my attitude toward the movement that had earned my fanatical devotion. My gradual metamorphosis from zealot to slightly detached observer was partially because the shock was over. Innovation had declined, and most of the revolutionary bands had come and gone. If punk wasn't exactly dead, it was terminally ill. The banality of repetition had dulled my senses, and the music wasn't only mine anymore; there were thousands of punkers and other people into so-called weird stuff in San Diego alone. Punk and its progeny were becoming institutionalized, and records went from being mysteriously hard to track down to bland audio smog. I could now see bands every weekend. When you get what you hope for, the suspicion sets in that longing is intrinsically superior. At the same time, a glut of records and fanzines led to the law of diminishing returns. I could go to Off the Record on El Cajon Boulevard and get any hardcore album available, and there were more and more of them every month. There was also Lou's in Encinitas. A mixture of fatigue and the sense that it was no longer relevant to me personally (or anybody else, for that matter) caused me to stop *Revenge Against Boredom* after the fifth issue and let my far-flung correspondence slack off.

Despite gnawing disenchantment, there was still a vibrancy I was lucky enough to partake in, even if it was a little late. Incandescent moments stand out, like D.C.'s Government Issue, with the incomparable punk showman and record-store employee John Stabb on vocals. I saw Jesus and the Mary Chain on their first tour of America at a small VFW hall, twenty minutes of blissful feedback with their backs turned to the audience, and then they just walked off. Venice's punk-metal crossover, Suicidal Tendencies ("I'm not antisociety / Society's anti-me . . . I'm not anti-anything / I just want to be free"), when they were at their most provocative, with songs like "Suicide's an Alternative" and "I Shot Reagan (and Would Do It Again and Again)." One of their rabid gang-affiliated followers tried to beat me up for coming too close to frontman Mike Muir while stage-diving at their show in San Diego.

In California, the violence wasn't as explosive as in Hawaii. It was ritualized, punks against punks. I went a little overboard with three Dead Kennedys shows in a row. The first night at L.A.'s Olympic Auditorium, with five thousand ne'er-do-wells bum-rushing the doors and a racist skinhead stabbing the black bassist of opening act Fishbone during their set; the next night in San Diego; the last in Tijuana, surrounded by a crowd of enthusiastic Mexicans singing along with Jello Biafra's acutely funny rants against hypocrisy and American stupidity. Greg Ginn's unique guitar playing gave Black Flag's sound a physiological impact as barefoot, muscular, sweaty Henry Rollins, with his stained shorts falling off, paced the stage like a wounded animal. X's John Doe, Exene Cervenka, Don Bonebrake and the incomparably cool Billy Zoom smiling away while playing his guitar were evocative chroniclers of L.A.'s abject under-side: "Every other week I need a new address / Landlord, landlord, landlord, clean up the mess / My whole fucking life is a wreck /We're desperate / Get used to it." The absurd poetry and jazzy brevity of the Minutemen had no parallel and was cut shockingly short by the even more absurd death of songwriter D. Boon in a car accident.

It wasn't just the music; there was an edge to being involved in a scene that existed on its own terms and hadn't been explained or sold to the public at large. The uneasiness that punk still engen-dered in 1985 was easy to see at Fairmont Hall, a no-frills dusty box in a poor neighborhood where, before every show, an old black man would sit on his porch with a shotgun across his knees, suspi-ciously eyeing the freak parade streaming past his door.

Hearing Grand Master Flash next to the ramp at Red Hill signaled a possible savior from my musical anomie as rap became a strong presence. At the beginning, rap was an exciting new voice that was incalculably refreshing. Part of the appeal was the whole white Negro thing all over again. The well-worn path of rebellious white youths' confused identification with the downtrodden went back to at least Norman Mailer and Jack Kerouac's "wishing I were a Negro, feeling that the best of the white world has offered me was not enough ecstasy for me, not enough life, joy, kicks, darkness, music, not enough night." I listened to Public Enemy's opinionated and galvanizing first two albums religiously. Not just rehashed Black Panther rhetoric, they had crunchy lockstep beats and John Coltrane samples underlying verse that really said something. Run-D.M.C., Schooly D., Eric B. & Rakim, Ice-T, KRS-One and especially N.W.A. emanated danger and were fresh in both senses of the word. Though N.W.A.'s "Fuck the Police" was about being black and oppressed in South Central L.A., it appealed to margin walkers of all stripes. Like hardcore before it, rap reflected a reality that wasn't pleasant or understood by mainstream society. At an N.W.A. concert, the gunshots in the parking lot certainly added to the ambience of menace, but worrying about getting killed because of the color of my shirt deflated my enthusiasm for what came to be vilified as gangster rap. Over time, hip-hop's promise wasn't kept, and for the most part, it has degenerated into formulaic pap. But for a time it was an electrifying mix of humorous braggadocio and straightforward reportage.

Hip-hop's emergence coincided oddly with the rise of speed metal. Black Sabbath and AC/DC were standbys who, no matter how much you rejected the seventies, were hard to get out of your system. They rocked; there was no way of getting around it. Then Metallica's "Kill 'em All" came out of the blue. It was loud, fast, musically complicated and physically moved you. There was a certain guilt attached to liking them, because by doing so, you were admitting that Crass and everyone else had failed to wreck the system. In listening to Metallica, you were endorsing a group unabashedly influenced by the music that punk sought to bring down. But Metallica were different; they were harder and integrated something of punk's spirit. They even did a Killing Joke cover. I saw them with a thousand headbangers at the Backdoor in San Diego, joyously getting crushed in the front row while trying to keep other people's hair out of my mouth. Metallica were the first to break out, though they owed much to forgotten groups like Void, China White and Corrosion of Conformity, who had brought metal into hardcore earlier. Despite their descent into lameness after the second record, Metallica must be acknowledged, along with two other metal standard-bearers whose music is indivisible from sweaty skate sessions: Motörhead and Slayer.

Metallica and the rest unfortunately set the stage for the hip-hop/heavy-metal mutations that have brought so much dreck into the world. Public Enemy did it first by collaborating on "Bring the Noise" with Anthrax in 1990. They can't really be blamed for spawning the current rash of corrosive excrement. Along with all the rhyming and guitar soloing, there were the unorthodox tunings of Sonic Youth, Live Skull's dense urban malaise, the four-and-a-half-octave-range Valkyrie Diamanda Galas and the German power-tool-wielding, fire-setting, banging-metal outfit Einstürzende Neubauten, completely contrary experimental noise that had its roots in everything from Minor Threat to John Cage to improvisational maestro Ornette Coleman. As the single-minded idealism of the hardcore scene petered out, it became easier to appreciate sounds that would have been dismissed out of hand during the doctrinaire phase.

Following my parents' departure for Lisbon, I nervously installed myself in the UCSD dorms on the cliffs above the Pacific with a stranger from Maine as my roommate. My preliminary disorientation quickly turned to an appreciation of thought-provoking classes, a varied stew of social types, girls unlike the La Jolla snobs and relief that Kent from Maine was all right. After my long immersion in a do-it-yourself philosophy that meant refuting the Western canon, college opened my eyes to the possibility that Shakespeare & Co. had something to offer. Classes on the empiricists, political science and elective film courses exposed me to ideas and a universe outside of the unconventional and sometimes limiting strain that encompassed *NO* magazine's perversity, a fascination for Survival Research Laboratories warring robots, skateboarding and Echo and the Bunnymen. Neorealist and French new-wave cinema and H. W. Jansen's *History of Art* opened windows to aesthetic concerns underrepresented in mass culture's pabulum. My awakening to archaic images and words was driven in part by punk's lesson to value inquiry and not take received wisdom at face value. Jean-Luc Godard's *Weekend* had more in common with hardcore than I would have guessed, and it actually made some of it seem pretty tame by comparison.

My high school alienation gave way to the intellectual stimu-lation and encouragement of college's fairly independent thinking. There were other attractions. One day I saw a saucy older woman wearing a leather jacket, boxer shorts and cowboy boots in the cam-pus record store. She made an impression and was in the art pro-gram, so I gravitated in that direction. The art and film crowd were smart people with bacchanalian tendencies, and not without some soul searching, my straight-edge streak came to an end. I still fer-vently believed in not letting drugs control your life and being politically informed, but after five years of abstinence I was ready to indulge. Soon I was smoking, drinking and doing drugs, and com-pletely at peace with the turn of events.

The way my intellectual pursuits clashed with nonpractitioners' perceptions of skating made me slightly self-conscious, and I rarely rode my board around during the day. That sensitivity was some-what misguided, since my bleached hair and straight-leg high-water-pants look wasn't really giving me a scholarly air. At night, with the fog moving through the eucalyptus groves, I would go to the art complex's ledges and planters and do rock-and-roll boardslides and bonelesses and street plants. If people approached, I would hang back in the shadows until they passed.

On Friday afternoons after class, I drove east to Russell's ramp in La Mesa. Russell, John Hogan, Steve Claar, Jeff Croteau and I would have small sessions, joking half the time, hanging out and skating for pure fun. Steve was still bailing inverts but was improving by leaps and bounds. Croteau was a wittily sarcastic handplant master whose reaction against "different" fashion's increasing popularity was to dress like an inconspicuous civilian. Like J. G. Ballard's comment that the most radical thing he could do was live an unremarkable middle-class existence in London's suburbs while writing his books, many skaters were coming around to how played out their formerly rebellious antics and plumage had become. To be truly subversive might mean blending in with the crowd.

John Hogan casually got me on the Gullwing team and I became a semisponsored amateur, getting boards and wheels for free and semiseriously entering contests. I was a decent vertical skater for the time, proficient but far from outstanding. The heights still seemed attainable, although seeing the McTwist had made me less sure. Getting sponsored was nice but not that important. I wanted it and had plenty of daydreams about my imaginary upcoming interview in *Thrasher*, but I knew that outcome wasn't grounded in reality unless I dropped everything and single-mindedly devoted myself to the goal of turning pro, a vague aspiration that was quickly seeming implausible and unimportant.

Davin moved to San Diego in the summer after my freshman year, and we went to Europe for our version of the grand tour. We had a typical plan, if it could be called that, to use Eurrail passes to travel around and experience new things. After a couple of jet-lagged days in Amsterdam, dodging American trust-fund pseudohippies, we went off to Belgium. Why Belgium? I have no idea. Although it wasn't a skating vacation per se, the idea of not bringing our boards was inconceivable, and in Antwerp we spent an afternoon at a vintage public cement quarter-pipe. In our cheap hotel, the manager burst in on us in the middle of one night, accompanied by a newlywed couple to whom he had promised the room as well. It was language-barrier-enhanced comedy of the highest order. In Brussels, we slept on the train-station steps while sketchy thieves lurked nearby. I contemplated getting a tattoo. Sailors and convicts had them then, but they hadn't yet become de rigueur for the alternative set, and luckily I didn't go through with the blue rose and snake design that had captured my imagination.

We saw Cologne's cathedral, and it was big. In the station bathroom, I came out of the stall to hear Davin whispering, "Check out the guy at the urinal." A man in a trench coat skulked around, and whenever someone walked up to relieve himself, he would peer over, hand furiously working in his pocket. The mise-en-scène of acrid smell and the masturbator was right out of a Fassbinder movie. While we were getting our bags together, a kid came over, and prompted by Davin's Independent Trucks T-shirt, said in his accented English, "Do you guys skate?" His excitement at unexpectedly encountering two members of the tribe was infectious. In the five minutes before our train left, he told us that there was a great ramp in Stuttgart. He had passed on the secret, and unbeknownst to him, his need to communicate had a profound influence on later events in my life. Although I didn't even know where Stuttgart was, I made up my mind to convince a slightly skeptical Davin that we had to make Bavaria our destination.

After a stop at a thirteenth-century castle, we continued down the Rhine, awkwardly flirting with the local Fräuleins, staying in hostels and missing curfews. At my imploring, we got on a train to Stuttgart, where all we had to go on was that the ramp was near a sports center. Taking a tram until we sighted a stadium in the distance, we got off and wandered around in the late afternoon. Like dogs cocking their heads at far-off frequencies undetectable to human ears, we picked up that telltale sound, the whoosh, silence, whoosh, silence, a clang and a racket and the rhythm starting over. We had hit the jackpot. The ramp was thirty feet wide and ten feet high, with a channel and extensions, covered by a smooth steel surface. Adrenaline pumping, we went through the oft-repeated ritual of getting our pads on as fast as possible before jumping on the ramp. Doing airs was just a matter of flying out and nonchalantly catching your board to float back in. Even though we didn't speak the language and we were five thousand miles away from California, we felt right at home.

Toward dusk, as I was taking my last runs, I saw Davin talking to a bespectacled guy who had been riding with us. I got down, and Davin introduced me to Thomas Hauser. He said we could spend the night at his place. Thomas was hospitable, funny, a few years older and wiser. We hit it off immediately. As Californians, we were a novelty from the land of milk and honey. Before globalization, video and the Internet, there was a large gap between U.S. skaters and the rest of the world that has all but disappeared. In the mid-eighties, there were a few European skaters—Tony Magnusson from Sweden, Claus Grabke from Germany, Nicky Guerrero from Denmark and Jeremy Henderson, Steve Douglas and Lucian Hendricks from England—but they were exceptions. They were at a disadvantage, getting the magazines two months late and paying dearly for imported equipment. Thomas rolled his eyes in amazement when we told him about U.S. prices. We talked and talked about every aspect of skating. That we came from the epicenter and knew people like Tony Hawk, Neil Blender and Chris Miller made us storytellers with firsthand knowledge of mythological personages. We ate and conversed and went to a disco, where we drank rum and Cokes while unintelligibly yelling at one another over pumping disco music. Davin and I made Thomas and his friends laugh with our stock phrase, "*Der Fernsehapparat ist wieder kaputt*," the only German Davin had retained from a high school class. We thought it meant "The refrigerator is broken again" and said it constantly, giggling at our non sequitur. Years later I found out it actually meant "The television set is broken again." It was a good night, and I still dream about that ramp.

Leaving Thomas behind, we went on to Switzerland, France and Italy. In Marseilles, we checked out the topless bathers and I got heat stroke. Unfortunately, it would be another three years before the legendary Marseilles bowl was built. In Nice we slept in storage lockers and got kicked out by the station police, then got rousted by the real police for sleeping in the bushes outside. We saw nuns by the dozen in Milan, and in Venice we drank cheap wine, saw the Doge's Palace and slept at an overcrowded hostel pungent with body odors. I drove Davin crazy by singing LL Cool J's "Radio" incessantly as we sat by the canals. The husband of a married couple with whom we shared a compartment during the thirty-hour passage to London persisted in rhapsodizing about how great Phil Collins was. He was a nice guy, but that crossed the line, and I could barely look at him after that; Davin was more diplomatic and said, "He's a good drummer." In England, we were greeted by August rain and cold, bought records at Rough Trade and creepers on Kings Road. We fraternized at the long-standing meeting point, South Bank, and rode Meanwhile II, a sloped half-pipe located under an overpass next to a grim set of train tracks. There was a gap of at least ten feet between two sections, and the locals told us that Mark Gonzales had recently been there and ollied it. That was just ridiculous, almost unbelievable. His deserved reputation was starting to spread. Davin went home, and I went to Paris and on to Portugal to find my parents. I arrived just in time, with hardly any money left, dirty and bedraggled.

Resuming my Del Mar citizenship, I met up with Phil E. and his cohorts Ace and Chaz. Phil and I dressed exactly alike—pegged thrift-store pants, oversize T-shirts and high-tops—and with our long, dyed hair we resembled an off-kilter set of twins. Phil had been part of the L.A. environment shown in *The Decline of Western Civilization* and had seen all the bands I dreamed about back in Estes. His father would pick up an embarrassed thirteen-year-old Phil from shows, yelling for his son to "Get in here!" as swarms of punks jumped up and down on the car's hood. There were endless stories about Phil's father's tantrums, like the time at a gas station when he tried to punch someone who had cut him off in line but instead put his fist through the pump's glass front. Phil's sardonic response: "Way to go, Dad." Tensions increased until Phil came home one day to find all his records and clothes thrown away. He ran away from home to live under a bridge, then moved to a Hollywood teen squatter house, where he slept in the bathtub and was woken up by his housemates' morning evacuations, coupled with a cheery "Good morning, Phil." Eventually he made it down to San Diego to live with his mother and her new husband, Jim, and when I met him, he was living the semblance of a normal life, if you can call eating Pop-Tarts as your main nourishment and skating all night normal.

Physically, he was pale and stooped. He had a way of hunching his shoulders and sticking his head out like an old, long-beaked bird. Smart, twisted, caustic, he had a weird giggle and a habit of constantly repeating phrases, "You bastard" and "I'm your momma" being two favorites. *I'm Your Momma* was also the name of his zine. Jim employed him to do custom painting and told hilarious stories about taking acid when he was younger and coming home to fall on the lawn and grab it for dear life because he thought the earth was slipping away. He wasn't the typical father figure. Phil and I worked for him one summer and made quite a team in our white painter pants, white T-shirts and Frazee paint-store hats that inspired Phil to maniacally utter "Crazee Frazee" in any situation. We worked on rich people's homes, whaling away on brand-new kitchen cabinets with two-inch-link chains for days to "weather" them. We saw bands, skated ramps, ditches and schoolyards and Del Mar, all the while discussing life and skating, skating and life.

The next summer I shared a house dubbed "The Hut" with six roommates. It was in the blue-collar suburb of Claremont and had puke-yellow shag carpeting. We sat in the driveway in our friend's convertible Corsair smoking pot, and did drunken donuts on the street at 2 A.M. after coming home from the Pink Panther Bar, where I could get in with a fake ID. Phil dyed his hair blue, and mine was a raspberry pink for a while, and when we lingered too long at a convenience-store counter, the cashier said, "Why don't you take some more drugs?" Our motley crew would go on missions to play basketball at a nearby school in a preposterous cavalcade of bicycles, skateboards and one indestructible moped. Toward the end, it got out of control. Tod, Phil and Davin's band Scarecrow would play in my living room at unhinged bashes, the house suffering attending amounts of damage. My roommate John's Suicidal Tendencies friends came down from Venice and jumped the moped off ramps in the backyard and wreaked havoc. Thomas and three of his friends from Germany stayed with us and bought Vans and boards in bulk. Exasperated, the neighbors banded together to send a letter imploring us to calm down for the sake of their children. Phil countered with a letter of his own stating that we all had cancer and "just wanted to have some fun before we died."

We localized a school in Mira Mesa that was later referred to as School W. It had small banks and foot-high balance beams that were good for boardslides. Ollies were getting higher, and we started popping up to axle stalls on planters. The thought of grinding along something after ollieing up to it was beginning to percolate. At another street affair in Oceanside I saw Mark Gonzales attempt a frontside boardslide on a three-foot-high wall. Like the McTwist, it was an evolutionary leap, something nobody had conceived of doing because it didn't make any sense. Mark didn't make it, but he was coming close, and not long after, he was the first person to do a railslide on a stairway handrail. Natas Kaupas and Johnee Kop were present when he crossed the border into handrail territory and soon were doing it also.

Del Mar temporarily closed in 1987, which didn't come as a big shock because there obviously wasn't enough business to support an enterprise on that scale. There was talk of exorbitant insurance rates and a hotel going up on the property. We heard the news and called. In answer to our anxious queries, the son of the owner came out with the unforgettably dopey line, "Yeah, it's a real bummer in the summer." It reopened a month later, but the death knell had been sounded. Del Mar hung on for a while and then closed for good. That left Upland, which held out for a year longer as the last surviving commercial seventies skatepark in California. So many good times and dreams of the future reduced to nostalgia. Right before Del Mar's bulldozing, Pete Busse and I went there at 7 A.M. and took a few runs on the banked slalom ditch before bailing in fear of the police. I never quite got over seeing that empty space by the freeway.

Del Mar's end was hard to swallow because skateboarding was in the midst of an upswing. *Thrasher* and *Transworld* were thriving, and there was *Poweredge*, along with a growing number of zines. Big ramps were built in Westminster, Fallbrook, Linda Vista, Eagle Rock and at Lance Mountain's house—and that was in Southern California alone. Somebody told me at the time that Gator's optical maze graphic board was selling at a rate of fifty thousand decks a month. Skating wasn't as huge as it had been in the glory days, but it was expanding beyond the early eighties' subterranean profile. There were new companies, bigger contests and more people turning pro; and it was less uncommon to see skate competitions shown on the television news as the novelty end of the sports segment.

With the Ranch's demise, some of my personal aspirations fell by the wayside. I was taking art classes, getting into photography, partying a lot and enjoying the exotic new development of a lovely girlfriend. Skating was no longer paramount. The sacrifice and satisfaction that came from being studious and making underexposed sixteen-millimeter films about blind people getting their seeing-eye dogs stolen made the choice between skating and other pursuits less clear-cut. I continued to skate as much as possible, but I knew that I couldn't keep up with the whole ollie revolution, and I definitely wasn't ever going to do a McTwist. I didn't see Steve Claar as much, but I saw pictures of him in *Transworld* doing waist-high ollies at the Fallbrook ramp. A couple of years before, we had been skating at Russell's or sitting in his room avidly listening to and deconstructing Joy Division's "Atmosphere," and now he rode for G&S and, along with Jason Jesse, was pushing aerials and ollies past the established limits.

During my junior year, I heard rumors that UCSD was going to construct a ramp. I didn't believe it, but thanks to a proactive skate club, it did get built. It was a pleasure to have a place close by to go right after class. Less in touch with the scene in general, I was content to luxuriate in the no-pressure backwoods atmosphere of the UCSD ramp. Ironically, I was skating better than I ever had or would again, doing back-to-back airs, one-footed inverts, backside disasters and long frontside lipslides, finding that transcendence described by mountain climbers, skiers, surfers and other pursuers of solitary athletic enlightenment. I entered the trance that becomes a clear-eyed dream where daily cares disappear, replaced by an overwhelming clarity of purpose.

Standing on top of a nine-foot-high ramp with your back foot on the board epitomizes the narcotic allure of skating. You wait for the person riding to fall or finish his run, and the moment that happens, you hear a clatter of boards being pushed over the coping in the tail-drop position. A second goes by before the silent understanding that you're next, and then you drop in down the first foot of flat wall. Down the curving slope, across the bottom at speed, bending your knees to pump up the other wall. You pop off the lip into the air, the board flying out with you on it; you catch it and, keeping it to your feet, turn back in and release, trying to avoid a disastrous hang-up. Grinding on the coping, the metal of the truck scrapes the metal at the top of the ramp with a rough, grating noise. Or you're going upside down, one arm extended on the lip, the other holding the board above your head; you stall, inverted, then come back in. Ollies, rock-and-roll boardslides, boneless ones, lien-to-tails, method airs, you and a thirty-inch-long piece of wood with some sandpaper on it to make you stick better, rolling on four tiny wheels. Hurtling through space, an escaped convict from rigid and normally unavoidable physical laws.

By 1989, when I graduated, Davin was into surfing and we had gone our separate ways. I didn't see Phil that much anymore. I was out of it and moving to L.A., with delusions of grandeur about my photography overriding the prospect of uncertain employment in film production. I wanted to move on. Maybe I was a little burned out. Toward the end of the UCSD era, I got to know a character at the ramp named Geth Noble, a science genius known to surf big swells at Black's Beach on acid. He could barely do a kickturn in the beginning, but soon he was living in a tent by the ramp and riding every day, becoming the best skater there. He was quiet and meditative and possibly psychotic. Sometimes we played backgammon, and he would nonchalantly figure out the equation for rolling double sixes. One chance in two hundred in sixteen, if I remember correctly. That was over a decade ago. Recently I heard that Geth helped build the new park in Aspen, Colorado, and is still ripping; a perfect example of skating as an addiction that subsumes everything else in your life. As John Hogan remarked to me not too long ago without the slightest note of condemnation, "These are people that ruined their lives for skateboarding."

Chapter Eighteen
The Philosophy
Is the Action

When I moved to Los Angeles after college in 1990, most of my friends were returning to the bosom of their parents' homes. I had no such refuge, and though I had no burning desire to become an Angeleno, L.A. seemed like the place to go. As to be expected for a recently minted Bachelor of Arts with artistic pretensions, I was full of delusional expectations. I foresaw a new car and living large in a downtown loft while my photographs racked up popular and critical accolades. Needless to say, all stayed well within the realm of fantasy. I worked a dead-end job writing "coverage" of inane scripts for a production company that never actually made any movies. Days slid languidly by in a fairly typical postgraduation letdown as I made espressos for my pot-smoking Stevie Nicks—manqué boss, talked on the phone, called in speed-metal song requests to my favorite radio station and bemusedly read *Variety*.

I wanted to make art and write, but I wasn't taking many pictures or putting pen to paper. Instead I drank copiously and went to shows every weekend to see firsthand that punk's fire had gone out. L.A. was alienating, and the routine of driving to work and to the store and back and encountering only scriptwriting-course-taking waitresses and car-wash attendants was demoralizing. The seaminess of the Industry was impossible to ignore. I was vacillating between an undying faith in wild success and being convinced of utter failure. Maybe I'd write a script that would sell for a million dollars, or maybe I'd become Madonna's new confidant and she would help me get an agent for an unrealized opus. Or I might become a truck driver. My vague glimmerings dovetailed with colossally unfocused ambition and the kind of ennui that in no way separated me from thousands of other deluded souls with half-baked ideas for artistic world domination.

Though I daydreamed about skateboarding incessantly, I didn't know how much it figured into my plans. Maybe I was tired of skating, maybe I was disappointed that I had never become a pro, maybe I felt left out of the whole street revolution. As a symbolic coda to my years in San Diego, I visited Joe Johnson on the way north. He was living at Tony Hawk's Fallbrook estate, and we skated Tony's ramp complex while reminiscing about Colorado and High Roller's unsung locals. But when I got to L.A., I stopped looking at the magazines and ceased knowing or caring what was going on in the scene. I skated Wilshire Boulevard sidewalks and parking lots by my generic apartment in Brentwood, but it was all pretty desultory. The only bright point was that I lived within three miles of the Kenter, Paul Revere and Bellagio schoolyards where it all began. The call of the past and banks was strong, since I had always liked long inclined asphalt planes where you can do new school tricks or carve soulfully and get back to basics.

Surely there were people riding in the city, but since I was in a vacuum, I had no idea who or where they were. L.A. is so spread out that except for a few beach cruisers and Suicidal Tendencies types at Venice, I didn't see anybody skating the whole time I lived there. The concurrent downturn in skating's popularity (which didn't last too long) might also have contributed to the dearth of visible action. I did find out about a mini-ramp in a gang-infested area near the University of Southern California that I would drive to after work; it was all right but lacked the energy of real knockdown sessions because there was hardly ever anyone there. Once when Johnee Kop was in town, we visited Christian Hosoi's house, and I dropped in to do a few padless kickturns on the ramp. That was the extent of my vertical riding in the City of Angels. Stirred by atavistic tendencies, I just went to Paul Revere and spun 540-slides like the pioneers had done way back when. I had become a shadow of my former skating self.

I needed a major change from the Southern California lifestyle, an environment where I could find a place for myself. The woman who had captured my heart moved to New York, and that was enough incentive to go there, along with a craving for the sophistication and stimulation and real urban experience that Los Angeles couldn't provide. One of those cold nights in Colorado, as Joe Johnson and I listened to PIL's masterwork, *Second Edition*, I asked if he knew where the band hung out. The way he said "New York" conjured up a host of mysterious and magical connotations. Seven years later, I was finally going to see what it was all about. California was no longer the Promised Land.

The sham production company went bankrupt just as I quit and happily left town. First I went to London, where my parents were on another stop of their never-ending world tour, for one last lark of going to museums and movies and slacking around without having to think about money and the demands of the real world. Besides soaking up the cultural offerings and the time's anxiety about the Gulf War, I went to a shop and saw that boards had dropped to eight inches in width. There was a decided concentration on clothes, shoes, hip-hop and "attitude." The fresh kids behind the counter were quite chilly. Perhaps it was British reserve, but looking back, it seems like the foreshadowing of increasing factionalism and diminished camaraderie in skating. At South Bank and Meanwhile, I skated alone under dreary gray winter skies. Way out east in Essex at the seventies-era Rom Park, there was a pool, a huge decaying ramp, one guy who could ollie pretty well and a lot of BMXers. As I did a grind in the bowl, I heard somebody say, "Yeah dude, surf's up," in a sarcastic imitation of an American accent. Mostly I localized a rarely used metal half-pipe in Crouch End at the bottom of a ravine near some public housing flats. It was always misty and damp down there, and the ramp smelled strange because skaters occasionally poured oil on the surface and lit it on fire to burn off the moisture. Between runs, I would nod and smile at the old men on the nearby benches who mumbled at me in impenetrable Cockney accents. Premonitions of aging came to the fore when a woman stopped by with her children. As one of the boys ran around on the ramp, she admonished, "Johnny, stop doing that and let the man skateboard." Being referred to as a man while I stood on the rollout deck was unsettling, to say the least.

Arriving in New York, I felt right at home and more alive than I had in a while. I knew it was where I belonged when, walking down Avenue B in the East Village one night, I saw a car in flames and not a single pedestrian paid it any attention. There was an invigorating sense of danger that made it like an American version of Beirut, and later the same night, I serendipitously wandered into a dingy bar called Downtown Beirut. Manhattan was a new universe of art galleries, heroin dealers, transvestite bars, three-card-monte shysters, homeless encampments and clubs opening at three in the morning frequented by freaks of all shapes and sizes and ethnic varieties. You didn't have a choice but to deal with humanity. Whether it was with a homeless person begging or a Pakistani immigrant selling newspapers, you interacted with actual human beings in a way that was impossible in the compartmentalized sterilization of L.A. I was living with my girlfriend, going out every night, seeing contemporary art shows and revival movies and having the time of my life. When the situation became desperate, I got one job bagging meals at a takeout Mexican restaurant and another calling lonely New School alumni for contributions.

The now unacceptably wide Matt Hensley board I had owned for far too long sat unused in the corner. But during that twilight zone right before falling asleep, the movie screen in my mind played extravagantly trick-laden runs in which I performed at a preposterously high level. I examined the city's architecture, thinking that a certain bank would be much better without the curb in front of it or that a subway tunnel turned upside down would make a great ditch. When I heard the sound of wheels on the street, I would whip my head around to look forlornly after the anonymous rider. I didn't know any skaters in the city or look at the magazines anymore, and in a way that was a relief; but the board taunted me from the corner and couldn't be forsaken.

Chelsea in the early nineties wasn't the art-gallery ghetto it is now but a grungy haunt of transvestite prostitutes and their clients. It was just one of the many picturesque districts I reconnoitered on my board. New York was full of quirky, distinct neighborhoods that hadn't yet been overrun by the normal Jacks and Jills from the suburbs, who came when it got safe and boring in the later part of the decade. There were numerous unknown, exotic and frightening nether regions to marvel at and explore. I did a lot of that on my own, but thanks to a fellow traveler named Justin Forbes, I made my first foray into the uncharted territory of the Bronx.

Justin was a skater from my generation whom I met through an L.A. connection. We hit it off immediately, and I ended up moving into his loft on Twenty-third Street, where he painted and lived the bohemian lifestyle to its fullest. We stayed out till all hours, indulging in as much alcohol and as many mind-altering substances as possible, which eventually led us to the urban decay across the Harlem River, where Justin knew of a skatepark. Riding the unfamiliar 6 train out onto the elevated tracks, we got off at 161st Street by Yankee Stadium. Mullaly Park had rows of low-rise projects on one side, the tracks on the other and a decent half-pipe, a pyramid and some other obstacles. Not that great, but it was something, and the ambience was worth the trip. Wolf packs of little rascals ran around calling one another nigger, constantly demanding, "Can I use your board?" Extended families barbecued up a storm, and Puerto Rican meringue music frenetically blasted out of apartment windows and slowly prowling cars. I expected a drive-by shooting at any moment, because they were so in vogue during the early nineties. Nothing really bad happened, but it seemed like shit could go down at the drop of a hat. One time I heard a whitey ask a local, "When does this place close down?" The guy responded, "When it gets dark, or when you get beat up and your stuff gets stolen."

But Mullaly was far away, and my heart wasn't in it. There weren't that many skateboarders there, since everybody was riding street. What Mullaly did have was a budding plague of bicyclists and Rollerbladers infesting skateboarders' domains. The traditional animosity between BMXers and skaters had simmered down with the arrival of a common eight-wheeled in-line enemy, and while I did admire the bikers for their aerial acrobatics, those thirty-pound machines they pedal around on are a real problem. It's like a football player running into the middle of a basketball game—all of a sudden one is silently almost running you over, and collisions do occur, with the skater always coming out the loser. That said, their offensiveness pales in comparison to the annoyingly ubiquitous hordes of Rollerbladers who won't go away. Frolicking on pseudo–roller skates is fine, but at places made by skateboarders for skateboarders, they are always dawdling on the coping and trying to act embarrassingly tough. It's an obvious case of overcompensation for deep-seated feelings of worthlessness. One white boy on his boot skates told me in his fake slang, "I mean, I give you guys respect, but this is what's happening now." It was a reprise of the girl's snotty remark at the roller rink in Boulder twelve years earlier. Whereas roller skaters like Fred Blood and Duke Rennie were philosophically aligned innovators, Rollerbladers are a different contemptible breed. They've adopted the clothes and style of skateboarding wholesale, and they "grab" their "tricks," but it doesn't mean anything, since the wheels are attached to their feet. And they're everywhere, like a cloud of irritating gnats.

Six inches of boxer shorts showing at the top of pants so baggy they looked like some kind of antigravity device held them up; small boards and tiny wheels; I saw these by the Cube at Cooper Square, and they had a destabilizing effect. One night after I hadn't trolled downtown with Justin, he returned and said, "Guess who I hung out with last night?" It was Mark Gonzales, whom I hadn't seen since Pete Finlain's ramp in Oceanside. Justin reported that Mark was living in New York and taking ballet lessons, and I realized I wasn't the only one who might be a little disillusioned. A few months later in Washington Square Park, I saw Mark, with his unmistakable grin, pushing around on a borrowed board fashioned from a water ski. He reiterated how little he was skating, and we discussed other topics like Isadora Duncan and his fascination with Howard Hughes.

Justin moved to New Orleans, so on my own I went to the Brooklyn Banks, a storied wave of red bricks in the shadow of the neoclassical municipal building. It's been ridden since the sixties. A contingent of homeless men—skaters, as societal outcasts, have always shared disused urban space with them—were lying around amid the stench of urine, and they and the cracks and tree planters made it an obstacle course. I rode and watched the youngsters trying ollie flip variations without making them. It was the first time I really didn't feel the brotherhood. They gave off a disdainful too-cool-for-school vibe that a friend who moved to the city around that time characterized as "big pants and big attitudes." They seemed to regard me with a mixture of ridicule and indifference. When I did a layback or boneless, I detected snickers, and deep down I knew that was the way it should be. It's the new generation's prerogative to dismiss its elders.

It became painfully apparent that I was a twenty-five-year-old dinosaur, one of those oldsters I had considered hopelessly out of touch when I was younger. Even though skating is an individual pursuit, having a group of cohorts to ride with is important, and without it you can't help but be a wallflower. The solitude of Estes Park had been hard to bear but was relieved by the knowledge that whenever I saw another skater, I would feel an immediate covenant. Now that was gone, and I couldn't be one of them even if I tried. W. Somerset Maugham's warning to the piano-playing, irresponsible George in his story "The Alien Corn" took on another meaning: "You can't go on leading the student's life. . . . Your friends here will grow older and go away." When George protests that he'll get new friends, Maugham says, "Yes, but you'll grow older too. Is there anything more lamentable than the middle-aged man who tries to go on living the undergraduate's life? The old fellow who wants to be a boy among boys, and tries to persuade himself that they'll accept him as one of themselves—how ridiculous he is. It can't be done."

I was coming to terms with that, and the fact that in light of recent trick advancements, I also wasn't very good anymore. I could do 180-ollies off a curb, but I wasn't going to be bounding up to any handrails. For a long time I had been able to hold my own, but that was no longer true. Not only were my skills not up to par, I was now on the outside, self-aware and long past being organically cool in the unself-conscious way only teenagers can be. Since that had defined my life for so long, it was hard to accept that I was essentially getting older and could never go back: a midlife crisis at twenty-five. I had a girlfriend, a full-time job and was settling down. I wasn't going out at midnight to skate with the crew anymore.

A little lost, I decided to try making something of the connection between my skating and photography. I'd never even thought of taking pictures of the activity that took up most of my free time. Plus there were plenty of photographers with more inclination and talent. I fervently believed in my conceptual, out-of-focus photographs, but they weren't putting any bread on the table, so I half-heartedly tried to earn a little money by shooting a familiar subject. Dave Swift had become the editor of *Transworld* and told me to send slides. My whole artistic stance was one of rebellion against technical skills—in particular, one Ansel Adams–trained professor—so I was unfamiliar with using a flash and woefully unprepared. Feeling uncomfortable because I had turned myself into an observer and, by extension, a pariah, I went to Washington Square one night, and on some level the experience represented a fall from grace. Jeff Pang, Peter Huynh and Ivan Perez good-naturedly made fun of my outmoded setup but were friendly enough and invited me to tag along.

Over on Broadway they prodigiously ollied off a propped-up metal grate as I pretended to know what I was doing. Along with all the flip tricks and board spinning, seeing Jeff Pang ollie with maximum pop from flat ground over a fire hydrant was an eye-opener. They took me to Ray's Pizza, where, over slices, I was more of an eavesdropper than a participant, since the people I knew, like Steve Claar and Jason Jesse, were already being relegated to irrelevant history. We went over to the Lower East Side, where drug dealers loitered on every corner, and it reminded me how skaters acquire a wider worldview than most through their willingness to go into normally shunned areas. On Orchard Street, they ollied off a bump in the sidewalk until eggs rained down on us from an apartment above. We retired to play pinball at a den of rampant heroin use that was one of the only bars hipsters dared go to below Houston Street. I went home completely depressed. Unsurprisingly, Swift said the pictures were too dark to be used.

Before those vague notions of an orthodox photography career dissipated, I went down to a contest at the Brooklyn Banks with my camera. There were young girls with lip piercings and skaters darting to and fro being chased by video-camera-wielding friends. For some inscrutable reason, one kid got chased and beaten up. As far as the skating went, the vast majority of attempts were only that. I could appreciate the difficulty factor, considering the perfect timing and pinpoint accuracy flip tricks entail, but the frequency of bails made it unsatisfying viewing. A few standouts ollied the Jersey Barrier onto the off-ramp from the bridge, which was impressive enough, but they also did kickflips over it while cars raced down the pike into the landing zone. I saw how outdated my conception of the state of the art was when Danny Way showed up, looking slightly out of place with his blond hair and almost jocklike demeanor. With everyone gathered around, he pushed hard and, after a few tries, did a switch noseslide down an eight-stair handrail. Commonplace by today's standards, but at the time all I could think was, "Holy shit." As when I saw the McTwist, it brought the paradigm shift home. In a few short years, skating had progressed from ollies up to benches and short handrails to high-speed leaps onto much more daunting waist-high edges. And Danny did it switch.

I saw some unseemly antics at the Brooklyn Banks, but none that compared to the outlaw scene that Chris Pastras perfectly captured in an article that appeared in *Paper* magazine. He described a contest held in the mid-eighties while three older black guys, with their boom box blasting and "the Cooley High look," played basketball on the courts up top. After the game, the three marched through the throng exuding disgust until one of them tripped over a kid's foot. "He then bellowed: 'Look the fuck out when I'm walking, and don't get in my damn way!' The kid realized he was more than underqualified to rebuke the order and was blank for a few seconds. Then it hit him that some 300 skaters with boards for weapons had his back. He turned around and screamed 'Fuck you' in typical wise-ass rebel/skater fashion. The thug took a deep breath before he bounced his basketball off the kid's head with a thump. The dazed kid hit the bricks and all eyes turned to the three hoods. 'Get 'em!' was all I heard as the whole crowd rushed the guys and started swinging their boards. As everyone closed in, one of the thugs reached into his jacket. . . . He held the gun in the air and let off a couple of shots. Everyone scattered Vietnam-style while the triumphant three stood there with old-school break beats as their soundtrack. They must have felt like movie stars."

In 1993 I went to St. Petersburg, Russia. It really is the Venice of the North, with all the canals and scores of pastel rococo palaces, the Bronze Horseman, Peter the Great's log cabin and the Hermitage on the banks of the Neva River. Nabokov's childhood home was across the courtyard from my parent's new apartment. Late in the evening, as the white nights faded, I would go over to the Astoria Hotel's parking lot to skate. During one of these rambles, a Russian guy happened along and, with a gleam in his eye, gestured excitedly toward my board. Putting my apprehensions about Petersburg's crime rate aside I pushed it over to him and he ecstatically set off tic-tacking and carving across the pavement. He came back smiling and thanked me profusely with "Spasiva," but by then we were communicating on a plane beyond words. The enthusiasm and pleasure he got from simply riding around was infectious.

On the flip side, I returned to the August mugginess of New York and my prosaic existence. The first night back, I tried to prolong that state of mentally remaining abroad, but restlessness made me go to the same heroin-soaked bar I had been to with Pang and the others. In due course, I'd become a regular. Nobody familiar was around, and seeing the same old ennui-addled demimonde got me down, so I slunk out feeling sorry for myself. If that wasn't bad enough, on my way home, I looked up to see Ivan Perez with a big grin barreling down the street and ollieing up to a long manual across the median. Next to him, with her long blond hair trailing, was a lithe vision of sporty femininity wearing short shorts striding along on roller skates. Even if it was almost a parody of carefree youth, it didn't strike me as very funny. I felt so old.

But that depressing encounter made me realize that even if I wasn't as immersed in skating as before, I wasn't going to start playing tennis or golf and grow up in the usual sense. The "skate for life" rhetoric that had previously seemed a little silly was revealing itself as an apt motto for an incurable infection. I went to an out-of-the-way shop in Chinatown to get with the program and buy a new modern board. Staring at the unfamiliar graphics and minuscule wheels, I was like a dad flummoxed by the prospect of getting the right gift for his child. The wheels were ridiculously small and hard; boards were symmetrical so you couldn't tell the front from the back; and riser pads had gone out of style because the lower carriage meant higher ollieing power. My chagrin came across in a diffident "Don't treat me like I don't know anything" manner. Escaping the humiliation I dropped the new stick down on the asphalt to discover that its size and light weight made ollieing much easier. I was enjoying myself. I'm sure the look on my face resembled the happy Russian's in St. Petersburg.

Ironically, it was the art world I had ambivalently immersed myself in that circuitously brought me back. An outfit called Creative Time put on exhibitions every summer in the anchorage of the Brooklyn Bridge, where the cables that hold up the span are secured. I heard that somebody had built a ramp there for one of the shows and skeptically went to check it out. To my surprise, there really was a nine-foot-high, twelve-foot-wide half-pipe that an artist named Maura Sheehan had built as a rideable sculpture. Urban warriors were uncertainly fakieing halfway up, boards were flying everywhere, and the attending aural chaos reverberated off the cavernous stone ceilings. After not being on a ramp for three years, the sight of it reawakened something deep inside of me. Donning some

pads, I ran up the wall to jump on and wobble around on my miniature sled. Even dropping in, a basic act that had been second nature,
was scary at first. Then the old feeling came back. Just doing a frontside
grind was life-affirming, and all my doubts about being over the hill
or unable to do the latest tricks evaporated. After numerous tries I
did an invert, a maneuver that in the past I could have done in my
sleep. As I landed, a sweet elixir surged through my veins and, like an
alcoholic falling off the wagon and rediscovering bliss in the liquor
cabinet, I wanted to imbibe without end. I couldn't believe I'd lost so
much time.

Seeing Sanford and Rich Lopez killing it doing six-foot-high
airs to fakie and kickflip indys was inspiring, but so was just watching a bunch of skaters of varying abilities and styles go off. There were
familiar faces from Mullaly and people who had been in the wood-
work even longer than I had. The collective exhortations, shouts,
whooping, clapping and banging of boards on the coping at well-done
or barely made tricks reminded me of how much I missed the shared
purpose and enjoyment of a good session. On the platform I met Andy
Kessler, who talked about building a skatepark in Manhattan's Riverside Park with city funds. Though doubtful it would come to fruition, I held out hope because I had an itch that needed to be scratched.

Then there was the trip to Cameroon. It had been three years
since I'd seen Thomas Hauser, and because his brother Stefan worked
as a soil scientist in the capitol city of Yaounde, we chose that especially undistinguished West African country. That it is a place no
tourists go was appealing and made Stefan's insider connections indispensable. With my board and one of Stefan's handmade models
from the seventies, we rode around behind the house as his adolescent daughter circled on her bike, laughing at the two grown men
playing on their toys. The locals selling warm soda and cigarettes at

their roadside stands grinned as we went by, amazed and bemused. Acclimatizing to the fetid atmosphere and genuine otherness of Yaounde, we talked about the old days and how much skating had defined our lives. All the stories, the weird characters and the shared heritage that had brought us together in the first place were crucial to our continuing bond.

Our skating was as much a novelty to Yaounde's small expatriate community as the fact that we inexplicably made it through customs without incident. Reports of a "skate-run" at the French Club sounded exaggerated, but we vowed to investigate upon returning from our backwoods tour of the country's northwestern quarter. On a diet of cold chicken dinners and warm soda, we trekked from poisonous lakes to volcanic black sand beaches, staying at cattle herders' compounds and at one point almost straying into Nigeria. Once we were back in Yaounde, the first order of business was finding out if the rumors were true. To our amazement, the seventies-vintage half-bowl improbably materialized as we came up the hill to the club. Faded graffiti read, "Jean-Luc is the best." An imperious woman sneered at my deficiencies in the French language and tried to charge a full-year membership until I cajoled her down to fifteen dollars and got a receipt for "skeet-ball." Appropriating a broom to sweep out the sand, we proceeded to reanimate the unused relic. With the club's waiters staring blankly and Stefan carving around in his Birkenstocks under the equatorial dusk, our little session bordered on the absurd, while also being representative of an unyielding allegiance to concrete embankments and their possibilities. Ten years and thousands of miles from the ramp in Stuttgart, Thomas and I were still friends and still skating.

Following my first aesthetically captivating (according to a select few) but fiscally disastrous photography exhibition in New York,

I impulsively quit my job. Darby Romeo, creator of *Ben Is Dead,* was in town with an RV full of "zinesters" in the midst of a cross-country zine tour. Seeing that I was at loose ends, she offered me a free trip from Baltimore to Chicago to Seattle to San Francisco, with stops at Mount Rushmore and Yosemite. All I had to do was help drive the RV. Postpartum blues after my show, along with a lingering affinity for do-it-yourself publishing, drew me to the idea of rambling across the United States with them. In each city I would assist the zinesters in setting up their wares at the local alternative bookstore before going off on my own for slightly disaffected and dubious observations of America circa 1996. The "what we have bought" homogeneity that Robert Adams documented so despairingly in his pictures of Denver's soulless subdivisions was ubiquitous. It wasn't only the tawdriness of the artificial landscape but the masses of sheep masquerading as humans that was so crushing. The trip was a sentimental education, the final implosion of youth's naïveté and idealism. This was particularly true in the realization that punk had "won" and there was a nation out there of "punks" and "skaters" who had been able to buy their identities instead of finding them through a transforming process of self-discovery. On the worst days, the land appeared a waste of sameness, with minimalls and kids who looked and talked the same, aping their favorite skate stars or the rappers they saw on television. Every contingency was represented and pandered to, their rebelliousness bought and worn.

Portland, Oregon, figured prominently in my plans because I had heard about a massive renegade wonderland there called Burnside, brought into existence by devoted locals. As soon as possible after arrival, I left the zinesters and went over the Burnside Bridge to the other side of the Willamette River, where telltale sounds of clacking boards emanated from underneath the bridge. What I saw when I looked over the retaining wall left me agog. Burnside was an extravagantly convoluted moonscape that, in its vastness, recalled a more organic and unregulated version of a first-wave skatepark. It was filled with skaters whizzing every which way in a ballet of barely controlled chaos. After some hesitation, I threw myself into the mix and took a shaky ride from slanted wall to corner to bump to corner to quarter-pipe to simulated backyard pool. The slightly sketchy scene made me feel right at home, and I seriously considered relocating to Portland. Disreputable teenagers scrounged change for beer, while the kind of skaters you rarely see in magazines exhibited absolute mastery of the terrain by grinding hard, ollieing on a dime and flowing around in a way that, for me, defines skating much more than stop-and-go flip trickery. A scruffy lunatic who resembled a refugee from the Steve Miller concert I attended in fifth grade turned out to be Burnside progenitor Mark "Red" Scott. His virtuoso high-speed perambulations were a joy to watch.

Burnside's rise from junkie lair to its current glory was due to ten years of sweat, toil and piecemeal ingenuity by local diehards whom Scott led to expand upon Osage Buffalo and Brett Turner's original impetus. Entirely unsubsidized, they laid down concrete and tested it as they went along until they achieved the desired result. It is a grassroots reclamation project that so positively changed the surrounding neighborhood that the city bestowed on Red and the rest a citation for civic improvement. Their successful mission to make something out of nothing has been as influential as any trick or board-design breakthrough. Burnside is an awe-inspiring pilgrimage site because the right fanatics built it for all the right reasons— the opposite of the deplorable travesties that occur when architects completely ignore their constituency to design flawed skateparks, or anything else for that matter. Burnside's atmosphere reflects the authenticity of its builders' impulses: as long as you're riding and not acting like an asshole, you've got a place in the lineup.

After roaming the nation, I slid into a lethargic stupor and, with no job and my so-called art career mostly a figment of my imagination, contemplated moving out of New York or going to medical school or some other drastic action. There was one thing that made me forget my troubles: the new ramps at Riverside Park, which had come into being against the odds. Crossing West End Avenue, I followed the birdwatchers' gazes to the peregrine falcons that come down from a nearby steeple, and then I saw the blue-painted ramps arrayed below. Andy Kessler had been skating since 1974, and he was still doing it with vigor. Through his own initiative, he made Riverside happen; he had effected change.

As I skated the park for the first time, I found that most of what I had been able to do five years before came fairly easily, but I was definitely out of practice. My feet would be in the wrong place, I'd be off balance and worst of all were some really gut-wrenching, contusion-inflicting meetings with the plywood. There are run-of-the-mill bails, and then there are the more damaging hang-ups on the coping, or the "Mr. Wilson" spills when the skater steps on his own loose board as he runs down the wall. Falling is inherent to skating, because even deceptively simple maneuvers have a narrow margin of error. Usually you twist your body instinctively so you can knee-slide or run out and not get hurt, but it isn't foolproof. I knew I was rusty because I would wake up the next morning with swollen elbows and my whole body hurting so much it took ten minutes to get out of bed. But I kept going back.

That other adults of different backgrounds and professions who shared a common legacy still had an itch to ride helped. One day I heard a familiar voice on the platform, and it turned out to be

Michael Laird, whom I'd met at Pflugerville thirteen years earlier. Jimmy Murphy, Coan Nichols, Rick Charnoski and Jack Fitzgerald were some of the incorrigibles in their late twenties or early thirties still bent on abusing themselves. It's funny in the context of skating's youthful image that so many crusty old guys still ride. But why not? Seventy-year-olds play tennis, ski and surf, so why not skate? Tony Alva, Steve Olson and Joel Chavez are still doing it in their forties, and plenty of the children of the sixties—Lance Mountain, Steve Caballero, Tony Hawk and Mark Gonzales are just a few of the more famous ones—are proving that radical and viable skating doesn't end with the bloom of youth. The formative years were so larval that no one knew if older bodies could withstand the punishment, and the idea of middle-aged practitioners was laughable, but with time's passing, Bill Dohr could turn out to be a prophet about skating into old age.

One salient feature of skating's broadening appeal over the last few years has been a dramatic rise in skatepark construction. Skateboarding has finally been legally defined as a dangerous sporting activity, which has lessened liability problems and coincided with the demand for and realization of hundreds of municipally built free parks. For-profit rinks are also proliferating. The parks are everywhere, some well designed, many not. It's quite a difference from the dearth of transitional terrain that used to be such a curse, but the trend is a mixed blessing. On one hand, it's fantastic to have the kind of concrete creations that encourage flowing and engaged skating; on the other, they foster complacency and the ghettoization of skaters. Whatever the downside, some of the most amazing manifestations of this flowering are in Oregon, where Mark Scott and Mark Hubbard and their Dreamland team have taken their Burnside experience and applied it to building city-funded parks that are better than anything else in the world. They are built by real skaters who ride what they sculpt with authority. My jaw dropped the first time I saw Newburg's lovingly rendered undulating forms, and to say that Oregon's Newburg and Lincoln City skateparks are masterpieces is not an exaggeration. These works put their builders in league with artists like Richard Serra, Robert Smithson and James Turrell: the parks are beautiful environments, awesome to look at and, on some level, superior to sculpture because they combine aestheticism with athletic functionality. Their specific purpose is fulfilled beyond even the highest expectations.

Within Newburg's deep cement swells, speed and weightlessness make for a ride more thrilling than any roller coaster. It expands the backyard pool's horizons so a skater can ricochet without pushing from bump to coping to corner until he or she falls off or succumbs to exhaustion. As you gyrate back and forth and go from one elevation to another, you achieve a oneness with the surface. Intimate knowledge of an inanimate object combines with athletic action on the threshold between thinking and primal instinct; you link tricks together in an improvisation that relies on thousands of hours of daydreaming and mental practice. Speed and flight take you through multiple dimensions as form and function become one. The philosophy is the action.

Chapter Nineteen
Awe Against Compromise

Outsiders peering into the closed world of skateboarding wonder where the devotion comes from. . . . To my mind, what is engaging about skating is that it is a metaphor for life. . . . It will teach you the difference between courage and vanity, it demonstrates that power is nothing without control. She rewards hard work and perseverance, and short-cutting in application will get you shown the horizontal door. Style over content are the emperor's new clothes, while quiet and clear truth resonates like a clarion. . . . Disappointment and frustration serve to temper our overleaping ambition and season our dreams of majesty with the earthy taste of humility. . . . The victory of optimism over experience is the engine room of skating. It underlines the importance of bringing a sense of awe and wonderment to a compromised and average adult world.

—Niall Neeson, *Slap*, June 2001

Neeson's eloquence touches on skateboarding's enduring noble aspects. At the same time, it can be more than a little dispiriting to see skating partially neutered and subdued by modern society's malignant forces, but what else is new? Isn't that what happens to every-thing in the end? The barbarians were inside the gate a long time ago, and this onslaught is just the latest corruption. All skaters used to be participants who collectively rebelled against the false values associated with sport, but the divide has gotten smaller. Does it matter? Not as long as skating remains challenging, different and fun. That's what matters.

One leitmotif in the history of skating and the punk move-ment is the stark contrast between the real counterculture of the past and the pseudocounterculture of the present—a present where teen-age rebellion is packaged and sold in a perpetual feedback loop of co-optation and regurgitation. Youth movements are picked over the moment they surface, and everything is "edgy" and "extreme" to the point that these concepts have lost all meaning. The quotes around those very words tell the story, and the overwhelming mood among the adults who pander to young people is one of calculated cynicism and hypocrisy. Before MTV and the Internet and the cur-rent vulturelike mentality of appropriation, youthful rebellions and experimentations could be off the radar of popular culture, thriving and developing organically. Punk and skating could be hidden—and their appeal and authenticity lay therein. That freedom to be underground has all but disappeared today.

It's become an old saw that society integrates formerly reviled movements by turning them into cultural consumer goods. They are commodified, studied, and explained—and all their unwhole-someness is stripped away. From the Marxism that originated this argument to Dada, surrealism and body piercing, this tendency has proven to be true. With punk it was due partially to the transience of the new and a mass audience coming around to a watered-down version that suited their taste. What was once a movement has become a style. There was a special era of noninterference in the ten or so years after the Ramones' first album, when certain music, clothes and opinions genuinely repulsed most normal people, instead of being calculated rehashings that desperately try to shock. Punk and skating used to have a fiercely independent and contrary worldview that couldn't be digested easily by society at large, and that gave them a special quality that is rarer and rarer. They weren't subcultural styles; they were subterranean.

Now skateboarding supports a huge industry full of as much backstabbing and duplicity as any other recreational sport or entertainment field, fueling a marketing machine that ensures skate stars' fame in the remote jungles of New Guinea. Tony Hawk is unquestionably the most renowned skateboarder in the world, not only because he has won more contests with his still-amazing skills than anybody in the history of the "sport," but also because of his multiple endorsements, autobiography and wildly popular video game. By promoting sundry products and maintaining a high media profile, Hawk and other stars have become the sole symbols of skateboarding for people who don't know better. And that is very misleading.

Skating is a fixture on the twenty-first-century equivalent of *Wide World of Sports,* pro vert skater Andy Macdonald met President Clinton, and video tours of roller celebrities' homes are regular occurences—these are just a few indications of how much skateboarding has changed. Today's situation feels ever more standardized and sportslike, with kids who pursue it seriously thinking they're failures unless they get sponsored after a year of doing kickflips.

There are at least twenty million skateboarders in the United States today and a booming resurgence in park construction. Other countries now have their own magazines and untold numbers of skaters who are just as good or better than their counterparts in

America. The divide no longer exists. Over the last fifteen years, skating has been transformed from an innocent underground activity with a premium on vertical to an increasingly mainstream sport with street trickery that boggles the mind. The level of difficulty of flip tricks and handrail stunts makes the moves of yesteryear seem positively tame. But as the painter Andre Masson wrote, "Traced, repeated over and over, the unusual vulgarizes itself"—and that was in 1945. When an art form is codified, it gets a little stale, and it would be disingenuous to claim that this book isn't part of that process. If there is one phenomenon that has emerged as a sign that the golden age really is over, it's that parents now actively encourage their children to skateboard.

For better or worse, skating has grown up and become institutionalized. There is money to be made, and a lot of water has passed under the bridge. Chris Robinson, Blaize Blouin, Phil Shao, Curtis Hsiang, and Ruben Orkin are just a few who died before their time, and Jeff Phillips committed suicide. Jay Adams and Christian Hosoi have been in jail for drugs and Gator is doing life for murder.

Skating is dangerously veering toward becoming as American as apple pie. That Vans honcho Steve Van Doren says, "We have to market the idea that these sports can be done at top level only in the best facilities, in specially designed skateparks and not on street corners" is just as depressing and inevitable as a recent *USA Today* article that stated, "Athletes like Tony Hawk are very hip. . . . Their equipment is cool. And let's face it, from a visual standpoint their sports are very cool, too." Unfortunately, skating has been woefully "cool" for too long, making it not cool at all and altering the exclusivity that attracted the kind of determined outcasts who made it what it is.

It is now more than twenty years since Robert "The Fly" Schlaefli said, "Skating's not nice. You don't grind to be nice." The sullying avalanche of magazines, pictures, videos, jocklike behavior, idiotic sunglasses endorsements and rock-star posturing of the present is embarrassing for skateboarding in general but thankfully can't entirely dilute what Schlaefli knew to be true.

The real skaters are the practitioners whose reputations are rooted in action and not the clothes they wear or their purported drunken escapades. The Reese Simpsons, Josh Falks, Ivory and Shelter Serras, Mark van der Engs, Evan Beckers, Rick Charnoskis and thousands of others are authentic in a way that gets lost in the current climate. They care about riding and their friends, not prostituting themselves for the almighty dollar. Mainstream magazines and television spectacles, with their advertisements and hype, and corporate sponsors and corny announcers, mutate something beautiful into the kind of sham that skaters historically have rejected. *Vive le résistance,* because what was a bracing corrective is succumbing to the mainstream and the loud, cheap, grasping, phony all-American pap it represents; in doing so, it becomes a "sport" with "heroes." That's badhood, as Neil Blender would say. Torger Johnson, Jay Adams, Steve Olson, Duane Peters and the rest were not "hip athletes," and they were not heroes.

But if the X Games and action figures and fingerboards and other petty developments encroach, it's too bad but not the end of the world, because it can't be taken too seriously. This planet has horrible problems with real people suffering and dying and complaining that things have gone to hell, and endlessly extolling the virtues of a bucolic past is pointless myopia. The joy of skating— the solitary quest combined with the camaraderie, the unending search for terrain—is paramount. It's still an unorthodox passion that brings together disparate races, creeds, sexes and ages, a pluralistic utopia in which improbably named individuals like Nanda

Zipp, Karma Tsocheff and Satva Leung can pursue happiness in a way most people will never comprehend. Elissa Steamer put it well: "A true skater can have more fun on a few feet of curb than six people can all day at Disneyland."

In 2001 I was in Berlin visiting Thomas Hauser and went to Cologne to see a publisher I know through Mark Gonzales. It's all connected. Capitola reminds me of Oceanside reminds me of Yaounde. It was business in Cologne, but there's always an overriding ulterior motive—I'd heard there was an indoor park called Wicked Woods in nearby Wuppertal. I'd never been there, and all I had was a scrawled address written on a napkin. It was getting dark, snow was falling and dour Germans were trudging purposefully under the aerial tram gliding silently overhead. I believed I could divine where the park was by some sort of sixth sense, but after half an hour of wandering in the gloom, I got a taxi and headed off toward a desolate warehouse district. The driver soon revealed that he had no clue. Then we saw a guy carrying a board who spoke English and helped build the park, so with him in the passenger seat, we made our way to Wicked Woods.

Inside it was warm and dry. There was a huge street course, a wide miniramp and a seven-foot-deep bowl with carveable corners and a hip. A couple of guys were ripping on the mini-ramp and doing hard flips to fakie and disaster to revert combinations and I joined in for a good session. We existed outside of time, slaking desire, skating for who knows how many hours. After a long frontside grind, I came down at an angle and flew onto a recessed transition I hadn't seen and slammed really hard. It knocked the wind out of me and hurt so bad that for a moment I thought I was going to vomit. Then it passed, and to sympathetic and understanding looks, I limped back up to the deck where I dazedly watched and held my arm for a while before going back to the bowl.

As the night wound down, it was just me and Isabelle, a sixteen-year-old girl with blond dreadlocks. She was going for it, committing herself, making some things and not others, not caring if anybody was watching, smiling inwardly and having a very personal kind of fun. She radiated real skating—the challenging of societal norms, the trying and failing and the moments when it all comes together. I stopped riding as exhaustion set in, and Isabelle was the only person left as they started turning out the lights. She tried a boardslide down a steep rail and almost made it, but her board got away on the landing and she slammed really, really hard. Then she got back up and tried again.

It's like the Fly said. Skating's not nice.

Afterword
(History Is Bunk)

Skating has been a constant in my life that has taken me to unexpected places and made me look at the world differently, an act and art and lifestyle that permeates and is my world. I have made new friends and revisited old ones because skating is a bond that, unlike most, lasts forever. I recently skated the Baldy Pipeline with David Fuller from Colorado, and I still talk to Joe Johnson and Johnee Kop, who now teaches tennis in China. Through skating I've met cognitive behaviorists, rare-book dealers, architects, high school honor students, burnouts, chefs, furniture makers, gun-toting maniacs, little Polish kids and countless others I probably would never have encountered in normal society. I've spent lazy summer days riding and watching the Hudson River boat traffic at Riverside, cruised hills on Menorca, skated to the store, ridden ramps in tenth-floor Brooklyn lofts as it snowed outside, bailed out pools in decrepit Asbury Park, New Jersey, and helped design a bowl in Holland.

So what does it all mean? Why spill so much ink on its account? On the urging of an anesthesiologist friend who used to frequent San Pedro pools, I wrote a story about witnessing Mike McGill change things forever with the McTwist. That ended up in *Thrasher* and became the kernel for this book. I was initially reluctant to write more, because skating is so special and personal that I thought it was a mistake to try to explain it to outsiders and that doing so was sacrilege—the fear of selling out the cause that *"traduttore traditore"* implies. But in the three years since I first began writing, skating has undergone such a massive transformation that it's now omnipresent. The doubts I had about betraying my brethren have turned into a desire to document and eulogize a time and a way of life that are fading into an irretrievable past. If the pain and sentimentalizing that invariably accompany nostalgia are one outcome, it's a risk worth taking. In the face of historical amnesia, I had to show that the present didn't spring from nothing. As Russell Baker wrote in *Growing Up*, "We all come from the past, and children ought to know what it was that went into their making, to know that life is a braided cord of humanity stretching up from a time long gone, and that it cannot be defined by the span of a single journey from diaper to shroud."

This book is a memorial to people and places and intangibles that went into making skating's now. It's less about a physical act than about the characters, visionaries and idiot savants who did this thing when there was no money to be made and nobody else cared about it. As *Big Brother*'s Dave Carnie wrote, trying to describe skateboarding is like attempting to explain an itch. "You can't give an ostensive definition of an itch: Try pointing at one and saying, 'This is an itch.' Skateboarding is an individual internal experience that is virtually ineffable. . . . Writing about skateboarding . . . [is] as hopeless as trying to define the color red." Photographs and moving images communicate more of the essence of skateboarding, and they're hard to compete against. The reason Aaron Rose's *Dysfunctional* is without a doubt the best book on the subject so far is because it intermixes depictions of action with images that say so much more: John Cardiel maniacally throwing up a two-handed devil horn salute in front of a Slayer banner, Ed Templeton's bruised ass and spiderweb-tattooed, bald-headed Andy Roy shooting a revolver elucidate skating's spirit in a way prose can't. With that in mind, I tried to write around and below and above the experience to illuminate its specific pleasures.

And then there's the problem of history. For many skaters, the history of their own pastime is boring, and that's a good thing, because too much reverence for the past hinders the innovation that skating thrives on. People are happier not remembering the past anyway, and most skaters are young and indifferent to anything outside of their own moment. This particular historical overview mostly encompasses the original phase of development that culminated with Blind's *Video Days* in 1991. That demarcation is overly simplistic, but as a milestone, the video is undeniable. Much has transpired in recent years, but most of it is an extension of what came before. People ollie higher and farther and do new, more complicated tricks, but the curve of progress has leveled off, and it must be acknowledged that we're experiencing the onset of an age without radical departures.

Skaters today are quantifiably better than the pioneers and are doing things that verge on the demented—but they have precedent to build on. That's not to suggest that the last decade hasn't been rife with outrageously talented individuals. They're jumping off of buildings, going faster than ever and pushing the envelope so far the cliché is justified. There was the incomparable Phil Shao, may he rest in peace. John Cardiel, Elissa Steamer, Eric Koston, Chris Senn, Dan Drehobl, Omar Hassan, Gershon Mosley, Ed Templeton, Donny Barley, Alan Peterson, Jaime Thomas, Mike Carroll, Rune

Glifberg, Rick Howard, Pat Duffy, Peter Hewitt—the list goes on and on and covers the spectrum from hesh-transition dogs to hand-rail kamikazes. Danny Way has done seventeen-foot backside airs and jumped out of a helicopter onto a ramp as high as a two-story house. Extreme? The word loses meaning in light of lipslides down eighteen-stair rails. It's impossible to find a comparison to that much skill and cajones.

Even the era of skating I've covered most fully is rife with holes, because any telling of history can't be all-inclusive. It isn't just the great men. It's not just Hammurabi and Charlemagne or Tom Penny and Wade Speyer, for that matter. What about the innovative chamber-maid or the blacksmith who contributed in some forgotten way to the narrative of civilization? Or Alfred Russell Wallace coming up with the theory of evolution at the same time Charles Darwin did, only to be forgotten? Does that make him any less important? Napoleon said, "What is history but a fable agreed upon?" We must accept that it is cyclical and mysterious and ultimately unknowable, something that never happened precisely as it's related, reported by someone who wasn't there. The paradox is that, with all of history's omissions and ambiguities, the influence of great people is inescapable. This is a tale about the meshing of the celebrated and the unknown, from the Scandinavian sliding down a slope to the Hawaiians' *He'e nalu* to the first youngster who broke the apple cart off the scooter to John Cardiel skating hell-bent for leather yesterday. And tomorrow some kid will get on a board and skate for the first time. That is the braided cord of humanity that is skateboarding.

Sources

Besides my own personal experience, there were many books, articles and conversations that I drew upon in the writing of *The Answer Is Never*.

Five books about the history of surfing were indispensable. They were *Hawaiian Surfboard* by Tom Blake (Paradise of the Pacific Press, 1935); *Great Surfing: Photos, Stories, Essays, Reminiscences and Poems* edited by John Severson (Doubleday, 1976); *On Surfing* by Grant W. Kuhns (Charles E. Tuttle, 1963); *Duke Kahanamoku's World of Surfing* by Duke Kahanamoku with Joe Brennan (Grosset & Dunlap, 1968); and *Surfing: The Sport of Hawaiian Kings* by Ben R. Finney and James D. Houston (Hugh Keartland Publishers, 1966). On the beginnings of skiing I consulted *The Ski-Runner* by E. C. Richardson (London, 1909); *A History of Skiing* by Arnold Henry Moore Lunn (Oxford University Press, 1927); and Charles M. Dudley's *60 Centuries of Skiing* (Stephen Daye Press, 1935).

An extensive conversation with Jack Barth informed the first half of chapter 2. The wonderful *1936–1942 San Onofre to Point Dume, Photographs by Don James* (T. Adler Books, 1996) is a photographic evocation of the generation that came before the era described, with a foreword by C. R. Stecyk. *The Quarterly Skateboarder*, published by Surfer Publications from 1964 to 1965, is the essential primary source on skateboarding's entrance onto the national stage. Noel Black's 1965 movie, *Skater Dater*, is an interesting and funny artifact from the steel-wheel days, as is Michael Brault's 1966 *Devil's Toy* with its kids skating through the streets of Montreal, drinking milk and throwing rocks at cops. The *Life* magazine articles quoted are "Here Come the Sidewalk Surfers" from the June 5, 1964 issue and "Skateboard Mania" from May 14, 1965.

Skateboarder magazine is referred to in chapters 3 through 9. It was published by Surfer publications from 1975 until 1980, when it became *Action Now*, which survived for a little over a year before closing. *Skateboarder* is the most compelling and inclusive documentation of the skateboard boom and bust of the seventies. *Skateboard, Skateboard World, Wide World of Skateboarding* and *Zero Gravity* were other magazines of the time. For technical aspects of early skateboard technology, Don Redondo's "History of the Skateboard" in the June 1989 *Thrasher* is invaluable, as is Kevin Thatcher's "The History of Skateboarding" in *Slap* (December 1999). The films referenced in chapter 3 are Bruce Brown's 1966 *The Endless Summer*, Mike Nichols's 1967 *The Graduate*, and Francis Ford Coppola's *Apocalypse Now* from 1979.

The "Los Angeles Against the Mountains" section in John McPhee's *The Control of Nature* (Noonday Press, 1990) and *Los Angeles, The Architecture of Four Ecologies* by Reyner Banham (Icon, 1971) both served as background for Los Angeles's geological and cultural aspects. Dogtown and the Z-Boys have been extensively covered, with a recent slant toward hagiography. "The Lords of Dogtown" by G. Beato in the March 1999 *Spin* and "The Ghosts of Dogtown" by Joe Donnelly in the August 24–30, 2001, *LA Weekly* are especially noteworthy. Additionally there is Stacy Peralta's *Dogtown and the Z-Boys* documentary (Vans Off the Wall Productions, 2002) and Glen E. Friedman's book (which includes Craig Stecyk's articles from

Skateboarder) Dogtown—The Legend of the Z-Boys (Burning Flags Press, 2002). Friedman's other books of defining photographs of the Dogtown scene as well as later skating and music developments are *Fuck You Heroes* and *Fuck You Too* (Burning Flags Press, 1994 and 1996).

Homo Ludens: A Study of the Play Element in Culture by John Huizinga (Beacon Press, 1986) influenced my argument in chapter 5. Becky Beal's "Disqualifying the Official: An Exploration of Social Resistance through the Subculture of Skateboarding" in *The Sociology of Sport Journal* (1995) and "Alternative Masculinity and Its Effects on Gender Relations in the Subculture of Skateboarding" in *The Journal of Sport Behavior* (Vol. 19, No. 3, August 1996) offer an interesting discussion of the role of women and the lack of emphasis on competition in skateboarding.

C. R. Stecyk's articles quoted in chapter 7 were all published in *Skateboarder*. "The Season of Divorce" appears in *The Stories of John Cheever* (Alfred A. Knopf, 1978).

The books relevant to chapter 8 are *Skateboarding, A Complete Guide to the Sport* by Jack Grant (Celestial Arts, 1976); *Hot Skateboarding* by Pahl and Peter Dixon (Warner Books, 1977); and *The Skateboard Book* by Ben Davidson (Grosset & Dunlap, 1976). There is also Laura Torbet's *The Complete Book of Skateboarding* (Funk & Wagnalls, 1976) and *Enjoying Skating* by the Diagram Group (Putnam Publishers, 1979). The films mentioned are Gregg Weaver and Spider Willis's 1976 (rereleased 1998) *Downhill Motion*, Hal Jepson's 1975 *Super Session*, Scott Dittrich's 1975 *Freewheelin'*, and George Gage's *Skateboard: The Movie (That Defies Gravity)* from 1977. *Over the Edge* was directed by Johnathan Kaplan and released in 1979. The Pacific Beach paragraph comes from reminiscences provided by Greg Lipman.

The material in chapter 9 would not have been possible without long and illuminating interviews with Terry Krekorian, Andy

Kessler, and James Cassimus. Their recollections were extremely helpful. The John Fante quote is from *The Road to Los Angeles* (Black Sparrow Press, 1985).

Thrasher is mentioned from chapter 8 on. It has been published continuously since 1981. Directed by Penelope Spheeris, *The Decline of Western Civilization* came out in 1981 and is the definitive cinematic document of the L.A. punk scene at that time. To my knowledge the writing that best explores the maniacal obsession and solitary satisfactions of surfing is "Playing Doc's Games" by William Finnegan. It appeared in *The New Yorker*, August 24 and August 31, 1992. Thad Ziolkowski's *On a Wave* (Atlantic Monthly Press, 2002) is also worth noting, as is Daniel Duane's *Caught Inside: A Surfer's Year on the California Coast* (North Point Press, 1997).

Kem Nunn's novel *The Dogs of Winter* (Scribner, 1997) is quoted in chapter 15. The movies cited are 1985's *Back to the Future* (directed by Robert Zemeckis), 1986's *Thrashin'* (David Winters) and 1989's *Gleaming the Cube* (Graeme Clifford). *Another State of Mind* follows Social Distortion and Youth Brigade on tour across the country and has some great footage of punkers practicing stage dives into a swimming pool. It was directed by Adam Small and Peter Stuart and released in 1984. *Hardcore California* (Peter Belsito, Bob Davis et al., Last Gasp Press, 1983) is a photographic and journalistic document of the Los Angeles and San Francisco punk scenes in the early eighties. It is particularly valuable because of its subjectivity and the fact that it was produced at the time both scenes were vibrant. The same goes for Glen E. Friedman's photo zine, *My Rules* (self-published, 1982). This author's "Damned to Be Free, The Photographs of Edward Colver" in the September 1998 *Thrasher* is an appreciation of one of the finest chroniclers of the L.A. scene at its headiest. Some other more recent work about American punk and hardcore include:

Bryan Ray Turcotte and Christopher T. Miller's excellent *Fucked Up and Photocopied: Instant Art of the Punk Rock Movement* (Gingko Press, 1999); *Forming: The Early Days of Punk* (Smart Art Press, 2000); Mark Spitz and Brendan Mullen's *We Got the Neutron Bomb: The Untold Story of L.A. Punk* (Three Rivers Press, 2001); and Steven Blush's comprehensive *American Hardcore: A Tribal History* (Feral House, 2001). Dick Hebdige's *Subculture, Meaning and Style* (Routledge, 1981) is only partially concerned with the early English scene but is germane to punk's path from transgression to irrelevance.

Transworld Skateboarding began in 1984 and continues to this day. *Poweredge* started publishing in 1987 and lasted about three years. *Big Brother* was birthed in 1992 and continues to amuse skaters and annoy parental types. Susanna Howe's (*sick*) *A Cultural History of Snowboarding* (St. Martin's Press, 1998) is graphically attractive as well as being an intelligent book about snowboarding.

"The Alien Corn" by Somerset Maugham (*Collected Short Stories 2*, Penguin, 1977) is quoted in chapter 18, as is Chris Pastras's article "The Standoff" in the November 1995 issue of *Paper* magazine. Darby Romero's *Ben Is Dead* was one of the most entertaining and interesting underground zines that reached magazine proportions; it ran from 1988 to 2000. Although not mentioned in the text, Hugh Gallagher's *Teeth* (Washington Square Press, 1999) is a novel that adroitly personalizes the commercialization and subsequent degradation of punk and skating culture in the early nineties. *Slap* has been publishing its brand of graphically inventive, earnestly die-hard skate reportage since 1992. The Russell Baker quote is from *Growing Up* (Signet Books, 1984).

Tod Swank's quote about Del Mar in chapter 16 is from the biographical section of *Dysfunctional* (Booth-Clibborn Editions, 1999), which includes a C. R. Stecyk introduction and many great images. It was the first book to seriously contextualize skateboarding as a physical pursuit in conjunction with its artistic and cultural aspects. It remains a classic.

Some other books of interest: Tony Hawk's *Occupation: Skateboarder* (with Sean Mortimer, Regan Books, 1999); Michael Brooke's *The Concrete Wave* (Warwick, 1999); and *Insane Terrain* by the editors of *Thrasher* (Rizzoli, 2001). For a more European outlook there is James Davis and Skin Phillips's *Skateboard Roadmap* (Carlton, 1999) and Helge Tscharn's book of photographs, *Possessed* (Tropen Verlag, 2000).

Finally, in the somewhat esoteric field of scholarly investigations into skateboarders and how they relate to modern architecture and public space, Iain Borden's *Skateboarding, Space and the City: Architecture and the Body* (Berg, 2001) is in an exhaustive league of its own. Some of his other articles on the subject are "Beneath the Pavement, the Beach: Skateboarding, Architecture and the Urban Realm" in *Strangely Familiar: Narratives of Architecture in the City* (Routledge, 1996) and "Chariots of Fire" in the July 2000 issue of *Blueprint*. Two other interesting views on skateboarders' unique appreciation of and interaction with modernist architecture are "The New Modern Lovers" by Marc Spiegler in the September 1994 issue of *Metropolis* magazine and the excellent "The Future of Skateboarding?" by Ocean Howell in *Slap*, January 2000.

Acknowledgments

Without my agent, William Clark, this book would never have been started or have gotten published. I am greatly indebted to his perseverance and unyielding support.

The same goes for Brendan Cahill, my editor at Grove, who believed in the book and edited it with extreme intelligence and exactitude. Thanks also to Beth Thomas for her excellent copyediting. Michael Crewdson and Jim Supanick were there from the beginning—their help and encouragement cannot be measured. The same goes for Mark Gonzales and Craig Stecyk. Luke Ogden, Jake Phelps, and Kevin Thatcher at *Thrasher* were also instrumental.

My thanks to Jack Barth, James Cassimus, Andy Kessler, Terry Krekorian, and Greg Lipman for being gracious and indispensable interviewees. And to Alex Baker, Danny Barger, Evan Becker, Douglas Blau, Rick Charnoski, Glen E. Friedman, Hugh Gallagher, John Hogan, Johnee Kop, Julian LaVerdiere, Coan Nichols, Ivory Serra, Shelter Serra, Sean Silleck, Terry Stacey, and Matt Tabor. This couldn't have come to fruition without them.

And thanks to Joanna Yas, for everything.

Index

340 Index